Confidentiality in Social Work

Confidentiality in Social Work

Issues and Principles

SUANNA J. WILSON

THE FREE PRESS
A Division of Macmillan Publishing Co., Inc.
NEW YORK
Collier Macmillan Publishers
LONDON

The Free Press
A Division of Macmillan Publishing Co., Inc.
866 Third Avenue, New York, N.Y. 10022

Collier Macmillan Canada, Ltd.

First Free Press Paperback Edition 1980

Library of Congress Catalog Card Number: 77-18475

Printed in the United States of America

Hardcover printing number

2 3 4 5 6 7 8 9 10

Paperback printing number

1 2 3 4 5 6 7 8 9 10

Library of Congress Cataloging in Publication Data

Wilson, Suanna J.
    Confidentiality in social work.

    Bibliography: p.
    Includes index.
    1. Confidential communications--Social case
work. 2. Privacy, Right of. I. Title.
HV43.W518   361.3'2   77-18475
ISBN 0-02-934750-5
ISBN 0-02-934850-1 pbk.

This book is dedicated to my father, Dudley W. Wilson, and to all who share his philosophy, which was taught to me at an early age:

"When somebody tells you something is impossible, that's all the challenge that's needed to go out and prove it can be done."

Contents

Preface   ix

Acknowledgments   xiv

1. Basic Principles of Confidentiality   1
2. Situations That Often Lead to Confidentiality Violations   8
3. The Federal Privacy Act of 1974   17
4. Confidentiality of Case-Record Materials   31
5. Release of Information to Others   55
6. Consumer Access to Record Materials   83
7. Privileged Communication: What It Is and Who Is Covered   97
8. Privileged Communication: Common Exceptions to
   State Statutes   111
9. Lawsuits, Subpoenas, and the Right of Privileged
   Communication for Social Workers   143
10. Confidentiality Problems Faced by Supervisors and
    Administrators   155
11. Confidentiality of Personnel Records   172
12. "I Have a Question. . . ."   188
13. Conclusions   202

Appendixes
   A. Self-Instructional Exercise   207
   B-1. NASW Policy on Information Utilization and
        Confidentiality   214
   B-2. A Model Licensing Act for Social Workers   220
   B-3. NASW Code of Ethics   231

B-4. Confidential and Privileged Communications:
Guidelines for Lawyers and Social Workers   233
C. A Model "Consent for Release of Information"
Form   236

Bibliography   *238*

Index   *269*

Preface

The judgment of the worker is, in the last analysis, a major factor in confidentiality, regardless of the nature of the agency policy and cannot be regulated out. In the absence of agency policy, perforce the worker carries the full burden of deciding what information shall be obtained, received and disclosed.[1]

National Social Welfare Assembly

CAN YOU ANSWER the following questions quickly and confidently?

1. Your client, who has been served by your agency for several years, suddenly asks to see his case record. In fact, he'd even like to have a copy of it. Should you grant his requests? Do you have a choice in the matter? What is the *exact* policy of your agency on this? [For discussion on this issue, see pp. 83–96.]
2. Your patient appears quite emotionally disturbed. He hates his brother for many reasons. In fact, he tells you that he plans to kill him and asks you not to tell this to anyone "or else." What should you do? What are your legal obligations, if any? [For the "answer," see Appendix A and pp. 115–121.]
3. What exactly is meant by the term "right of privileged communication?" Do you or your clients have this right? [See Chapter 7 for the "answer."]
4. A client in your private agency has just told you he's been cheating the local welfare program and asks you not to tell anyone. What should you do? [See pp. 190–191.]
5. Your patient doesn't appear very alert mentally. You need his permission to release some information from his record, but he doesn't seem to know what you are talking about. There is no emer-

---

[1] *Confidentiality in Social Services to Individuals: An Examination of Basic Concepts and Everyday Practices, with Suggestions for Overcoming Current Problems*, Ad Hoc Committee on Confidentiality, National Social Welfare Assembly (New York: John B. Watkins Co., 1958), p. 22.

gency involved. Can you accept his wife's permission to go ahead and release the information? [See pp. 64–67.]

6. Your agency has just adopted a policy permitting employees access to their personnel records. However, the files contain old references submitted in confidence before the policy took effect. Should your staff be allowed to see this material? [See pp. 155–162.]

If you had difficulty with any of these questions, you need to read this book. You are also in very good company, for many counselors, administrators, field instructors, and faculty cannot answer these and similar questions.

The topic of confidentiality is becoming a primary area of concern for many of the helping professions. The consumer's increasing sensitivity to confidentiality and his desire to assert and protect basic privacy rights are giving rise to complex legal and ethical problems which were not imagined only a few years ago. For example, the Federal Privacy Act of 1974 established legal guidelines regarding the rights of clients to see their federal records; it also set controls for the release of information, providing a legal solution to issues which social workers have been debating since the beginnings of the profession. It is highly possible that the provisions of the Privacy Act will one day become mandatory for the private sector, as well.[2] Computerized data systems have become highly sophisticated, and there is increasing pressure for social workers to contribute their share of confidential consumer information to these massive data banks which, in one way or another, affect virtually everyone.

In spite of these developments, there is little specific literature for the social-work practitioner to turn to for guidance or even for identification of key issues, although these issues have already generated much thinking and writing by other professions. As social workers become licensed and gain the legal rights and responsibilities of privileged communication, they too must focus attention on these areas. This book attempts to meet the need for identification and assimilation of the key issues and principles pertaining to confidentiality in social work practice.

It is recognized that one author cannot define principles of confidentiality for an entire profession. It is time, however, to centralize key concepts and offer some practical guidelines that can be applied to a large number of the day-to-day confidentiality questions that arise in social work practice. Not everyone will agree with the concepts presented; others may react to the fact that some thoughts are being expressed that have traditionally been discussed only in hushed verbal exchanges, safe from the ears of "clients" and others.

---

[2] The Federal Privacy Protection Study Commission in Washington has been holding hearings on this subject, and social service organizations were given an opportunity to testify during January of 1977. See Chapter 3.

The author is not an attorney, and legal advice is not given in this book.[3] Although it does contain references to articles, cases, and experiences along with the author's analysis and opinion, individual confidentiality situations may require legal interpretation, which may be given only by a lawyer. Examples of confidentiality cited here cannot and should not be relied upon as legal guidelines.

The book was originally intended to be an informal, somewhat "folksy" discussion of confidentiality which would make easy reading for students in schools of social work. However, what started out to be simple has turned into an in-depth research project. It was soon obvious that confidentiality is far from a simple topic. I have encountered agency executives, educators, practitioners and even attorneys who were also unaware of its complexity. Herein lies a serious problem for social workers: we plod along in blissful ignorance, assuming we know a great deal more than we do. Then one day the closet door is opened by the courts and we discover an entire room full of knowledge that could have revolutionized our method of practice had we only known it existed. We can no longer avoid looking behind that closet door—to do so is to invite injustices to our clients, violations of state and federal laws, and to risk having to make payments for damages out of our own pockets when we are held liable for infractions.

I started work on this book by reviewing the social work literature and soon felt comfortable in my knowledge of confidentiality . . . until curiosity demanded a review of psychiatric, medical, legal, psychological, guidance, nursing, and other literature to see what these related "helping professions" were doing with confidentiality issues. Suddenly the few efforts of social workers to study confidentiality over the past few decades seemed inconsequential by comparison. In fact, a serious deficiency became evident: some social work literature on the topic not only proved to be inaccurate and misleading because of its incompleteness but, in several instances, actually gives wrong advice to the reader on how to handle confidentiality and privileged-communication issues.[4] Bibliographies and footnotes are often scant, and aspects of confidentiality are dealt with so superficially that the reader is

---

[3] The material has, however, been reviewed by several attorneys.

[4] A recent ACSW exam (November 8, 1976) even contained an erroneous question dealing with confidentiality issues. It read as follows:

A group of 9th grade students approach a school social worker and offer to share details of their extensive drug use, but only if the information will be kept confidential. An appropriate response by the social worker would be to explain to the group that:

a. He respects the right of the individual to complete privacy as the most important element in preserving the fostering of trust in a relationship.

b. He would need to reveal the information to parents, school officials, or law officers when and if in his professional judgment it would be in the students' best interest.

c. The information would be revealed to other relevant persons or authorities only with the students' approval.

d. Such information will not be shared with others even if requested and initiated by the students unless the social worker first obtained legal counsel.

lulled into a false sense of security, believing that he has been fully informed. It is time that these deficiencies were corrected.

It is frightening to realize that many of the settings where mental health professionals practice have no written policies on confidentiality or merely state "we must maintain confidentiality" without providing interpretations or guidelines for employees to follow. As we shall see, even the National Association of Social Workers provides rather incomplete guidelines and fails to address several key issues. In the absence of any comprehensive and accurate study of confidentiality in recent years, one wonders where social workers and related professionals have been turning for guidance in making agency-level decisions on confidentiality policies. It is imperative that the social work profession take time to examine the issues fully before establishing guidelines and legal mandates that may prove unworkable. Along with this, a massive educational effort must be underaken to acquaint social workers with the importance and ramifications of confidentiality as it affects all areas of social work practice.

There are those who will overreact, converting these concepts of confidentiality into a veritable straitjacket, so that these helping professionals cannot carry out their day-to-day operations without fear of confidentiality repercussions. On the other hand, a full understanding of this complex topic should bring about an informed freedom; because he knows the limits and possible consequences along with the grey areas, the practitioner can use intelligent discretion in daily practice as he applies the principles of confidentiality in the best interests of his clients. This may mean seeking for loopholes and using them appropriately. Without awareness of the complexities, it would appear easier to pretend they do not exist and continue with the present *modus operandi*. However, we can no longer afford this luxury.

There is cause for some legitimate concern when federal legislation begins determining confidentiality practices for social work professionals. In moderation, these can increase consumer and employee rights and guarantee some consistency in the handling of confidential material. However, if regulation is carried to excess, services to consumers could actually be hindered. We are in an era of acute sensitivity to consumer rights, and confidentiality and openness of files have become important issues which will undoubtedly receive even more attention before the tidal wave reaches its peak. When confidentiality policies begin interfering with basic services to the consumer, it will then be time for the wave to recede so that professionals can go on about their business of servicing those who come to them for help.

The question is poorly worded and fails to mention legal statutes in the state the worker is practicing in that might dictate his response. A further reading of this text will reveal that none of the "answers" provided are correct.

There seems to be a trend toward making the skimpiest possible recordings in an effort to avoid confidentiality problems. This is not the answer. If more attention were paid to how data are gathered, recorded, and handled, there would be less need for concern regarding confidentiality. This may necessitate some changes in basic practice methods. To achieve openness in recording with the view of sharing records with consumers, there must be more honesty in the therapeutic relationship from which the records are generated. The implementation of confidentiality principles requires their integration into the basic therapeutic process. Perhaps, then, our efforts have been directed toward dealing with confidentiality after the fact rather than intervening on a preventive level. It is the preventive level on which the social-work profession must concentrate if concepts of confidentiality are to be successfully internalized and implemented in future practice.

This book has been organized in a manner that takes the reader from basic definitions of confidentiality (Chapter 1) through the intricacies of federal legislation (Chapter 3) and privileged communication (Chapters 7-9). Several chapters present guidelines for handling confidential data in daily practice (Chapters 4-6), and two (Chapters 10 and 11) focus on the special problems faced by supervisors and custodians of personnel records. An informal question-and-answer chapter (Chapter 12) presents some problems that may be encountered in daily practice. A self-instructional exercise (Appendix A) presents one method of teaching confidentiality concepts. Selected NASW statements comprise Appendix B and illustrate some of the profession's current thinking on confidentiality and privacy issues. An exhaustive bibliography provides additional reading for those who wish to study the topic in greater depth.

Acknowledgments

THE COOPERATION AND ASSISTANCE of many people have made it possible for this text to become a reality. Special appreciation must go first of all to Diana P. Doyle, Director of the Medical Social Service Department at Jackson Memorial Hospital. Her support and faith that I could write this book were important factors. What is most significant is that she allowed me to be creative and withstood the sometimes neurotic work habits that are necessary for a full-time practitioner to undertake a text of this magnitude.

Robert H. Cohen, ACSW, LL.B., deserves special appreciation for his continuous encouragement, helpful review, and pertinent suggestions.

I am grateful to Gladys Topkis, my editor, whose enthusiasm, frank critique, and competent guidance helped make this book possible.

Donald Doyle must be thanked for his assistance in proofreading and for his comments, which were sometimes painful but essential in changing a "folksy" manuscript into a professional text.

Daniel A. Sorrentino, BA, J.D., was most helpful in reviewing the material from a legal viewpoint, and his comments on the privileged-communication chapters are greatly appreciated.

I corresponded and talked with many people during the data-gathering process who provided invaluable input. They are too numerous to list individually. However, Charles R. Knerr, Assistant Professor in the Department of Political Science at the University of Texas; Hermann Schuchman of the University of Illinois at Chicago Circle; Ralph Slovenko, professor of Law and Psychiatry at Wayne State University; Helen Pinkus, Social Work Professor at Virginia Commonwealth University; Jeffrey J. Lampos, Project Manager for Privacy, Confidentiality and Security for the Blue Cross Association; and Carole Parsons and Susan Bennett of the Privacy Protection Study Commission in Washington deserve special mention.

A word of appreciation must also be extended to the many persons who have attended my lectures on confidentiality during recent years. It was their searching questions that forced me into seeking answers and eventually producing this text.

Finally, my brother, Freestone F. Wilson, must be thanked for his moral support, patience, and helpful attitude.

S.J.W.

1. Basic Principles of Confidentiality

What exactly does the social caseworker promise when he promises confidentiality? Does he actually promise that what the client tells him will be known to no one but himself? If he does, it is unethical because it is not true. What the client tells him will be known to the typist who transcribes his record, to the supervisor who reads it, to the workers who follow after him. . . . All the caseworker can truthfully promise is that what the client tells him will be used responsibly, and will be guarded against misuse.

Helen Harris Perlman[1]

SOCIAL WORKERS, PSYCHIATRISTS, psychologists, physicians and others have long argued that absolute trust is essential between client and helping professional if the treatment process is to be effective. Trust cannot be fully achieved unless all personal information shared during the counseling process is kept "confidential." Thus, various professions and social-work settings have adopted stances and incorporated into their professional codes of ethics statements regarding the necessity for maintaining confidentiality. For example:

> I respect the privacy of the people I serve. I use in a responsible manner information gained in professional relationships.[2]

> Confidential information has been defined as those personal facts or conditions pertaining to the client's life which he has communicated to the agency for definite purposes related to the service he is requesting or receiving from the agency. It is the client's right and expectation that such information will be respected and safeguarded by the agency and all of its personnel: professional, administrative, secretarial, and clerical staff; field-work students, volunteers.[3]

[1] Helen Harris Perlman, "The Caseworker's Use of Collateral Information," *Social Casework,* Vol. 32, No. 7 (July 1951), p. 326.

[2] NASW, *Code of Ethics of the National Association of Social Workers* (Washington, D.C.: NASW, adopted by the Delegate Assembly of the NASW October 13, 1960, and amended April 11, 1967). See Appendix B-3.

[3] Frances A. Koestler, ed. "The COMSTAC Report: Standards for Strengthened Services," mimeographed (New York: Commission on Standards and Accreditation of Services for the Blind, 1966), p. 33.

[Confidentiality means] safeguarding information about an individual that has been obtained by the psychologist in the course of his teaching, practice, or investigation [and] is a primary obligation of the psychologist.[4]

Confidentiality means that disclosures by the patient or client to the professional will not be revealed to others except under certain circumstances and then only for the purpose of helping him.[5]

Thus, there is widespread recognition of the need to keep certain information confidential. However, the fact that an obligation to maintain confidentiality is recognized does not necessarily mean that any such right is guaranteed by law. Records can be subpoenaed and court orders may force disclosure of confidential material in many social-work settings. It is not unusual for social workers to confuse "confidentiality" with "privileged communication" and assume that, because they believe in the principle of confidentiality, they also have legal protection from having to disclose confidential material.

Some professionals' communications with their clients are safeguarded by legislation providing the right of privileged communication. These laws vary from state to state; when present, they enable the client, if he desires, to prevent his counselor from testifying in response to a subpoena. Social-work counselor-client communications do not have this legal protection in most states. Thus, while the profession recognizes the importance of confidentiality, such awareness is no guarantee that attorneys and courts cannot gain access to sensitive information.

Confidentiality is almost universally defined, in modern lingo, as meaning "keep your mouth shut and don't blab about your clients' personal affairs." Unfortunately, this is easier said than done. In actual practice, social workers encounter many situations in which absolute confidentiality cannot exist. When violations do occur, they are often the result of carelessness or ignorance regarding the more complex and subtle aspects of confidentiality. Now that ethical and legal actions against those who make unauthorized disclosures are occurring with increasing frequency, social-work practitioners who wish to avoid legal penalties need to understand the full definition and application of confidentiality.

The Two Kinds of Confidentiality

It would be nice to know that when one talks of keeping something "confidential" it means just that—no one else will ever find out what was communicated. However, as the quotation at the beginning of this chapter illus-

---

[4] American Psychological Association, "Ethical Standards of Psychologists," *American Psychologist* Vol. 23, No. 23 (May 1968), p. 358.

[5] Mildred M. Reynolds, "Threats to Confidentiality," *Social Work Journal,* Vol. 21, No. 2 (March 1976), p. 109.

trates, this is not necessarily realistic or desirable in actual practice. Thus, two kinds of confidentiality must be considered: absolute and relative.

ABSOLUTE CONFIDENTIALITY

The security of information is absolute when data learned or observed by a social worker stay with that individual and are *never* passed on to anyone or anything *in any form*. Such information would never be shared with a supervisor, written in a case record, fed into a computer, or discussed orally. The student or beginning practitioner tends to think in absolutes, and often naively promises his client such "absolute confidentiality." A few private practitioners having the right of privileged communication can actually maintain absolute confidentiality in some situations. Agency-based practitioners may acquire information that is never passed on to anyone else, but this situation is extremely rare, since considerable intra-agency sharing of information is necessary for the functioning of most service-delivery systems.

RELATIVE CONFIDENTIALITY

The majority of social workers in practice today function as part of a larger department or agency. In such an agency, much of the communication between client and social worker is shared with others in the system as part of the service-delivery process. Students and employees share details with supervisors as they seek guidance. In many settings interdisciplinary exchanges of information occur. Thus, the promise of "confidentiality" must be a relative one. Social workers have traditionally recognized the need for obtaining permission from the client before releasing information about him to sources outside the agency. However, his permission is almost never sought for the internal sharing which is so commonplace. Many clients have no objection to this process and recognize its necessity.

Practitioners can become uncomfortable assuring their clients that confidentiality is maintained when in reality intra-agency sharing occurs. It is an error to assume that the persons served are aware that this process occurs; in fact, many are not and should be informed of it during their initial contact with the agency. The Federal Privacy Act of 1974, which governs confidentiality practices in federal programs, makes it quite clear that information regarding consumers (and staff) *can* be shared with "those officers and employees of the agency which maintain the record who have a need for the record in the performance of their duties."[6] Unfortunately, some settings guard information so jealously that staff who need the data to provide

[6] Federal Privacy Act of 1974. Public Law 93-579, December 31, 1974 (effective September 27, 1975), section 552a (b) (1).

a service to the consumer cannot get them. Such strictness appears unnecessary; with the precedent established by the Federal Privacy Act, it appears highly unlikely that an agency could be held liable for responsible internal exchange of selected information.

Should I make it a standard part of my first session with a new client to assure him that I will keep whatever he tells me confidential?

What Information Must Be Kept Confidential?

This subject will be defined in more detail in subsequent chapters. However, there are two broad types of information that a social worker deals with which must be handled confidentially. The first of these is quite obvious; however, little conscious thought is usually given to the second:

1. The worker must keep confidential all information learned and observations made regarding clients or consumer groups served. This principle, with slight modifications, also pertains to supervisory, administrative, and other indirect-service personnel who work with employees, students, community groups, and others.

2. The agency, institution, or setting within which the social worker practices is entitled to confidentiality regarding its inner workings and difficulties. All settings experience times of internal upheaval as they strive to provide the best possible services to consumers. Social-work employees and students may see and personally experience some of the less-than-perfect aspects of their agencies. It can be tempting for the frustrated social worker, struggling with an "inefficient bureaucracy" and "a few dodos who should have been fired long ago," to take his observations and reactions out into the community to be heard by other agencies and potential clients, thus damaging the agency's reputation.

There are various ethical principles that dictate proper handling of such information about agency affairs. This obligation is definitely suggested in the NASW Code of Ethics:

> I treat with respect the findings, views, and actions of colleagues and use appropriate channels to express judgment on these matters.

One author addresses the concept of professionalism in social-work practice and quotes from an early version of the NASW Code of Ethics as she presents her arguments for confidentiality of internal agency matters:

> We are usually clear about the relation of the principle of confidentiality to our work with the people we serve. We may not fully realize, however, that this principle covers all agency operations. . . . It protects all internal operations of

the agency, including statistics and reports which are not explicitly intended for release to the public.

. . . "If agency policies and procedures violate professional standards, the social worker should accept the obligation to make all due effort to effect change through appropriate agency and professional channels; refrain from irresponsible public criticism of agency's policies. . . . " Upon termination of employment with an agency for whatever reason, "the social worker should have a continuing obligation to act responsibly in accordance with professional ethics regarding disclosure of information obtained during employment."[7]

Thus, agencies and social-work departments are entitled to a certain measure of protection from gossip and irresponsible publicity. On the other hand, there may be situations where a community is in need of protection from unethical practices within an agency. One tenet of the NASW Code of Ethics addresses this matter directly:

I accept responsibility to help protect the community against unethical practice by any individual or organization engaged in social welfare activities.

The professional determined to take this role must do so in a responsible manner, using as constructive an approach as is possible under the circumstances. Furthermore, it is obligatory to

distinguish clearly, in public, between my statements and actions as an individual and as a representative of an organization.

The student placed in an agency is in a delicate position. He is there to learn, and to do so he must critically evaluate the service delivery system and become acquainted with reality. He is often fitting together pieces of information obtained in the field with ideals learned in the classroom, and may literally as well as figuratively scurry back and forth between agency and academia sharing data, making observations, and raising questions. Thus, some sharing of internal agency affairs with campus faculty is necessary for student education. If the process is handled in a mature, constructive manner, there is little to fear. However, the overzealous student can get into difficulty if emotionally laden material is taken out of the agency into the community without full awareness of possible repercussions.[8]

---

[7] Jeanette Regensburg, "Some Thoughts on Being a Professional Social Worker," *Social Casework,* Vol. 40, No. 3 (March 1959), p. 224.

[8] In one situation known to the author, a graduate student was taking a course in institutional racism and was encouraged to write a paper for class on his observations of its existence or absence in his field placement setting. The student did so, found what he believed to be evidence of institutional racism, and submitted his paper to the editor of the local NASW newsletter for publication. The editor discovered upon talking with the student that no one in the agency knew he had prepared this paper or that he was seeking to publish it. The editor agreed to print it, but only if the student would first agree to share a copy with his agency administrator and inform him of his desire to have it published. It had not occurred to him previously to do so, and a frank discussion ensued regarding possible repercussions, both positive and negative, for the student, the administrator and the agency as well as the clients being served. After the student became aware of his responsibilities to the agency and the possible repercus-

An interesting point must be raised: One of the basic premises of confidentiality is that the client should control the release of confidential information to others—disclosure should not occur without his full knowledge and permission. Should agencies, employees, and service-delivery systems have this same privilege? In practice, many settings require that staff and students obtain clearance before being interviewed by news media, writing "letters to the editor" as representatives of the agency, or otherwise officially publicizing information concerning the program. Social-work settings have very limited control over informal sharing by employees among themselves and with others in the community. Therefore they must rely on staff's judgment and allegiance to basic professional ethics for the protection of confidential activities. An occasional student or dissatisfied employee planning to resign may argue, "I've only got to stick it out a little while longer before I'll be gone, so it doesn't matter what I say." Some seasoned practitioners can, with great sadness, recall situations where someone had strongly negative reactions to an agency or an individual and his indiscriminate, thoughtless sharing of negative feelings destroyed the reputation of the agency or the individual employee. A given student's or employee's experience with a setting may be transitory, but the agency and those working there must continue functioning after the disgruntled person has left the scene, and they must bear the after-effects of violations of the agency's right to confidentiality.

Who Is Bound By the Principle of Confidentiality?

All persons acquiring either of the two types of confidential material described above must be bound by this ethic. Those who might have routine access to confidential information in a typical agency or institutional setting include:

1. social-work practitioners, supervisors, and administrators
2. students
3. members of other disciplines
4. volunteers (and their parent organizations)
5. agency-based secretarial staff
6. outside clerical staff (i.e., transcription pools and secretarial services)
7. consumers
8. computer and data-processing personnel

sions involved, he nevertheless made a decision to go ahead—but at least it was with full knowledge of what might happen. See *The Sandpiper* (newsletter of the South Florida Chapter of NASW), April–May 1973 and June 1973 issues for several articles and letters to the editor regarding this incident.

9. consultants
10. agency legal counsel
11. board members
12. persons involved with peer-review and accountability mechanisms (i.e., Professional Standards Review Organizations as well as "in-house" reviewers)
13. accrediting and licensing authorities
14. third-party funding sources (Medicare, state health-insurance programs, private insurance carriers, grant sources, others funding the agency or its clients)
15. researchers—from both inside and outside the agency
16. agencies with which the setting officially cooperates in the exchange of certain data

Agency confidentiality policies should spell out clearly who does and who does not have access to various kinds of information. Those having even limited access must receive formal training (preferably as part of their "orientation" when first hired) on the principles of confidentiality and related personnel policies. Definite disciplinary measures should be prescribed for those who violate confidentiality. Students must receive special attention. Schools of social work vary widely in their classroom emphasis on confidentiality, and some fail to teach the topic at all. Even if the principle is covered in depth by the school, the lecture may be timed so that the student does not receive it until he has already started field placement. In addition, clerical staff, often trained or experienced in the business world, usually do not understand the peculiar confidentiality requirements of social-service agencies. They may talk disrespectfully of clients served or even duplicate copies of case records because the material "is so interesting." Thus, the need for training all personnel cannot be overemphasized.

2. Situations That Often Lead to Confidentiality Violations

Some doctors would rather go to jail than reveal their patients' secrets. But some gossip with their colleagues—they say the last patient cannot handle money or was married too many times; they take their telephone calls in front of both family and friends, they entertain at parties with juicy case histories wherein the characters are only loosely masked. If either curious spouse or hungry lawyer stands among the seemingly innocent listeners, the results may be disastrous for both patient and physician.

APA Conference on Confidentiality of Health Records[1]

THE QUOTATION INTRODUCING THIS CHAPTER is certainly applicable to social workers as well as physicians. Although few practitioners consciously and deliberately violate confidentiality, violations do occur, usually as a result of ignorance or carelessness on the part of the social worker or his agency. The intricacies of privileged communication and formal disclosure of information to others are not fully understood by many helping professionals, and it is easy to understand how one might slip up in these areas. However, there are many simple, everyday situations that lead to confidentiality violations as social workers let their professional guard down and verbalize without thinking. The offense usually goes unnoticed because no one overheard who should not have done so, but there have been situations in which the careless professional is not so fortunate. Negative repercussions can be both frightening and expensive (if the consumer initiates legal action for alleged damages). As the social work profession strives to achieve full "professionalism" through licensing and by gaining the right of privileged communication, it must also follow with greater fidelity its ethics of confidentiality. Consumers and the courts will expect full adherence to the principles being espoused and will exact stiff penalties for lapses.

[1] *Confidentiality: A Report of the 1974 Conference on Confidentiality of Health Records,* American Psychiatric Association (Washington, D.C.: 1975), pp. 5–6.

Legal action against social workers for confidentiality violations is virtually unheard of; however, such action has affected other helping professions. In one recorded instance, a patient overheard a conversation between her doctor and another member of the medical team while they were standing in a hallway. They were discussing her case situation in a rather unprofessional manner, and it upset her so much that her surgery had to be cancelled. She sued and collected damages from the physician for mental anguish suffered because of his thoughtless remarks. In making its decision, the court obviously took into consideration the fact that the physician had violated his profession's code of ethics, which requires him to maintain confidentiality regarding his patients.[2] With the recent Watergate episode involving conscious violations of privacy, the attempted theft of Daniel Ellsberg's psychiatric records, and with rising consumer concern over computerized data banks and "big-brother" operations, there is increasing awareness of the need for confidentiality. At the same time there is a move toward educating the consumer regarding his right of access to information and control over its use. One author, discussing confidentiality and psychotherapy, even suggests that "perhaps the time is right for a psychological-consumer advisory committee—a Ralph Nader of psychology clients."[3] Careless confidentiality violations must be avoided if helping professionals are to retain the respect of their clientele.

Some Problematic Situations to Avoid

Following are some of the most common instances in which confidentiality violations occur. Inappropriate disclosures in these situations seem to take place almost daily in many large social-service settings and among private practitioners:

DISCUSSING CLIENT/WORK SITUATIONS WITH FAMILY AND FRIENDS

This is undoubtedly one of the most frequent violations. The offending social worker often rationalizes, "It's OK as long as I don't use names, and, besides, they don't know the people I'm talking about." The argument appears logical, so what exactly is wrong with discussing clients or work situations with these individuals?

[2] Frances Ginsberg and Barbara Clarke, "Patients Need Privacy—and May Sue if They Don't Get It," *Modern Hospital,* Vol. 118, No. 6 (June 1972), p. 110.

[3] Stanley L. Brodsky. "Shared Results and Open Files with the Client," *Professional Psychology* (Fall 1972), p. 364.

In dealing with this problem the social worker who is tempted to share information must first ask himself a basic question: "Is my friend or relative bound by the same rules of confidentiality that I am?" If the answer is "no," then that person has no moral, ethical or legal restraints to prevent him from passing the information on to a third person and perhaps doing so in a most unprofessional and highly undesirable manner. If the person whose privacy is violated should learn of the incident, the social worker, rather than the friend or relative, would be held responsible. The person to whom the friend or relative repeats that interesting story may be someone who knows the individual being discussed or recognizes him from the details provided. He may even be the consumer himself.

If others hear a social worker glibly discussing personal information about his clients or his agency, they might appear very receptive during the telling but basically be losing respect for the individual and for social workers in general as professional helping persons. If the listener should later require professional counseling he may not seek it, fearing that the counselor will discuss his personal affairs and feelings with others, as his social worker friend had done. Furthermore, once details about clients or supervisory/administrative responsibilities are shared inappropriately in a social setting, the listener will eagerly seek the next installment, thus creating a vicious circle that can be difficult to break. It is acceptable and desirable for practitioners to share *feelings* experienced as a result of daily activities, but here too names and specific details regarding clients and others should not be disclosed. Emotional reactions to confidential material rather than the confidential information itself can be shared. It certainly is permissible to state, for example, "Boy, I had a frustrating day today—nothing went right," or "A patient of mine had a psychotic break and it took everything I had to deal with it," or "A man I've been working with for months died today and it really wiped me out," without revealing identifying data. Indeed, such release of feelings generated by social-work activity is essential if friends and family are to provide the emotional support and empathy every professional needs from time to time.

Occasionally, a social worker's spouse is also bound by professional confidentiality ethics and regulations. Both may be social workers, or one might be an attorney, a clergyman, or a psychiatrist. Such individuals will often consult each other about their work. If the process is handled properly and professionally, no harm is done and service delivery may actually be improved. However, such discussions are technically a violation of confidentiality because the consumer has no knowledge that information is being shared with an outsider and has no control over its disclosure. Thus, the practice goes against many of the concepts of confidentiality being defined today by the helping professions and by the courts.

Unfortunately, some practitioners simply cannot keep "secrets"—personal or professional. Their own need to exaggerate, attract attention, and dramatize case situations prevents them from maintaining confidentiality. If a practitioner does not have enough respect for the persons whom he serves to refrain from discussing their confidences in public, then that individual should not be practicing social work.

The social worker who is tempted to share material inappropriately might ask himself this question: "If *I* were the client or the supervisee, would I want the social worker discussing *my* situation with his family and friends?"

INFORMAL DISCUSSIONS WITH COLLEAGUES

The busy professional is often in the midst of grappling with a problem as he stops to join some colleagues for lunch or a coffee break. There will be a natural tendency to ventilate feelings and discuss unresolved problems during the break. Information can be shared within the agency without violations of confidentiality if this is done in a professional manner and for the purpose of serving the consumer. But what about the people who might be sitting at the adjoining table while such a coffee-break discussion is taking place? Could they be friends or relatives of the consumer being discussed? Perhaps other clients are overhearing, and if so, could they become upset over the content or the manner in which the material is presented? How might the courts rule if legal action were initiated?

Sometimes indiscreet conversations are held while walking down a busy hallway. This is often the only way to consult with a busy colleague. Bear in mind, however, that problems similar to those in coffee-break discussions can arise and that at least one lawsuit has been successfully won against a physician who engaged in an inappropriate hallway discussion (see p. 9).

The elevator discussion, to take another instance, comes complete with its own unique psychology. Consider the following vignette, which describes a common experience in most hospitals:

A group of impatient people, mostly strangers, are crammed into a crowded square that forces them into the discomfort zone because of physical closeness to others. Some are desperately studying the ceiling configurations or staring down the lighting panel in a concerted effort to avoid eye-to-eye contact with— gasp—a stranger standing only inches away. All are bored and in a hurry. Suddenly the tension is broken—two physicians are discussing their patient! All ears perk up as names, identifying data, diagnoses, and even prognoses are tossed about as freely as leaves falling in autumn. No one lets on that he is listening, but every word is eagerly absorbed.

Confidentiality—who ever heard of that?

INAPPROPRIATE CONVERSATIONAL REMARKS TO CONSUMERS OR EMPLOYEES

It is very easy to violate someone's privacy as the next client or a supervisee walks into the social worker's office. "Hello, Mr. Jones—I'm sorry I had to keep you waiting so long—the person before you just seemed to go on and on." Or consider the following exchange between a supervisor and another employee:

> _Supervisor:_ Oh, hi, Peter, what can I do for you?
> _Worker:_ I wanted to ask you about something—but say, what was wrong with Mrs. Smith? She sure looked upset when she left your office as I was coming in.
> _Supervisor:_ Yeah, she's uptight again today.

Secretaries are often guilty of this violation as they give out unsolicited analyses of employees and superiors and pass the word that "Sara was crying in the boss's office today—something really bad must have been done to her." Such remarks may cause troubled employees to turn to the one with the loose tongue for the latest "inside story," and this then can lead to morale problems and behavior that can disrupt the functioning of an entire program. When the problem becomes serious enough to warrant administrative intervention, the passer of the unsolicited remarks usually ends up wishing he had handled himself with more maturity and self-restraint.

INCOMING PHONE CALLS DURING COUNSELING SESSIONS AND CONFERENCES

Interruptions during a counseling session or conference are annoying because of the resultant break in rapport, but they are sometimes unavoidable. Meanwhile the counselee usually sits silently and uncomfortably _listening_ while the worker conducts his business by phone. In most instances the topic of discussion is not confidential or the conversation is so one-sided that the counselee cannot discern any identifiable information. However, sometimes the listener can be adversely affected by the experience, or he may broadcast the juicy details rather freely. Such potential problems can be avoided by instructing the secretary to hold all calls during conferences. Should a call get through, the response should be, "I'm in conference now, but I'll call you back as soon as I can." A less desirable alternative would be for the social worker to take the call in another room or ask the client to wait outside for a few minutes. Supervisors whose conferences with supervisees are similarly interrupted will need to apply these suggestions as well.

VIOLATIONS WHILE DICTATING

Dictating into a tape recorder requires going off into a corner and talking to oneself. Most persons feel awkward enough about this process that they insist on privacy. However, not all social workers and students have private offices, and some may be tempted to take dictation home when they get behind in their work. Who then overhears the dictation? Is a violation of confidentiality occurring as curious family members gather around?

COCKTAIL PARTIES

One author who described ways in which physicians tend to violate confidentiality through gossip discussed this phenomenon quite frankly. The offending professional becomes "lubricated" with a generous dose of alcohol and subsequently spills attention-getting tales about his professional pursuits, including well-known persons he has treated.[4] Similar dangers exist for social workers.

ACCIDENTAL OVERHEARING OF CONFIDENTIAL REMARKS

This occurrence can cause real discomfort for the social worker who happened to be in the wrong place at the wrong time and overheard something he should not have heard. What does he do with the interesting tidbit that has accidentally come his way, that no one knows he knows? Absolute confidentiality is usually the best course of action, though it can be very difficult not to take the "ego trip" of regaling fellow workers with what one has learned. The individual whose comment was overheard may need to be informed that he had unseen company. If the accidentally acquired information is anxiety-producing for the hearer, he may need to reveal what has happened in order to get help in dealing with his feelings.

THE ATTENTIVE REPAIRMAN

Let us suppose a social worker is discussing something confidential on the phone, speaking face-to-face with a client, or holding a supervisory conference when a man walks in to change the filter on the air conditioner or repair a broken light. Does the social worker's conversation stop until the repairman finishes? Is he asked to return at a more convenient time, or is he treated as if he were either severely retarded or deaf and blind, while the

---

[4] Ralph Crawshaw, "Gossip Wears a Thousand Masks," *Prism,* Vol. 2, No. 6 (June 1974), pp. 45–47.

discussion of confidential material continues uninterrupted? How many repairmen, janitors, construction workers, and others have taken a little longer than necessary to do their job because they just could not pry themselves away from the fascinating (and confidential) discussion they were overhearing? How many have rushed through a difficult task because they were uncomfortable being present while the social worker continued delicate conversations as if no one else were there?

THE SECRETARY-CONFIDANTE ROUTINE

Social workers, administrators, and others often work very closely with their secretaries. Most clerical workers are intelligent, mature individuals who understand that their bosses often share things with them that are confidential and not to be passed on. But must *everything* be confided to the secretary? Must all the social worker's analyses of behind-the-scenes events be shared? The secretary may find it fascinating to get the inside story but can experience real discomfort trying to figure out what to do with the knowledge and may secretly wish the boss would not share it. Again the question must be personalized: If *you* were, for example, a supervisee experiencing problems with job performance and you had just had a rough conference with your supervisor, would you want your supervisor to share the details with a secretary who is not professionally involved and with whom you may also have to work on a day-to-day basis?

Handling Others Who Carelessly Violate Confidentiality

The social worker who finds himself in a situation in which he overhears others discussing confidential material inappropriately can become quite uncomfortable; he wishes the person would stop talking, but is not quite certain whether he should intervene, or how to do so. Options will vary depending on the people involved and the circumstances.

If the offender is another social worker, a simple interruption of "Say, can we discuss this later when we get back to the office?" or "Ahem! I've had enough of work—let's make a rule not to discuss work during break today because my head feels like it's about to come off" may solve the problem. Direct confrontation may be the best approach—e.g., "I feel uncomfortable discussing this in public" or "I don't think that's any of my business, and I'd rather not discuss it." If the colleague persists, one may leave the scene entirely, as a last resort, and take the colleague aside later to discuss the incident further.

A non-supervisory employee who is aware of habitual confidentiality violations by a peer is often hesitant to "rat" on his colleague. Yet, this action may be necessary if all else fails. The individual must weigh his responsibility to the clients and the larger agency system against his natural desire not to get involved or get anybody "in trouble." He may have real insecurity about the probable actions of the supervisor or administrator should the employee be reported. Would the source of the complaint be kept confidential?

Social workers holding supervisory positions have a somewhat different responsibility when confidentiality violations come to their attention. Maintaining confidentiality ought to be a requirement for satisfactory job performance, and failure to do so should be cause for disciplinary action. Likewise, students in field placement who violate confidentiality should be counseled, and, if the pattern persists, the supervisor's concerns should be reflected in the performance evaluation process. Thus, for the protection of consumers served by the social work profession, the supervisor not only must intervene to stop the improper disclosure of confidential information while it is occurring but must also take action to prevent the offender from continuing his behavior.

If the individual violating confidentiality is a member of another profession, i.e., a physician or psychiatrist, the matter can become quite delicate. Public relations are important, and the careless colleague would not appreciate public embarrassment. It may be necessary to interrupt with a straightforward "Let's discuss this later" or to introduce a quick change of subject. Additional comments could be made later in private. Bold, creative individuals can often come up with unorthodox, though effective, measures to stop inappropriate discussions. For example, one such action was suggested by a mature social worker with years of experience in a medical setting who had spent many hours riding elevators crowded with physicians, patients, relatives, and others. Her answer for dealing with the problem of physicians who loudly air their patients' names, diagnoses, and terminal prognoses was simple and direct: "I'd step down good and hard on that doctor's foot. That'd change the subject in a hurry. I'd do it too—I really would!" Conscious awareness mixed with such creativity can go a long way toward resolving these situations.

Handling the Need to Talk About Confidential Material

Social workers are human beings first and social workers second. Thus, there *is* going to be a natural tendency and a desire to discuss confidential material. Professional helping persons come into contact with challenging, annoying, depressing, joyful, frustrating, and fulfilling situations almost daily. They will have strong emotional reactions to these experiences. Social workers must be empathic and capable of deep feelings in order to be effective; yet they are expected not to discuss or react to incidents that arouse these feelings. The most elementary principles of human behavior dictate that keeping these emotional reactions locked up inside is about as effective as trying to contain a bottled carbonated beverage that is being vigorously shaken—eventually something must give. Thus, confidentiality becomes an issue. To whom can the social worker safely ventilate reactions about confidential material without violating someone's privacy?

It is generally recognized that employees in an agency setting need to share information with one another as part of the service-delivery process. Such exchanges can take place without violating confidentiality if they involve only those persons who have a legitimate need to know, and if they are in the best interests of the client. Sharing in order to help a social worker be more effective in his professional role would certainly meet these criteria. Thus, in the course of such sharing, feelings and reactions can be safely ventilated to selected individuals within the agency. If the supervisor-supervisee relationship is warm, open, and trusting, the supervisor can serve as a sounding board for the practitioner's feelings. If the relationship is not conducive to such disclosures, the worker must turn elsewhere. Social work personnel and colleagues often "sound off" to one another, and this process can be legitimately combined with peer consultation if done in a professional manner. If the emotions being shared are negative and in response to a problem within the agency, the "sharer" will need to guard against reacting so strongly and so often that others are prevented from doing their work effectively.

The more that feelings and reactions can be ventilated within the agency-work setting, the less intense will be the need to verbalize to family and friends at night. If a social worker has a constantly impelling need to air confidences in both arenas, a close self-examination may be indicated to determine whether expectations need to be altered or other changes made in order to protect his clients' or agency's confidentiality.

3.   The Federal Privacy Act of 1974

While many of us are vaguely aware of something called the Privacy Act of 1974, precious few of us, even in the sophisticated professional community I represent, [know] much about the Privacy Protection Study Commission nor its interest in things state and local. [1]

Jerry A. Shroder

SEVERAL MAJOR PIECES OF LEGISLATION[2] have been passed in recent years which regulate the handling of record materials and confidential information in federally funded and administered programs. One, the Federal Privacy Act of 1974, clearly requires that the consumer have access to his records, and establishes exact procedures as to how this must be done. Such laws put into black and white "thou shalts" and "thou shalt nots" on issues which the social work profession has been debating for years.[3] The Privacy Act is destined to affect large numbers of social-work settings. While its regulations currently pertain to records maintained by federally funded and administered programs, it obviously lays the groundwork for extension to the private sector as well. The Privacy Act requires consumer education regarding the right of confidentiality and access to records, and these same consumers will undoubtedly expect similar rights from non-governmental agencies maintaining similar records. As a result, pertinent questions are being raised that are causing many private programs to review their existing confidentiality policies or set up new ones. In addition, the Privacy Act established the Privacy Protection Study Commission to determine whether

[1] Statement of Mr. Shroder, representing the Community Council of Greater New York, presented to the Privacy Protection Study Commission, Washington, D.C., January 13, 1977.

[2] For example, see the Freedom of Information Act, 5 U.S.C. 552. 1966; see also U.S., Department of Health, Education and Welfare, Office of the Secretary, "Privacy Rights of Parents and Students" (Part II), Final Rule on Education Records, *Federal Register,* (June 17, 1976), pp. 24662–24675.

[3] For an interesting and detailed history of the development of legal regulations as well as attitudes toward confidentiality, see Joseph T. Alves, *Confidentiality in Social Work* (Washington, D.C.: Catholic University of America Press, 1959). This is a doctoral dissertation available through University Microfilms, Ann Arbor, Michigan.

the existing record-keeping practices of local governmental and private programs need to be covered by the Privacy Act regulations. Hearings have
been held on this topic, and a wide variety of settings, both social-
service-oriented and private-industry, had an opportunity to present their
views. It appears very likely that private programs will soon come under
some type of federal regulation regarding confidentiality, record keeping
and consumer access.

Summary of the Federal Privacy Act of 1974

This law[4] was passed out of a concern that consumers were not adequately
informed of the records being maintained on them and were not able to
have full access to these files. The act pertains to federally funded and administered programs only, though some non-federal programs receiving
federal grant monies may have to abide by the regulations in the cases of
consumers receiving services through such monies. The Social Security Administration, Veteran's Hospitals, Supplemental Security Income (SSI) programs and others which employ social workers are affected. It is possible
that the act may undergo some changes as a result of the hearings before the
Privacy Protection Study Commission. A brief summary of the highlights
of the act is presented below; however, it should be borne in mind that certain aspects may change if the law is revised or amended.

The following general provisions are just that—broad guidelines only.
Individual federal programs were given a deadline for submitting a description of their system of records and for developing specific procedures to implement the Privacy Act guidelines. They were then required to publish this
information in the *Federal Register*. Issues of the *Register* during 1975 contain a large number of proposed and finalized implementation procedures.[5]

The definitions of two basic terms are important to the full understanding of this act:

"Record"—any item, collection, or grouping of information about an individual that is maintained by an agency, including, but not limited to, his
education, financial transactions, medical history, and criminal or employment
history and that contains his name, or the identifying number, symbol, or other

[4] Referred to as Public Law 93–579, 93rd Congress, December 31, 1974, Privacy Act of
1974. It amends Title V, United States Code by adding Section 552a. The Act was approved
December 31, 1974, and contains nine sections. Sections 3 and 4 are amendments which did not
take effect until September 1975, 270 days after the Privacy Act was enacted. (*Federal Register*
[October 8, 1975], Part V–VI)

[5] For example, see "Adoption of Notice of Systems of Records," Civil Service Commission, Privacy Act of 1974: *Federal Register,* Vol. 40, No. 226 (November 21, 1975), pp.
54356–54363; also see Public Welfare—Title 45 (Subtitle A), Department of Health, Education
and Welfare, General Administration, Part 5b—Privacy Act Regulation, *Federal Register,*
Vol. 40, No. 196 (October 8, 1975).

identifying particular assigned to the individual, such as a finger or voice print or a photograph. (Federal Privacy Act, §552a[a])

The "individual" on whom such a record might be maintained is:

a citizen of the U.S. or an alien lawfully admitted for permanent residence. (Federal Privacy Act, §552a[a])

Notice that this wording clearly includes records on employees as well as consumers served by the program.

1. *The individual on whom a record is maintained has the right to*
   a. find out what records are being maintained on him and how they are used and disseminated by the agency;
   b. prohibit those records which are to be used for a particular purpose in the agency from being used for any other purpose without the individual's written consent;
   c. have access to his records and bring with him a person of his choosing, whether as counsel or as support;
   d. have copies made of any or all of his records, though the agency may set a charge for this service;
   e. correct or amend his record as he feels necessary to render it complete and accurate.

2. *The agency must secure the individual's written consent before it can release information from that person's record to another person or agency.*
      However, there are some exceptions and situations when this written consent is *not* required:
   a. when information is being released or exchanged among employees in the agency who must use the record to carry out their duties;
   b. when information from the record is conveyed to researchers in disguised form so that no particular individual is identifiable;
   c. when the information is being released to another governmental agency for law-enforcement activity;
   d. in emergency situations where this release is necessary to protect the health or safety of an individual. *However*, notice of this disclosure must be sent to the last known address of the individual whose record-information is being released;
   e. when there is an appropriate court order (subpoena).

Publications pertaining to the Privacy Act are occasionally indexed by the *Federal Register.* For example, *Protecting your Right to Privacy—Digest of Systems of Records, Agency Rules, Research Aids,* Office of the *Federal Register,* National Archives and Records Service, General Services Administration (Washington, D.C.: Government Printing Office, no date—but appears to be February 1976). Also see the *"Federal Register* Privacy Act Publications: Table of Dates and Pages," *Federal Register,* Vol. 41, No. 21 (January 30, 1976), pp. 4710–4714.

There are eleven other exceptions, some of which are quite technical.

3. *When an agency makes a disclosure of information, it must keep records of*
   a. the date of the disclosure;
   b. the nature and purpose of the disclosure;
   c. the name and address of the person or agency to whom disclosure was made.
   d. In addition, (a) through (c) must be retained by the agency for a minimum of five years *or* the life of the record, whichever is longer.
   e. (a) through (c) must be available to the individual whose record is involved.
   f. The agency keeps note of all amendments or corrections made by the individual to his record. If the information involved has been disclosed to someone prior to the addition of the corrections or amendments, the agency must inform all persons to whom the disclosure was made of the additions or corrections.

4. *The individual has the right to correct or amend his record.*
   a. The individual has the right to request that this be done.
   b. The agency must respond in writing within ten working days after receipt of the request.
   c. The agency either must make the corrections within this time period, *or*
   d. the agency may inform the individual that it refuses to honor his request to make the changes and must state
      (1) the reason for the refusal;
      (2) procedures for the individual to request a review of the agency's decision to refuse to grant his request;
      (3) the name and business address of the head of the agency or his designee who is authorized to review the refusal decision.
   e. If the individual disagrees with the agency's decision to refuse to amend or correct his record, the agency has 30 days, from the date the individual requests a review of this decision, to complete the review and make a decision.
   f. When a disclosure is made regarding information in a record over which there has been a dispute, details surrounding the dispute, the individual's request, and the agency's decision must be released along with the information itself. This assures that the recipient of the information has the complete picture.

5. *Agencies must follow certain guidelines in gathering material for their records:*
   a. The agency must keep only information that is relevant and necessary for agency purposes.
   b. It must collect the information directly from the individual him-

self if it is information that might lead to negative decisions regarding federal benefits or rights.

c. The agency must inform those people from whom it collects information
   (1) by what authority the agency is allowed to gather the information;
   (2) whether the information can be disclosed to the individual whose record is involved;
   (3) the purposes for which the information is to be used;
   (4) the effects on the informant, if any, of not providing all or part of the requested information.

6. *The agency has a responsibility to set policies regarding the handling of records and the safeguarding of confidentiality.*
   a. There must be provisions for maintaining records with fairness to the individual.
   b. The agency must have provisions for making reasonable efforts to be certain of the accuracy, completeness, timeliness, and relevancy of any records before they are released.
   c. If a record is subpoenaed, the agency must make reasonable efforts to notify the individual on whom the record is maintained that this has occurred.
   d. The agency must establish rules of conduct for all persons handling any records and must provide training for them.
   e. There must be established safeguards—administrative, technical, and physical—to insure security and confidentiality of records.
   f. The agency must have a system for advising persons who inquire if the agency maintains any records regarding them.
   g. There must be times, places, and requirements specified for verifying the identity of individuals who ask to see their records.
   h. The agency must develop a procedure for disclosing the records to the individual, including special procedures, if necessary, for release of medical (including psychological) records pertaining to the person.
   i. There must be established procedures for reviewing requests from individuals to amend or correct their records.
   j. The agency must determine and set fees, if any, for making copies of records for the individual.

7. *If an adult individual has been declared incompetent and has a legally appointed guardian; or if a minor is involved, the legal guardian and/or the parents of the child can act on behalf of the individual whose record is involved.*

8. *There are situations where an agency is allowed to maintain records on an individual which it does NOT have to disclose to the individual:*
   a. Material that would reveal the identity of a source who gave the

information to the government under promise that identity of the source would be kept confidential does not have to be disclosed to the individual on whom the record is kept.

b. The agency does not have to disclose to the individual information which was gathered prior to the effective date of the Privacy Act *if* at the time an implied promise of confidentiality of the identity of the source was made.

c. An individual does not have to be given access to any information "compiled in reasonable anticipation of a civil action or proceeding."

d. Records maintained by the CIA do not have to be disclosed to the individual.

e. Records maintained by an agency concerned primarily with the enforcement of criminal laws do not have to be disclosed to the person.

9. *An agency cannot require an individual on whom it keeps records to disclose to the agency his or her Social Security number.*

a. No federal, state, or local governmental agency can deny any benefits or rights because a person refuses to give his Social Security number.

b. Any agency which requests a Social Security number from an individual must inform the person
   (1) whether giving this information is mandatory or voluntary;
   (2) under what authority it is being requested by the agency;
   (3) what use will be made of it.

c. There are exceptions whereby an agency *can* require an individual to provide his Social Security number:
   (1) when this is specifically required by federal law;
   (2) if Social Security number disclosure was required by the agency *prior to* January 1, 1975, in order to verify the identity of an individual.

10. *A Privacy Protection Study Commission is established which*

a. is appointed to monitor application of the Federal Privacy Act;

b. studies "data banks, automated data processing programs and information systems of governmental, regional, and private organizations to determine the standards in force for protection of personal information";

c. recommends additional legislative action as needed to protect privacy rights of the individual;

d. looks for violations of the Federal Privacy Act;

e. studies the information systems of governmental, regional and private organizations to determine the procedures in force for the protection of personal information. Following this, the Commission must recommend the extent, if any, to which the principles and/or requirements of the Privacy Act should be applied to those organizations not currently subject to them.

Draft Recommendations of the Privacy Protection Study Commission

The Privacy Protection Study Commission has concentrated its review efforts on the record-keeping practices of five public-assistance and social-service programs: Aid to Families with Dependent Children (AFDC), Medicaid, the social-services program authorized by Title XX of the Social Security Act, the Foodstamp program, and the Supplemental Security Income (SSI) program.[6] The Commission has not undertaken an equally detailed study of private social-service programs;[7] however, private as well as government-funded programs were invited to submit written statements in response to the Draft Recommendations and to appear at the public hearings for state and local government public-assistance and social-service agencies held on January 11–13, 1977, in Washington, D.C.

The Draft Recommendations[8] added several interesting concepts and proposed regulations to those already outlined in the Federal Privacy Act. Only the major and most controversial points are presented here in outline form:[9]

1. *In determining eligibility for services, agencies often collect information about applicants from collateral sources (third parties—i.e., banks, schools, neighbors, other agencies). This is permissible; however,*
   a. the agencies' policies regarding the collection and use of collateral information must be made known to the applicant;
   b. applicants for Title XX Social Services have a right to request that collateral contacts be handled in a manner that would not reveal the type of service the individual is applying for;
   c. applicants should be able to learn the sources of information obtained from third parties so they can insure its accuracy, trace inaccurate information back to its source, and correct it at that level if desired.

[6] The first four of these programs have not been under the jurisdiction of the Privacy Act; the S.S.I. Program has been since the act took effect.

[7] According to a comment by a representative of the Privacy Protection Study Commission office in Washington, the Commission is definitely concerned with private social-service programs, though it has not studied these as intensively.

[8] Published in the *Federal Register* (December 8, 1976).

[9] The Draft Recommendations will probably be revised by the time this text appears in print. Thus, this section is designed to illustrate some of the issues being considered which may eventually become part of state or federal legislation.

2. *Clients must have access to their own record materials:*
   a. Applicants and recipients who request a hearing on an adverse determination should have the right to inspect the contents of their case files prior to the hearing.
   b. Agencies should be allowed to adopt special procedures for the disclosure of medical records to consumers.
   c. Several key questions are raised for consideration, among them:
      (1) If a case file contains information about more than one individual, who should have access to the record and under what conditions?
      (2) When should a minor be allowed access and should parents or guardians be allowed access with or without the minor's consent?
3. *Agencies must maintain their records with "accuracy, relevancy, timeliness, and completeness" so that they do not cause inequities in determining eligibility for services.*
4. *Records and information about AFDC applicants and recipients can be disclosed to Child Welfare, Work Incentive, Child Support Enforcement, SSI, Medicaid, Title XX Social Services and Food-stamp programs without consumer consent.*
5. *When AFDC records are subpoenaed, the agency maintaining the record should bear the burden of contesting a subpoena compelling its disclosure. However, the subject of the record should also be notified when a subpoena is received, and given opportunity to contest it.*
6. *Public disclosure of the fact that an individual is an applicant for or a recipient of AFDC, and the amount received, should be prohibited.*
7. *There were some additional questions on which the Commission sought comment:*
   a. Should there be different disclosure regulations for different kinds of recorded information (i.e., medical-psychiatric records as opposed to financial information)?
   b. Should subjects of child-abuse reports be allowed to see and correct such reports?
   c. What legal obligations should be imposed on keepers of central child-abuse registries?
   d. What limits or regulations should be applied in the collection and disclosure of information used to locate absent parents?
   e. What additional regulations on the use of the Social Security number are needed?
   f. What special problems are presented by data-bank systems?
   g. Should the Privacy Protection Study Commission recommendations be implemented through federal statute, federal regulation, state law, or voluntary compliance?

h. "The Commission wishes to learn more about the impact that federal regulation has on the total record-keeping activities of private organizations maintaining records about clients whose services are funded privately, as well as those for whom federal funding has been secured. Do private organizations tend to apply the same kinds of safeguards to records about their private clients as they are legally obligated to extend to records about recipients of federally assisted programs?"[10]

Testimony of Social-Service Agencies Before the Privacy Protection Study Commission

The material generated from the Privacy Protection Study Commission public hearings mentioned above (January 1977) is too voluminous to present in detail here. However, a review of the testimony and a number of the submitted written statements[11] turned up some rather interesting responses to the Commission's Draft Recommendations. The material also documented, rather dramatically, the lack of consistency in approaches to maintaining confidentiality and handling disclosures among major social-service programs.

Most groups felt that the names of AFDC applicants and recipients should not be made public and agreed that outside disclosure of information about all consumers should take place only with client consent. This is generally accepted social work practice. However, the National Welfare Fraud Association opposes such thinking, feeling that

> . . . provision of the names of recipients and the amount of assistance given are part of the law, and such a change would be unfair to taxpayers, who have the right to know who is spending their money and in what amount.

Commenting on disclosures without client consent, the statement goes on:

> If we are concerned with the fraud and abuse inherent in our system now, as was the 94th Congress, we cannot place this kind of restriction on release of information. Furthermore, Federal law permits the disclosure of the names of recipients and the amounts they receive as long as the information is not used for commercial or political purposes.[12]

There was some disagreement as to whether a client's permission must be obtained for exchange of data between related governmental agencies.

[10] Taken from a copy of the "Draft Recommendations" obtained directly from the office of the Privacy Protection Study Commission (Washington, D.C.: Privacy Protection Study Commission, n.d.—but appears to be late 1976), p. 16.

[11] See the Bibliography for a list of those whose testimony and written statements were reviewed by the author.

[12] Statement by Dorothy M. Forney, National Welfare Fraud Association, Harrisburg, Pennsylvania, before the Privacy Protection Study Commission, January 13, 1977.

There was some concern over the fact that some of these programs operate under the Federal Privacy Act and others do not, thus creating inconsistencies and, in some cases, difficulty in obtaining needed information.

The matter of securing collateral information from third parties generated considerable response and much controversy. Some groups felt that "we shouldn't be using collateral sources in the first place—the *client* should be the primary source of information," while others argued that collateral information is essential to the eligibility process and necessary to prevent fraud. Some felt that the names of sources of collateral information should be protected while others insisted that this data, along with the content of information gathered, must be shared with the consumer. Some felt it was acceptable to use neighbors for information gathering or verification purposes "as long as their information was believed reliable," but others disagreed. Several agencies felt it would be impossible to request collateral data without revealing the service the individual was applying for, while others, such as drug and alochol programs, felt this requirement was necessary and could be met.

There was lack of agreement on who should have access to a record if it contains information on more than one family member. Most groups recommended that the head of household have access to the entire file; others felt that data on any given individual should be protected from perusal by other family members; and still others felt that everyone in the household should see everything in the record. There was also disagreement as to whether minors should be allowed access, and whether data on minors should be protected from disclosure to adults.

Most agencies recommended that social-service programs be permitted to establish special procedures for disclosure of medical-psychiatric information to consumers, so that possibly damaging material could be withheld if necessary. Some predicted an avalanche of requests from consumers seeking access to their files, thus creating an administrative nightmare. However, several groups which testified had already experienced openness of records at the state level; they admitted that they had entered into the policy with similar apprehensions, but said they found that their fears did not materialize. Client requests for access to records were very few in number. For example:

> We anticipated that far more clients would ask to see their record than we could possibly process. To our surprise, this multitude did not materialize. As we look back on it now, we attribute the lack of interest to the openness by which most of the counseling, therapy, and casework operations are carried out by our local agencies. Our agencies have kept clients reasonably well informed during our involvement with them . . . to the extent that most clients probably didn't feel the record would tell them anything they did not already know. Many clients have told us this.[13]

[13] Testimony of Dennis Erickson, representing the Minnesota Department of Public Welfare, before the Privacy Protection Study Commission, January 11, 1977.

Several groups expressed concern about old record materials gathered in the days when client access was denied:

> One area not addressed in the draft recommendations, but which is of concern to our agency, is the potential liability of the agency for material contained in case records prior to implementation of any changes in current regulations. For years agencies such as ours have had a number of untrained, short-term workers who may have written inappropriate subjective reports for inclusion in a case file. If these new regulations are approved, we feel we should have the right to either "purge" our records or to begin open access only after a given date. In addition, we strongly urge this commission to review the area of agency "liability" and we strongly recommend a "hold harmless" clause be included in the laws or regulations adopted. In addition, we would like to emphasize the excessive cost involved in any review and possible purging of records, and the impact of such a review on current workload. It would appear that to hold the agency harmless prior to a set date and to promulgate standards governing future record-keeping practices would be more cost-beneficial.[14]

The problem of client-employees is addressed by one large financial assistance program—how should these records be protected to maintain confidentiality? What special safeguards are needed? How can the agency avoid treating these individuals differently than they would non-employee recipients?

Most groups agreed that clients should be notified when subpoenas are received requesting material from their records. However, a few felt that clients would not be capable of responding meaningfully to the subpoena. For example:

> It is guessed that, by the very nature of the programs to which these recommendations would apply, the appropriate persons, or eligible applicants, would not understand or realize the import of a subpoena and would probably not have resources to contest it if they did.[15]

Most agencies that testified indicated that they were using computerized data systems of some type in their service-delivery process. Many recognized that such systems were essential and a reflection of modern technology; others expressed concern that such systems could lead to serious abuses of privacy because confidentiality of computerized information is so difficult to protect.

Several state-administered social-service programs described elaborate state laws dealing with the confidentiality of their record materials and felt that these regulations were already adequate. There was a concern that federal legislation might conflict with existing state laws. There were recommendations that all states set up their own regulations, or that all such laws be abolished so as not to conflict with federal regulations.

[14] This agency prefers to remain anonymous.

[15] Testimony of Maudine R. Cooper, Deputy Director, National Urban League, before the Privacy Protection Study Commission, January 12, 1977.

It is significant that there was little mention of existing privileged-communication statutes and the fact that some employees functioning within social-service programs have this coverage. How would these statutes fit in with Privacy Act regulations?

The wide diversity of opinions is perhaps best illustrated by the conflict over the basic necessity for preserving confidentiality of social-service information. One group feels that disclosures should take place rather freely:

> Access to records [by outsiders] *is* a deterrent to fraud. Removal or curtailment of such access will only increase fraud, and further handicap the poor.
>
> The proposed regulations would: subvert efforts to control fraud; restrict investigators and prosecutors; erode the power of subpoena.
>
> Therefore, if the regulations become effective or legislation is enacted as suggested, enforcement and prosecution will be seriously handicapped, the welfare rolls will further escalate and encourage the break-up of families, and the national debt will continue to rise.[16]

On the other hand, the National Clients' Council questions the ability of social workers to handle information responsibly and wants strong restrictions placed on the collection and disclosure of consumer data:

> We of the National Clients' Council hold that to be an applicant/recipient of any public benefit program in this country today is to be *forced* to surrender all privacy rights.
>
> We do not accuse welfare workers of being evil, venal, or unintelligent. They are poorly trained in most jurisdictions and they lack a code of professional conduct similar to that of the lawyer or a member of the voluntary organizations which attempt to guide the behavior of persons with graduate social work degrees. We do well to remember that the overwhelming majority of welfare department employees throughout the country are, at best, college graduates. There is no correlation between one's education and one's ethical standards. The only point we make here is that there is, very often, nothing except the individual worker's own personally arrived-at standard which dictates how information can, will, or should be given out.[17]

Finally, there is the ever-present concern that additional regulations will increase paperwork and hamper the delivery of services. Surprisingly, however, this viewpoint was expressed by a minority of those submitting statements to the Commission. The following comments are typical of this minority opinion:

> Some agencies feel that there is a general Federal unawareness that requirements placed on the voluntary sector can produce such a drain on resources and energy as to render the agency's service role self-defeating. That is, the agency may not be able to render the program it is funded to operate adequately, because such a high percentage of its energies are spent on being "accountable."

[16] Dorothy M. Forney, *op. cit.*

[17] Testimony of a representative of the National Clients' Council before the Privacy Protection Study Commission, January 12, 1977.

Several agencies have raised the question as to whether their capacity to do treatment or perform related services won't be severely jeopardized by expanded access to their records. What they are saying basically is that if judgment of their professional staff is constantly questioned, it will inevitably result in less use of professional judgment; ergo, less treatment.

. . . [A]gencies depending on some kind of professional judgments for their means of assisting people with problems could find themselves in a position in which they will face one of two alternatives, either: (1) dealing in placebo-type counseling, in which agency policy will result in instructions to otherwise skilled staff not to do anything which could possibly set in motion any form of litigation, thus reducing their treatment or counseling function to mere pap; or (2) finding themselves constantly being hauled into Court by litigious clients and that portion of the legal profession which will find in the added access to judgmental information new opportunities to institute contingency cases with "aggrieved" clients.[18]

Finally, one group which testified felt so strongly that the confidentiality rights of social-service consumers should be protected that it recommended a strong control mechanism:

The time has arrived at which an "information watchdog" agency is warranted. Such an agency should be well publicized and should receive complaints from persons who are the subject of records. It should be able to act on its own initiative, or at the prompting of interested groups, to assure that principles of privacy and fairness are being implemented.[19]

Summary Comments

Most of the issues presented in this chapter are discussed in detail elsewhere in this text. What stands out is the lack of agreement within the social work profession regarding the handling of confidential materials, including the issue of consumer access. The Federal Privacy Act imposes uniformity on federal settings, and it appears likely that many private and local government settings will also eventually be forced to comply with some type of state or federal guidelines. Although the National Association of Social Workers was represented at the hearings, it may be too late for the social work profession to implement its own internal regulatory mechanisms prior to federal intervention. The limited and not particularly representative number of social-service groups which testified or submitted statements to the Commission indicates a lack of interest in or awareness of the complexi-

[18] Jerry A. Shroder, Community Council of Greater New York, *op. cit.*

[19] Edward P. Scott, attorney for the Mental Health Law Project, Washington, D.C. Letter to the Privacy Protection Study Commission dated January 7, 1977.

ty and ramifications of the proposed regulations. The paucity of statements from fully private organizations perhaps reflects a failure to recognize that they, too, are being considered for inclusion under some type of federal privacy regulations. Can the social work profession achieve unified input into the upcoming legislation? This remains to be seen.[20]

[20] As this chapter is going to press, the 600-page official report of the Commission has just been published. It presents specific recommendations for maintaining confidentiality and concerns access to records in governmental financial assistance programs, files maintained by private employers and medical records as well as other areas. The recommendations are quite detailed but basically recommend the same kinds of rights and regulations presented in the Federal Privacy Act, with some modifications. The Commission's recommendations will probably be acted upon in 1978 or 1979, and some will undoubtedly become federal law. See *Personal Privacy in an Information Society* (Washington, D.C.: U.S. Government Printing Office, July 1977), and Privacy Protection Study Commission, "Final Recommendations of the Privacy Protection Study Commission as Contained in the Final Report" (Washington, D.C.: Privacy Protection Study Commission, n.d.). This is a summarized version of *Personal Privacy in an Information Society.*

4. Confidentiality of Case-Record Materials

We leave records behind us like litter—litter that is permanently attached to us, from which we can never shake free. Some call this an "information prison" in which an individual is bound by what he was and has done—not necessarily by what he now is or can be.[1]

Senator Sam Ervin, Jr.

IN ORDER TO STUDY THIS TOPIC, we must examine several concepts: (1) What exactly is a "record"? (2) Once a record exists, how should it be handled to safeguard confidentiality? and (3) Should there be social-service records at all?

What Is a "Case Record"?

In social work practice, a "case record" is usually a written document, often filed in a special folder. It contains recorded notes, correspondence, copies of pertinent forms, and other written materials concerning delivery of service to a client or client-group. With today's modern technology, this definition must now be expanded to include tape-recorded interviews, microfilms, videotapes, and computerized data storage as types of "records." Furthermore, records do not even have to be recorded to be considered records. At least one recent federal law regarding confidentiality of records has defined the term to mean "any information whether recorded or not. . . ."[2]

[1] Senator Sam J. Ervin, Jr., "Civilized Man's Most Valued Right," *Prism,* Vol. 2, No. 6 (June 1974), p. 16.

[2] "Department of Health, Education and Welfare, Public Health Service: Confidentiality of Alcohol and Drug Abuse Patient Records—General Provisions." Found in the *Federal Register*, Vol. 40, No. 127 (July 1, 1975), Part IV, page 27804, Section 2.11(o).

The Traditional Written Social Service Case Record

A case record is a compilation of papers which documents the sorrows, struggles, accomplishments, and joys of a human being. One wishes that some kind of built-in mechanism would cause it to self-destruct after a certain time period, but unfortunately no such device exists. As a result, most agencies retain written records for at least three to five years, with retentions of five to ten years not at all unusual. Some settings have no guidelines for record retention and just keep them until they run out of storage space. Many large service-delivery systems have a central storage warehouse, bulging at the seams with yellowing records that the system no longer needs or has room to store. Some agencies resort to microfilming as a more expedient method of long-term record storage and/or feed the information into computers for specialized purposes. One wonders if the average grass-roots–level social worker is sufficiently aware of the permanence of what he is saying about another human being in such files. [3]

Much highly personal material which finds its way into social-service records could become the focal point of confidentiality violations or various legal issues. This is one reason why verbatim ("process") recordings should never be kept in a case record. Should that file be subpoenaed by the courts, such material would have to be included—it cannot be removed at the last minute. Immeasurable damage could be done through improper handling or misinterpretation of process-recorded interviews. Although worker and supervisor may want to work with these papers for a time, they should be returned after use to the supervisor, who should then see that they are destroyed. A summarized version of what took place in the process-recorded interviews is then placed in the official case record.

Social-service files often contain reports that were obtained from other agencies or members of other disciplines, perhaps furnished as part of an inter-agency exchange-of-information process or sent upon specific request. In either event, once this material finds its way into a given social worker's hands, that person becomes responsible for maintaining its confidentiality. These reports often come with a "confidential" stamp, clearly mandating that the receiving agency is not to pass them on to a third party. If the material is coming from a federally funded or administered program, a written statement may accompany the report, specifying that it is against federal law to disclose the contents to anyone else.

---

[3] In spite of the importance of proper recording, it is interesting to note that a recent survey found only two schools of social work reporting that they teach techniques of social work recording in the classroom. Helen Pinkus, "Recording in social work," *Encyclopedia of Social Work* (Washington, D.C.: National Association of Social Workers, 1977), p. 1166. Even though a large number of schools of social work were contacted in the survey, only a small percentage responded. This might indicate lack of interest in or involvement with recording, or simply a disinclination towards completing the questionnaire.

Physically Safeguarding the Written Record

Agencies and individual practitioners must have some kind of mechanism for guarding their case records. Federal programs have no choice—the Federal Privacy Act of 1974 requires them to

> establish appropriate administrative, technical, and physical safeguards to insure the security and confidentiality of records and to protect against any anticipated threats or hazards to their security or integrity which could result in substantial harm, embarrassment, inconvenience, or unfairness to any individual on whom information is maintained.[4]

The provisions regulating confidentiality of alcohol and drug-abuse patient records for programs which are federally administered or receiving federal funds to provide services to these persons are quite specific:

> Appropriate precautions must be taken for the security of records to which this part applies. Records containing any information pertaining to patients shall be kept in a secure room, or in a locked file cabinet, safe, or other similar container when not in use.[5]

The National Association of Social Workers has not yet provided basic guidelines for social workers to apply uniformly. Thus, it is necessary for private practitioners, agencies, and schools to draw upon their own experience and knowledge to establish steps for physically preserving confidentiality of record materials. In the absence of clearly defined guidelines, the following procedures are suggested:

1. All records should be kept in a locked file-cabinet or in a room with a secure, preferably deadbolt, lock. Any door that can be opened with nail-file or knife should not be safeguarding case records. If an employee or student has an office in a high-traffic area, confidential notes and materials must be kept out of sight whenever the person is away from his desk.

2. Problems can arise when partly finished case-record material and notes are left lying on top of the desk at the end of the work day. Cleaning personnel are active in many offices after working hours and others could easily obtain access to confidential material. Likewise, the busy supervisor who is called away from his desk while in the middle of writing an employee's performance evaluation may return to find that someone who came into the office looking for him eagerly read it while awaiting his return.

3. No case-record materials should ever be taken home. Period. Unfortunately, this guideline is frequently violated. Supervisors are often the

---

[4] Federal Privacy Act of 1974. Public Law 93-579, December 31, 1974 (effective 9-27-75), Section 552a (e)-10.

[5] "Confidentiality of Alcohol and Drug Abuse Patient Records," *op. cit.,* p. 27808, Section 2.17.

worst offenders—and they should know better. The number of mishaps that can occur seem to multiply geometrically once the file leaves the security of the office: auto accidents and theft while in transit, curious family members reading it unknown to the worker, young children using it for their latest art project, etc. It can be left behind on the bus, papers can fall out of the record while it is being carried down the street, and so on *ad infinitum.*[6]

4. All social-work settings should have clearly established regulations as to who in the agency can have access to case records, and there must be some way of making certain that everyone, whether he is allowed access or not, is acquainted with the policy. Students and newly-hired practitioners should become familiar with the guidelines early in their experience so they do not unknowingly allow some unauthorized person access to files.

5. Confidentiality violations can occur when friends and relatives of staff members come to visit them at the office. These persons may be kept waiting while their social-worker friend finishes a phone call or completes a recorded entry. During that time, the guest may inadvertently overhear confidential conversation and perhaps even read confidential material. The practitioner should ask the visitor to wait in a public waiting area or outside the office if necessary.

6. Case records and the information in them must not be used for any purpose other than that mandated by the agency. This seems all too obvious; however, students and clerical staff have been known to duplicate selected records or segments to gather "interesting material for class" or for other unofficial purposes. This activity is a gross violation of the individual's right to privacy and in some settings would be a violation of federal law, punishable by fine and/or imprisonment.

7. The social worker must avoid having a client's case record sitting conspicuously on the desk when interviewing someone. If the content is not being shared with the client at the moment, the record's presence can create a real barrier to the interview as the consumer ponders silently, "I wonder what's written in there about me?"[7]

8. There should be definite guidelines specifying how long records should be kept before they are destroyed. Otherwise, a policy of "Well, we

[6] At a workshop on confidentiality and recording, an agency administrator volunteered how he had learned the hard way the perils of removing records from the office. He had taken a rather thick record home to work on it, and had an armful of other things to carry besides. When he reached his car he set the case record on the roof while fumbling for his keys. He unlocked the door, got in, and drove away. Only after traveling some distance did he suddenly realize that he had scattered loose pages of his case record over several city blocks.

[7] Security problems can also arise. In one instance a relative who wanted to create problems for the client contacted the social worker seeking the individual's address. The worker dutifully pulled the case record to read up on the situation, then invited the relative into his office for an interview (with the case record on the desk). During the conversation, the worker received a phone call and excused himself to take the call in another office. Upon his return, both the relative and the case file were gone. The record was never found.

just keep records 'til there get to be too many floating around, and then we weed some out" tends to prevail.

DESTRUCTION OF CASE-RECORD MATERIALS

Confidential case files cannot be emptied into the nearest wastebasket and carted off to the garbage dump as would other waste materials. Records should be put through a shredding machine, doused with water to render them illegible, or burned. There are private businesses that specialize in the destruction of confidential materials. Some large settings send records out to be microfilmed, and the firm performing this service then physically disposes of the old files. But shredding machines are expensive, and burning is not handy for agencies which do not have their own incinerators; thus, disposal can be difficult for smaller social-service programs and the private practitioner. Many settings simply lack any guidelines for destruction of outdated case materials, and even those having such regulations can run into embarrassing difficulties if the operation is not closely supervised.[8] The average social worker will seldom have to grapple with this problem individually. Supervisory and administrative personnel usually work in cooperation with clerical staff to effect record destruction. They should be prepared to answer sincere inquiries as to how this process occurs in their particular setting.

Confidentiality Guidelines for Students Who Take Case Material from the Field into the Classroom

Unfortunately, many agencies simply have no guidelines for students to follow. Likewise, many schools of social work either do not cover this topic at all in their curriculum or do so belatedly—after the student is already in field placement. Students should inquire whether any policies exist in their agency. These should be studied before a situation arises where the student wishes to use agency record materials in the classroom. Some basic guidelines are presented here, but they should be used in addition to, rather than as a substitute for, any guidelines stipulated by the student's school:

1. All names of clients, relatives, and significant others mentioned by name in a case record or recording must be altered. Fake names or incorrect

---

[8] In one instance, a firm was engaged to haul hundreds of old records to the incinerator for destruction. A large box of records fell off the truck en route. The mishap was not discovered until some time later when concerned passers-by began contacting the administrator with reports of "Look what I found—does it belong to you—I don't think it should be lying in the street!"

initials can be used. If names are changed rather than simply erased or obliterated, a notation should appear clearly indicating that this has been done.

2. If the interview or case material concerns a highly unusual or much-publicized situation that could be identified easily even after the client's name has been changed, the nature of the primary diagnosis or presenting problem, proper nouns, and certain identifying information may also need alteration. True, this may affect the reality of the situation and make it more difficult for the student to adequately present what really happened, but if it comes to a choice between presenting accurate recordings in the classroom and preserving the privacy and confidentiality of the consumers served, the client's needs *must* take priority.

3. Material of a highly confidential or incriminating nature should not be taken into the classroom at all. If a student is not certain whether his recording fits into this category or not, he should consult his field instructor for guidance.

4. Process recordings are the property of the agency and should not be copied or retained by the student. They should be turned in to the student's field instructor when their usefulness has ended or at the termination of field placement and should be stored separately from the official case record.

5. All material which students wish to take into the classroom should be reviewed first by the field instructor to insure that proper measures have been taken to preserve confidentiality.

6. Tape and video-recorded material cannot be adequately disguised to preserve confidentiality. Thus, the client's permission must be secured before a student takes it into the classroom. Furthermore, certain technical steps should be taken to conceal identity even when the client has given permission for use of the material. Students should seek specific direction from their supervisor.

Material That Should Not Be Recorded

Regardless of the type of recording method used,[9] there are certain kinds of data which simply do not belong in black-and-white in any case record. One reason would be the potential use of such material against the best interests of the client or the agency should the record be subpoenaed. Second, the possible effect upon the client himself should he see the entries must be considered. Thus, the following kinds of material should not be found in case records:

[9] For a comprehensive discussion of techniques of social-work recording, see Suanna J. Wilson, *Recording: Guidelines for Social Workers* (New York: Free Press, forthcoming).

1. Process (narrative) recordings should not be stored in a case record, even temporarily.

2. Any information regarding a client's political, religious, or other personal views does not belong in a case record *unless* it has direct and very important bearing on the treatment process.

3. Intimate, personal details which have little or no relevance to the helping process should be omitted.

4. Extreme details about a physical illness are usually not recorded in social-work files. Consider the following example, extrapolated from an actual case record in a public-welfare setting (names and identifying details have been changed in all quoted examples to preserve confidentiality):

> When I visited Mrs. Hollis, she told me she had just gotten discharged from the hospital after having a mastectomy. She told me that her nipple had been swollen and painful for the past several weeks, and she had a vaginal discharge that smelled terrible.

Social workers may record client statements regarding physical problems in charts to be read by medical staff. Such entries often aid in interdisciplinary communication and so could be quite pertinent. Otherwise, a brief summary style of recording would be more appropriate.

5. "Gossipy" information about other clients does not belong in a case record. It is not unusual for persons receiving the services of a large agency to know one another and to occasionally try to convince the worker, for example, that "I should get more money than that Mr. Smith down the street who just drinks up all his welfare check." The beginning worker or student often includes these kinds of remarks along with more relevant material in his eagerness to achieve totally accurate and complete recording.

6. Recording too much "process" must be avoided. The worker's plans and the results are more important than the detailed steps gone through in accomplishing something. This is especially true if one is describing a routine service that many staff perform repeatedly for their clients. When a worker is totally absorbed in resolving a problem, he may easily become enamored with his success in overcoming the hurdles and want to see the success story recorded in detail. Consider the following highly typical example of this kind of recording:

> Mrs. Atkins told me she had applied to get a Social Security number but had not heard from the Social Security office yet. I said I would contact them and find out about her application. On 12-5-74 I called and talked to the secretary, Mrs. Brown, who told me that the man I needed to talk to was Mr. Alvarez. I called his office but he was not in and was supposed to return in a half hour. I called later that day around 2 P.M. and reached Mr. Alvarez who said he would check on it and call me back. On Wednesday he called and said that Mrs. Atkins had applied for a Social Security number on 10-29-74, and one was being issued to

her and that she should receive it in the mail within the next 10 days. I thanked him and then called Mrs. Atkins and gave her this information.

Of what significance will all this detail be six months or three years from now? I myself confess to having filled many public-welfare case records with this type of recording in my early days of social work practice. Only when the tables were turned and supervisory responsibilities demanded a reading of such entries did full realization of their awfulness really sink in.

The fact that contact was made with the Social Security office in behalf of Mrs. Atkins is important enough to be recorded somehow. However, it should be presented in a very brief, summary style:

> Mrs. Atkins indicated she had applied for a Social Security number in August and had not heard any more regarding it. On 12-5-74 I talked with Mr. Alvarez, Social Security representative, who advised that Mrs. Atkins was being issued a Social Security number and would receive it by December 20th. I informed the client of this.[10]

7. Problems and frustrations in contacting and relating to other social workers, agencies, and members of other disciplines do not belong in writing. The case record must not become a showcase for all the worker's gripes and frustrations as he experiences difficulties, personality clashes, or delays in attempting to provide service to someone. Likewise, the worker must refrain from putting into writing his criticisms of the operation of his own agency's service-delivery system. The case record is not the place to document these problems. They are dealt with more effectively by bringing them to the attention of supervisory or administrative staff so that proper evaluation and action can be taken. When staff and students enter such problems into case records, it is usually an indication that the practitioner has become quite emotional over the incident and is therefore using his recording as an inappropriate outlet. He may also have clearly sided with the client against "the system" and be handling his feelings ineffectively. If a genuinely unpleasant incident has occurred, what is usually the most important and appropriate thing to record is the effect upon the consumer. The following is an example of inappropriate recording:

> I tried contacting Dr. Smith in the morning in order to discuss my patient's medical situation. When I talked to the ward secretary, she said that Dr. Smith is notoriously bad about responding to messages and she thinks it is because he just doesn't care about his patients. He was supposed to call me back by noon, but he never did. My client kept asking what was taking me so long in getting in touch with his doctor. I left another note on the ward for Dr. Smith to call me but he still didn't reply. Finally, my supervisor suggested I talk to his attending physician so he could get after Dr. Smith to return my call.

[10] It is important to record the name of the person contacted—if Mrs. Atkins fails to get her Social Security card as promised, someone will need to follow up on it. Notice that exact dates, rather than days of the week or time-periods, are recorded. It is also important to note that the plans were conveyed to the client.

This rather unpleasant experience might have been better said as:

> I had considerable difficulty in reaching Dr. Smith, and I can understand now why my client also gets frustrated trying to contact him.

Another example of inappropriate recording is the following entry, written by a busy social worker assigned to the emergency room of a hospital:

> Mr. Jones showed up again today in the ER. I had sent him to the XYZ Boarding Home yesterday and they had agreed to take him. Today they sent him back in with a note saying they feel he needs to be in a nursing home. I don't know how many times I've explained to them that this emergency room is *not* a hotel for people awaiting nursing home placement. I called Harry Bowden at the Boarding Home and explained this once more. After some grumbling, he finally agreed to take Mr. Jones back until we could arrange for him to go into a nursing home.

One wonders how Mr. Jones would feel is he were to exercise his right to see this medical record! A better way of describing this activity might have been:

> Mr. Jones was sent to the XYZ Boarding Home on 3-18-73. On 3-19-73 the Home returned him to the ER, expressing their feeling that he needed to be in a nursing home. Following a contact with Mr. Bowden at the boarding home, arrangements were made for patient to return there until we can arrange placement elsewhere.

Once again such inappropriate entries clutter up the record with unnecessary details, and take excess time to read. They could also be of considerable interest should legal action be initiated for some reason against any of the parties involved. Most social workers would not relish, for example, having to appear on the witness stand to testify that "the ward secretary said that Dr. Smith didn't care about his patients" should Dr. Smith be sued for malpractice at a later date. One way to avoid such unpleasantness would be to concentrate on recording direct observations and substantiated facts rather than hearsay information.

8. Any details which might be misinterpreted or misused by others in the agency with formal or informal access to the case record are better left unrecorded or at least altered. This can be a problem in multi-disciplinary settings where non-professionals as well as skilled practitioners may all be handling the record for various purposes.

9. Any information that could conceivably be used against the client in a court of law should not be recorded. This is a highly complex area, and recorders are encouraged to study it further. Social workers practicing in states which do not grant them the legal right of privileged communication need to be especially cautious, as virtually all records (those maintained both by them individually and by their agencies) could be successfully subpoenaed and revealed in court should the right occasion arise.

10. Material that could be damaging to the client if he were to exercise his right to read his record should be omitted.

11. Entries that might be incriminating to the agency should the client bring a suit for any reason must not be recorded. Most agencies and their attorneys will insist that staff follow this practice. For example, if a consumer tells a medical social worker that "Dr. Jones prescribed the wrong medicine—the nurse told me so—and that's how I got sick last night," this might be brought to the attention of pertinent supervisory staff, but should not become part of a written record. Extreme discretion must be used, and students or inexperienced practitioners should seek supervisory guidance on how to handle these situations. *If in doubt, don't record it!* Occasionally, social workers will become involved in cases where it is already known that a suit is pending against the agency, institution, or individual staff member. The practitioner should seek approval from his supervisor before making any entries, and he may work closely with administrative staff and agency attorneys before taking any controversial actions or recording material related to the suit.

If the agency is engaging in a questionable practice or has been careless in providing services, the staff member must determine the best way of bringing it to the attention of the proper authorities. He may decide to ignore the usual policies regarding recording and document the incident in official agency records. However, if he choses to do this, he must be prepared to bear the repercussions, which could range from a verbal scolding by a superior to loss of job. On the other hand, some settings (e.g. medical hospitals) require that "incident reports" be prepared and submitted to administration whenever an irregularity, a mishap or "an error" occurs. Thus, staff are provided with a very specific mechanism for documenting what happened and should not use patient charts or case records for this purpose.

Tape and Video Recordings

The Federal Privacy Act's definition of a "record" is worth reiterating:

> Any item, collection, or grouping of information about an individual that is maintained by an agency . . . that contains his name, or the identifying number, symbol or other identifying particular assigned to the individual, *such as a finger or voice print or a photograph* [emphasis added].[11]

Since tape and video recordings obviously come under the scope of a case record, many of the principles already described for the written record must apply to them also, as demonstrated in previous sections above. However, tapes do present some unique problems because of the fact that the interviewee's actual voice and image is being recorded, which makes such mate-

[11] Federal Privacy Act of 1974, Section 552a(a)4.

rial much more difficult to disguise. A person's voice is recognizable and very difficult to alter on tape. Video recordings are almost impossible to disguise unless this is carefully planned and carried out during the filming (the individual's face and identifying features might be masked or simply not shown). It would appear that the only way to avoid legal and ethical problems in the use of these devices is to always obtain the person's permission to record his interview or activity, and to fully inform him of exactly what will be recorded, how it will be used, and who will be seeing or hearing it. As long as the material will be used only within the agency, there may be no further need for clearances. However, if it is to be taken into a classroom or shared with persons outside the program, specific written permission for doing so must be secured from the client and the interviewer.

Several important factors and incidents have suggested the importance of this requirement. One is the federal Privacy Act legislation which demands that consumers have control over the use and release of their record material. Some less obvious situations can occur, however. In a letter to the editor of a journal, one physician described the common practice of filming childbirth in the delivery room for use in training physicians. Patients often did not know this was occurring and thus did not have the opportunity to give or deny consent. The physician urged consideration of the patient's right to confidentiality and the legal ramifications of this activity.[12]

Benjamin Youngdahl, in a letter to the editor of the *Social Work Journal*,[13] raised several questions for the American Civil Liberties Union to respond to. First, he wanted to know whether it would be a violation of confidentiality for students to observe interviews behind a one-way mirror without the client's knowledge and consent. Second, what if only the sound coming through the mirror microphone were to be tape-recorded, with identifying data changed, and the recording then used in the classroom for social-work student education? In both situations, the Civil Liberties Union responded that this type of disclosure "would constitute a serious invasion of the client's privacy" because he was unaware that the interview was being observed or recorded.

The National Federation of Societies for Clinical Social Work, in its "Ethical Standards for Clinical Social Workers," includes a statement that the clinical social worker must inform the client of the purposes of the interview and the ways in which the information will be used. The clinical social worker also

> makes known to the prospective client the important aspects of the potential relationship that might affect the client's decision to enter into the relationship.

These include recording of the interview, use of interview material for train-

[12] H. C. McLaren. Letter to the Editor entitled "Confidentiality in Gynaecology," *Lancet,* Vol. 1 (February 16, 1972), p. 487.

[13] Benjamin E. Youngdahl, Letter to the Editor entitled "A Civil Liberties Problem?," *Social Work Journal,* Vol. 5, No. 4 (October 1960), pp. 109–110. See also the reply by Alan Reitman, Associate Director of the Civil Liberties Union, pp. 109–110.

ing purposes, and observation of the interview by other persons. Furthermore,

> when confidential information is to be used for professional educative purposes, every effort should be made to conceal the true identity of the individuals discussed.[14]

A recent article on the use of videotape in social work programs presented the following guidelines for maintaining confidentiality:

> Ethical and legal issues are of major importance in programming which includes videotape recording. Informed consent of all participants (staff and client) is always required. The need to avoid any appearance of coercion dictates that service may not be withheld for refusal to be videotaped.
>
> Protection of privacy should be maintained. Recorded tapes must be stored securely and their content erased after they have been used for an intended purpose. Participants should be informed of who will have access to their videotapes and have the right to see—and order erased or edited—any information they do not wish shown to others. This right is especially important if videotapes can be subpoenaed for legal processes.[15]

Thus, it would appear that video and tape recordings can be made without violating confidentiality if (1) the client is informed that this process is occurring and how the results will be used; (2) his written permission (informed consent) is secured for making the recording; (3) his specific written consent is obtained each time the material is to be released to other persons; (4) his identity is disguised (*unless* the client gives specific written permission to use the material as is); (5) he has the right to see or hear the finished product to either approve it for use or make corrections and deletions; (6) permission for recording and use of the material is also obtained from the interviewer or other involved staff members; and (7) tapes are stored securely. Tapes should be erased as soon as they are no longer useful so they cannot become the subject of a subpoena or other action that might not work to the client's benefit.

Computerized Data Storage

It has been estimated that the average American is the subject of ten to twenty dossiers—both governmental and private.[16] A special Senate Constitutional Rights Subcommittee discovered the existence of over 900 different

[14] "News of the Societies: National Federation of Societies for Clinical Social Work: Ethical Standards of Clinical Social Workers," *Clinical Social Work Journal,* Vol. 2, No. 4 (Winter 1974), p. 313.

[15] David Katz, "Videotape Programming for Social Agencies," *Social Casework,* Vol. 56, No. 1 (January 1975), p. 50.

[16] Verne R. Kelley and Hanna B. Weston, "Civil Liberties in Mental Health Facilities," *Social Work Journal,* Vol. 19, No. 1 (January 1974), pp. 48–54.

data banks containing personal information in the federal government alone.[17] In addition, as of 1974, there were enough individual records in the federal government's files to provide at least five for every living American.[18] A bibliography for the brief period from 1965 to 1967 listed more than 300 references regarding all aspects of the problem of privacy in the computer age.[19]

The National Association of Social Workers in its policy statement on information utilization and confidentiality sums up the problem rather well:

> The "Big Brother" of Orwell's fantasy is becoming a reality a decade sooner than he had foreseen. In this context, officially sanctioned governmental invasions of privacy, the compilation of "enemies" lists, the abuse of FBI functions, the violations of IRS information files, CIA excursions into private lives, the revelation of insurance company data exchange banks, of credit blacklisting, and of countless other intrusions into the personal affairs of virtually every citizen, is cause for alarm. The danger of even greater abuses—deliberate or inadvertent—in collection, maintenance, and utilization of personal data by government and industry, pose a threat to our basic liberties of unprecedented dimensions.[20]

Business and industry, the federal government, and social-service agencies are making widespread use of this latest technological wonder. Perhaps in social work the earliest predecessor was the "social-service exchange." While it did not use computerization, this was a method for storing basic data on clients so that it could be readily available to a network of agencies. Similar practices under various names are in use today,[21] but they are much more massive and far-reaching due to computerization.

A quick review of the current literature in various disciplines makes it evident that there is much concern about confidentiality regarding such records and some genuine cause for alarm. In 1972, two social workers lost their jobs because they refused to feed into a massive computerized data system detailed information regarding the diagnoses and history of psychiatric patients, including criminal and sex offenders. The workers in ques-

---

[17] Sam J. Ervin, Jr., *op. cit.,* p. 16.

[18] *Ibid.,* p. 17.

[19] Annette Harrison, "The Problem of Privacy in the Computer Age: An Annotated Bibliography" (Santa Monica, Calif.: The Rand Corporation, December 1967).

[20] NASW, "Policy on Information Utilization and Confidentiality," Policy adopted at the National Association of Social Workers 1975 Delegate Assembly, May 30–June 3, 1975, Washington, D.C., p. 1. See Appendix B-1.

[21] For example, in 1946 there were 320 social service exchanges in the United States. Even though the number had decreased to 175 by 1962, they still exist today in one form or another. The social work literature of the 1940's and 1950's is heavily laden with articles discussing the merits and hazards of the social service exchange and many expressed virtually the same concerns regarding confidentiality that the profession is grappling with today. Freda A. Reinitz, "The Social Service Exchange and the Challenge of the '60's," *Journal of Social Work Process,* Vol. 13 (1962), p. 52. See also Charlotte Towle, "The Client's Rights and Use of the Social Service Exchange," *Social Service Review* (March 1949), pp. 15–20.

tion refused to cooperate because no effort had been made to insure the confidentiality of the information once it got into the system; no one had defined who would be authorized to have access to the information—in fact, there were no written rules or regulations governing access. No means were established for identifying those persons who sought access to the computerized data, nor was there any mechanism for social workers who fed data into the computer to inform their clients about the use made of it. Finally, there were no limitations set on the potential use of the data.[22]

The use of computerized data systems is difficult to contest legally, and persons seeking to bring about changes to protect consumer confidentiality must be prepared to present very specific data in support of their concerns. In a recent case before the Supreme Court of New York State, several physicians and a social worker affiliated with a crisis-center program brought suit against the state's Department of Mental Hygiene. They had been required to send patient names and other identifying data to a computerized data system used by the state. The plaintiffs

> sought a declaration that the use of such a centralized computerized system, without adequate safeguards, is violative of section 15.13 of the Mental Hygiene Law, the doctor-patient privilege and plaintiffs' constitutional right to privacy.[23]

The plaintiffs asked that the use of the system be discontinued and that all data already stored in the computer be destroyed. The Court ruled that "plaintiffs' cause of action, as alleged, is without merit" and concluded that

> [the] action of Department of Mental Hygiene in maintaining computerized records concerning psychiatric out-patients did not violate patients' right of privacy, patient-physician privilege or right of hospital staff personnel to practice their profession.[24]

Apparently the plaintiffs lacked the specifics necessary to support their claim. However, a dissenting opinion expressing concern about the majority decision of the court was recorded:

> It would be an unquestionable denial of justice to force plaintiffs to wait until a leak in the allegedly confidential system costs them their jobs or worse, or to dissuade a potential patient from seeking needed psychiatric counseling for fear of this computerized system, merely to afford them a factual basis on which to oppose summary judgment.[25]

A special Health, Education, and Welfare "Secretary's Advisory Committee on Automated Data Systems" submitted a report in 1973 stating that

---

[22] "Must Social Workers be Informers Too?," *NASW News* (December 1972).

[23] *Volkman v. Miller*, 383 N.Y.S2d 95 (Supreme Court, May 13, 1976), p. 95.

[24] *Ibid.*, pp. 95, 96.

[25] *Ibid.*, p. 97.

they found no consistent body of law to regulate computerized data systems and recommended special laws to protect privacy. The committee's survey of various states showed that most collected data fully identified individual clients while other states used a coding system. Some states had clients give signed permission to release information to the computer, while others did not (in these cases clients did not even realize that they had become part of a computerized data bank).[26] At least one author has observed that other nations are much more progressive than the United States in enacting specific legislation designed to protect the confidentiality of data-bank information.[27] It seems we have just begun to become aware of the problem, and protective measures are in their infancy.

Today's data-bank systems are so massive that the social-service exchanges of two decades ago seem inconsequential by comparison. For example, a ten-state computerized information system was developed several years ago for storage of data regarding psychiatric patients (MSIS—Multi-State Information System).[28] The planners were aware of many of the potential confidentiality problems and took elaborate steps to prevent unauthorized access to or disclosure of information. The built-in safeguards were quite specific. Each participating facility had access only to the information it had stored. The computer recorded every transaction occurring in the system—both input and output. Guards were posted twenty-four hours a day at the computer. A special state law specifically declared all records of the MSIS system confidential and specified that its records could not be subpoenaed by any court. The law denied governmental inquirers—i.e., state auditors and investigators—access to the files. All records became private corporate records and were removed from any connections that might cause them to be considered state, governmental, or public in any way. One person was designated to do an annual review of the system to make certain it was operating properly. MSIS was permitted to release data for research as long as all personal identifying data was removed.

The precautions certainly seem elaborate. However, as might be expected, the system has come under criticism. One important concept appears to be totally missing from the description of the system's safeguards: Is the client informed that data on him is being fed into the MSIS? Does he know how this information is being used and does *he* have access to it?

It has been suggested that computerized data should be collected in unidentifiable form, thus eliminating the need for elaborate coding devices and security systems. Each agency would code the information before sending it to the data bank and it alone would know how to decipher the code to

[26] Verne R. Kelley and Hanna B. Weston, "Computers, Costs, and Civil Liberties," *Social Work,* Vol. 10, No. 1 (January 1975), pp. 15–19.

[27] F. Holton, "What Other Nations are Doing to Protect Personal Information," *Prism,* Vol. 2, No. 6 (June 1974), pp. 60–66.

[28] William J. Curran, Eugene M. Laska, Honora Kaplan, and Rheta Bank, "Protection of Privacy and Confidentiality," *Science,* Vol. 182 (November 23, 1973), pp. 797–801.

retrieve the identity of any given individual. Kelley and Weston in a recent article in *Social Work Journal* outlined a number of guidelines for preserving the confidentiality of computerized systems:

1. Account to funding sources in a way such that collection of identifying data isn't required.
2. Identify all data by a code number known only to the center sending in the information. Do not use Social Security numbers for coding.
3. Get the client's permission to send the data to the computer system and inform him of the purpose for which it will be used.
4. Place a copy of the signed release in the consumer's record along with the name of the professional responsible for releasing the information.
5. Release information to third party payers only with the signed permission of the client. The consumer should receive treatment regardless of whether he signs or not.
6. Erase the computer information when its purpose is over.
7. Assign administrative responsibility for giving and receiving computer information to a professional who is bound by professional ethics.
8. Protect the data by laws and safeguards, and exercise control over who uses the information.[29]

NASW's Policy declaration set up similar, though not quite as comprehensive, guidelines:

There is a need for adoption of the principles of a Code of Fair Information Practice along the lines recommended in 1973 by HEW's Advisory Committee on Automated Personal Data Systems. NASW therefore recommends that, as appropriate, legislation be enacted, regulations promulgated and policies adopted to ensure that:

a. there be no personal data record-keeping systems whose very existence is secret
b. there be a way for an individual to find out what information about him is in a record and how it is used
c. there be a way for an individual to prevent information about him that was obtained for one purpose from being used or made available for other purposes without his consent
d. there be a way for an individual to correct or amend a record of identifiable information about him
e. efforts be made to curb the proliferation of universal identifiers, including use of Social Security numbers, wherever not currently mandated by law.
f. any organization creating, maintaining, using, or disseminating records of identifiable personal data must assure the reliability of the data for their intended use and must take precautions to prevent misuse of the data.[30]

[29] Verne R. Kelley and Hanna B. Weston, *op. cit.* Articles on this topic are extremely rare in the social work literature, though they can be found by the hundreds in the literature of other professional groups.

[30] NASW "Policy on Information Utilization and Confidentiality," pp. 4–5. (See Appendix B-1). NASW has taken these guidelines almost verbatim from *Records, Computers and the Rights of Citizens,* Report of Secretary Advisory Committee on Automated Personal Data Systems, Mass.: U.S. Department of HEW, 1973, p. 41.

It is interesting to note that while the NASW policy statement does recognize the importance of the individual knowing that information about him is in a data bank, no reference is made specifically to the important concept of the client's right to grant or refuse permission for the data to be there in the first place.

Thus, various suggestions have been made as to what must be done to protect the confidentiality of data being stored in computers. By combining the recommendations of several different organizations and authors, some basic principles for preserving the privacy of data-bank information can be suggested:

1. The client must be informed that this process is occurring and what data are being stored.

2. His permission should be secured before information about him is fed into any data bank or computer.

3. The consumer must be aware of how the information is disseminated and have control over its use through an informed consent process.

4. The information must be maintained in a disguised manner to protect the identity of the individual.

5. The client must have full access to information pertaining to him which is stored in the system.

6. There must be a mechanism by which the consumer can correct, amend, or delete any data that is inaccurate or incomplete.

7. There must be a time- or purpose-limited definition of when the data is to be removed from the system, so that it does not remain there indefinitely after its original purpose has been accomplished.

8. Social-work services should not be denied because a consumer refuses to permit identifying data to be fed into a computerized system. Likewise, employees in such settings should not have their employment status jeopardized for refusing to feed data into data-bank systems that do not effectively implement the guidelines specified here.

9. There must be laws enacted specifically protecting the confidentiality of data-bank information so that it is accorded the same, if not greater protection, than that provided for other forms of social-service records.

"Why Have Written Case Records at All?"

There are so many factors to keep track of in order to preserve confidentiality that one sometimes wonders if it wouldn't be simpler just to do away with social-service records entirely.

Various suggestions have been made for reducing or eliminating threats to the confidentiality of written record material. One alternative would be to keep the existence of such records a secret. This sounds absurd, and it is, but some settings actually do this. The federal government, for example, has come under heavy criticism because of its tendency to keep records on persons without letting them know that the files exist. This makes it impossible for the consumer to make certain that such records are accurate or properly used. Thus, the Federal Privacy Act of 1974 made it illegal for federal programs to keep secret records. This would, of course, include federal settings where social work is practiced. These agencies may keep records, but they must go through rather elaborate procedures to let everyone know what kind of files they maintain, who can have the right of access, and how those persons can go about exercising that right.

Another possibility that has been suggested is to simply create an expense or risk factor so great or so inconvenient for those who want to get at the case records that it would not be worthwhile for anyone to ask to see them. This works well until someone comes along who wants the material badly enough to pay the cost and undergo the required inconveniences. Such a practice would be illegal in existing federal programs.

A different approach would be to keep social-service records in such a way that only the guardians of the files could understand their contents. This could be accomplished via coding, computerization, or similar mechanisms. It could also be effected by removing all identifying data except for one master code-number. However, detailed encoding is largely impractical for most settings. Thus, while this approach might appear ideal, it is not very realistic.

A serious suggestion has been made, and is being carried out in some social-work settings, that there simply be no records at all. Advocates of this tactic prefer that all old files be destroyed and no new recording be done on social-work activity. Students have been known to have field placements in settings that require no recording whatsoever. What appears to be pure heaven to the student and agency is, however, actually fraught with potential problems. Most social workers do have to do some type of recording, and if a student does not learn this skill during field placement he will be at a severe disadvantage when he secures his first employment. The total absence of case records can make it most difficult for an agency to provide adequate continuity of services to its clientele. Some governmental settings have laws prohibiting or strictly regulating the destruction of old case records, even though the law might permit them not to generate new files. In interdisciplinary settings such as medical hospitals the social work department might not keep separate case records of its own, but the American Hospital Association, the Joint Commission on Accreditation, and other regulatory bodies may require the maintenance of a medical chart which must contain social-work entries. Also, settings dependent on third parties (insurance companies, Medicare, etc.) which reimburse them for services provided must be able to demonstrate that the services were in fact rendered. This cannot be done without written records.

The absence of records also prevents vital research, makes quality control much more difficult, and interferes with student education. In addition, records can become therapeutic tools as well as a means of helping the practitioner organize his thoughts and achieve greater depth and consistency in service delivery. Finally, an absence of records can actually complicate rather than obviate legal actions. Thus, having no records at all may initially appear to be Utopia, but the realities associated with social work practice will not permit it in most settings.

It has been suggested that persons who generate confidential records might keep two separate sets: one containing "less confidential material" that can be rather freely released to others, and a second file containing highly confidential records to be kept by the practitioner for his use only. A recent position statement of the American Orthopsychiatric Association describes one such system:

> Principle No. 6: A dual record system, utilizing *Working Notes* and a *Health Care Record* (or *Social Service Record*) is appropriate and shall be instituted by health care and social service providers. The Working Notes are the work-product of the provider and should be the property of and maintained in the possession of the provider. They would contain all the information necessary to the provider for serving the consumer, including tests, diagnoses, treatments, guesses, hunches, doubts, possibilities and questions to be dealt with at another time. These notes shall not be available to any other person or institution except as may be required to defend the provider against claims against him brought by or on behalf of the consumer; they shall be destroyed when (1) no longer relevant to current service delivery and (2) no longer required for the protection of the provider.
>
> The *Health Care Record* (or *Social Service Record*) would be compiled jointly by the provider and consumer and contain the legal record of all tests, procedures, diagnoses and treatments. The consumer should have access to and contribute to the record and should have the right to challenge, rebut or amend it. The Health Care Record (or Social Service Record) should not be available, in whole or part, to anyone outside the provider-consumer unit without specific written permission of the consumer and without adequate discussion to be certain the consumer understands the meaning and implications of what is to be shared.[31]

Adelle Hofmann[32] and others have been quite outspoken in their concern for confidentiality of children's medical records, and dual records have been recommended:

[31] American Orthopsychiatric Association Inc., "Position Statement on Confidentiality of Health Records," June, 1975, p. 6. For other examples, see Carmault B. Jackson, Jr., "Considerations of the 'Active Working Record' versus the 'Permanent Record': The Preliminary View of the American Society of Internal Medicine," *Psychiatric Opinion,* Vol. 12, No. 1 (January 1975), pp. 29–33. See also Roy H. Behnke, "The Confidentiality of the Patient Record," *Journal of the Florida Medical Association,* Vol. 62, No. 2 (February 1975), p. 40.

[32] Adele D. Hofmann, "Confidentiality and the Health Care Records of Children and Youth," *Psychiatric Opinion,* Vol. 12, No. 1 (January 1975), pp. 20–28.

There should be a *working record* containing hunches, tentative diagnoses, unproven guesses, conflictual confidential material, highly sensitive and developmental data of questionable significance—the property of the provider and shared by no one. And there should be a *permanent record*—the property of the consumer. . . . It contains test procedures and therapy results and clear, definable examination data.[33]

As might be predicted, an official recommendation has now been made that social workers maintain two kinds of records. The suggestion comes from a group representing a cross-section of major social-service agencies and reads as follows:

Agency workers need two kinds of records. One, the official record, will include facts, periodic summaries of diagnoses, treatment and outcomes. Aggregate data, needed for agency administration, for planning, budgeting, research, and community interpretation, can be compiled from such records. These records are also retained to safeguard information, as in child adoptions, and are useful for archival purposes. The other, less formal, will include personal information, preliminary diagnosis and treatment plans and will serve for supervisory purposes. It is of time limited use while the worker and the client work together on the problem that brought the client to the agency.[34]

In Illinois, a "Mental Health and Developmental Disabilities Confidentiality Act" has been drafted. It also permits the therapist to maintain a private record:

[The] record does not include the therapist's personal notes containing his impressions, his opinions, or information received from third persons concerning the recipient if such notes are kept in the therapist's sole possession for his own personal use and are not disclosed to any other person. If at any time such notes are disclosed, they shall be considered part of the recipient's record for purposes of this Act.[35]

The following comments are contained in the act regarding the above paragraph:

[It] makes the distinction between records kept by a therapist which are open to the recipient, and may be open to scrutiny by the courts, government agencies,

---

[33] *Confidentiality: A Report of the 1974 Conference on Confidentiality of Health Records,* Key Biscayne, Florida. Prepared by Natalie Davis Spingarn. American Psychiatric Association (Washington, D.C.: 1975), p. 12.

[34] "A New Look at Confidentiality in Social Welfare Services," The National Assembly for Social Policy and Development, Inc. (New York: Cambridge Press, November 27, 1973), pamphlet, unpaged. Social service organizations comprising the Assembly were Red Cross, National Conference of Catholic Charities, Child Welfare League of America, National Accreditation Council for Agencies Serving the Blind and Visually Handicapped, Family Service Association of America, Traveler's Aid-International Social Service of America, National Urban League, the Salvation Army, National Council for Homemaker-Home Health Aide Services.

[35] Quoted by Willard Lassers, "Availability of Records," Chapter 7 in *Confidentiality of Health & Social Service Records: Where Law, Ethics & Clinical Issues Meet,* Proceedings of the Second Midwest Regional Conference (Chicago: University of Illinois at Chicago Circle, December 1976), p. 151.

and others, and the therapist's personal notes which do not circulate to anyone else. This is to free the therapist to keep notes and jottings for his own use without having to write them in a way which would be suitable for perusal by anyone else, including the recipient.[36]

A "Model Law on Confidentiality of Health and Social Service Information" has been developed based on these guidelines. The task was spearheaded by Sandra Nye, an attorney–social worker, and contains a section permitting "personal notes" which do not have to be disclosed:

a. A service provider is not required to but may, to the extent he or she determines it necessary and appropriate, keep personal notes regarding a client wherein he or she may record:
   (i) sensitive information disclosed to him or her in confidence by other persons on condition that such information would never be disclosed to the client or other persons excepting, at most, other service providers;
   (ii) sensitive information disclosed to him or her by the client which would be injurious to the client's relationships to other persons; and
   (iii) the service provider's speculations, impressions, hunches and reminders. No authorization to disclose confidential information shall be effective with respect to such personal notes of a service provider except on authorization to disclose the same to another service provider occupying a professional service relationship with the client by reason whereof it would serve the client's interests for him to have the personal notes and whereby he is bound to observe confidentiality.

   Upon receipt of such personal notes by such other service provider, they shall be deemed to be his personal notes except to the extent that he transfers information from such notes to regular health and social service records pertaining to the client.

b. The keeping of such personal notes shall not relieve a service provider from any obligation to record and maintain in an official record information pertaining to such matters as diagnosis, treatment, progress and all other information required in an individualized treatment plan.[37]

Those in favor of dual record-keeping systems view them as essential for safeguarding information from outsiders and also from the consumer himself. Certain information would be rather freely released (with client permission, of course) and other data would simply not be available to anyone except the person who recorded it. Such a practice implies that the more private record would be somewhat "secret," and this invites the legal and ethical difficulties discussed earlier in relation to hidden records. Another difficulty with dual record-keeping is that many professionals, especially social workers (who generally do not rate recording as a favorite activity), would object to maintaining two separate files; entries in the "official" file could

---

[36] *Ibid.*

[37] Sandra G. Nye, "Model Law on Confidentiality of Health and Social Service Information," Appendix B in *Confidentiality of Health & Social Service Records, op. cit.,* pp. 275–276.

become quite skimpy as a result. Some unavoidable duplication would undoubtedly occur, resulting in inefficient use of time and materials.

Although favoring dual records, the 1974 *Conference on Confidentiality of Health Records* expressed its concern that the service provider's own "private" record might be difficult to separate from the "formal" record. In other words, how does one determine what information makes up "working notes"—i.e., is "private"—and what data is essential for diagnosis and treatment? Other concerns are that relevant professional judgments might not be documented, with dual record-keeping leading to meaningless recording as key data (needed by persons who *must* use the record) being omitted.[38]

The advantages of dual record-keeping are quite obvious, and would certainly appear preferable to a move to do away with all records. Practitioners would not be *required* to keep private working notes, as long as an official record was maintained. Thus, those wishing to avoid duplication could easily do so. Dual records would also permit more effective control over disclosures to the consumer and others and would give the professional "breathing room" for handling data that is not "sharable" at the moment. Unfortunately, the Federal Privacy Act currently prohibits the dual-record system in federal programs; perhaps subsequent revisions of the act could incorporate this feature.

In reality, many social workers, especially those in private practice, do keep highly personal notes which are brief, often rather disorganized, and not part of any formal case record. (The difficulty is that this is the *only* type of record kept by many practitioners.) Such a practice can effectively prevent unauthorized disclosures, especially if the individual's handwriting is illegible. However, there is no guarantee that such notes could not be subpoenaed by a court, along with any formal records. It is not unusual for courts to subpoena calendars, appointment books, and any scraps of paper on which the professional might have written down notes regarding a client. If a formal record can be produced, of course, the court would not need these informal, hand-scribbled notes even if it knew they existed. But if no formal record can be produced, the court will suspect that most professionals have to have *something* in the way of notes on their cases and may therefore aggressively pursue the informal material. While this problem has affected psychiatrists and psychotherapists primarily, it is foreseeable that social workers could face similar pressures.

This leads to a final argument in favor of doing away with records. It too is fraught with fallacies, however. Some practitioners argue: "If my record gets subpoenaed, I'll just say I can't remember what happened on the case. There's no record, so nothing can be revealed and I'll be safe." In an

---

[38] *Confidentiality: A Report of the 1974 Conference on Confidentiality of Health Records, op. cit.,* pp. 11–12.

article discussing this very argument in the field of psychotherapy,[39] Andrew S. Watson argues strongly that only the most naive would believe that the courts are unaware of this game, and he presents some valid arguments to support his contention that professionals who try this approach usually end up with their credibility challenged. Watson cites a case in which a psychiatrist's record was subpoenaed by a court. It was a delicate situation, and the therapist spent some time in jail over his refusal to comply with the court order to produce his record. Part of his argument was that the material the court was requesting was not relevant to the matter at hand, and thus he claimed his right not to release it. Someone asked if it would not have been easier had he kept no records and then simply stated that he could not remember the details of the case. In considering the purpose of case records (in the practice of psychotherapy), the following argument is presented:

> In relation to legal matters, they [records] have two purposes: (1) to refresh our memory about what we are doing for a patient in order that we may maintain our own working contact with a patient accurately. (This purpose, he observed, is not much used by the analyst in day-to-day work with the patient.) (2) In the event the therapist is called to account legally for his work with the patient, records add substantially to what lawyers call his *credibility*. Mere absence of records will not keep one from being subpoenaed. There are evidentiary dangers in saying that you do not remember things about a patient whom you have treated. . . . a good cross-examining lawyer would then tax the analyst's narcissicism rigorously as he began to explore the implications of nonmemory about the case. That could cause the therapist considerable embarrassment when he found himself in the position of saying he treats patients but does not remember anything about them. In other words, one should not fool oneself into believing that the problem of testimony will be solved by "not having any records." Neither will it be possible to readily convince the judge that he should pay attention to your notions of relevance, when you cannot demonstrate what you did through some kind of record. In short, if you jeopardize your credibility with the judge by playing games about memory, it is very likely he will pay no attention to you when you attempt to argue that certain matters are irrelevant and also damaging to your patient, so far as privilege is concerned. Therefore, such a tactic would be basically foolish and self-defeating.[40]

The Joint Task Group on Confidentiality of Computerized Medical Records, in setting forth guidelines for data centers, presents a very valid argument in favor of maintaining records. It is applicable to social work as well as to medicine:

> Adequate documentation is an essential part of clinical care. The comprehensive and accurate primary record shall serve as communication among those who

[39] See Andrew S. Watson, "Levels of Confidentiality in the Psychoanalytic Situation," *Journal of American Psychoanalytic Association,* Vol. 20, No. 1 (January 1972), pp. 156–176.

[40] *Ibid.,* p. 173.

contribute to the care of the patient. The physician and his team shall maintain an adequate primary record.[41]

In explaining the meaning of this tenet, the guidelines state that

> this tenet is intended to assign morally equal importance to patient care and documentation. Good clinical care requires the availability of good records. Moreover, peer review will depend on the accuracy and comprehensiveness of the primary medical record. Ethical practice of medicine calls for adequate primary records.[42]

One attorney has even pointed out that there are cases on record in which courts have found that "treatment is inadequate if the record is inadequate."[43]

Thus, social workers must maintain case records of some kind. At the time this is being written, many settings are just becoming aware of the implications of confidentiality and of legal actions that could result from violations. The relatively new concept of consumer access to records is also having an impact. Unfortunately, the trend now is toward doing away with all meaningful records, as the pendulum swings precariously to one side. With time, social work should develop a more realistic and workable solution to the implications of confidentiality and consumer access to files. It is obvious that we must now concentrate on the nature of our relationship with those we serve (openness vs. secrecy) and the way in which we gather data and maintain and safeguard records. If proper attention is given to these areas, social workers will be functioning on a *preventive* level, thus avoiding many of the nightmares that advocates of doing away with all records envision and many others they do not foresee.

---

[41] "Ethical Guidelines for Data Centers Handling Medical Records," Joint Task Group on Confidentiality of Computerized Medical Records, E. R. Gabriel, Chairman. Adopted by the House of Delegates of the Medical Society of the State of New York, March 1975; adopted by the Board of Directors, Society for Computer Medicine, November 1975. This position statement has also been adopted by the National Association of Blue Shield Plans. Page 2.

[42] *Ibid.*

[43] A. Budd Cutler, Attorney and President of the Health System Agency of South Florida. Talk given at the Florida Chapter of the Society for Hospital Social Work Directors, Orlando, Florida, November 12, 1976. His topic was "Legal Problems in Health Care" with special emphasis on social work in the medical setting.

5. Release of Information to Others

*Though information has a life cycle like us—a childhood, an adolescence,
and an aging process—unlike us, it never dies unless someone kills it.*[1]

Arthur Miller

IT SHOULD BE OBVIOUS THAT IF RECORDS EXIST, someone other than the
consumer may eventually seek and gain access to information contained
therein. Thus, guidelines must be developed specifying the confidentiality
rights of consumers, the conditions under which data will be released, and
the content which can be disclosed. As we have noted, the Federal Privacy
Act of 1974 has already done this for federal settings, and there is a likelihood that its provisions will soon become mandatory for the private sector
as well.

In the absence of any national policies, various professional groups have
developed their own guidelines for release of confidential information.
These mandates are as diverse as the groups that have produced them. A
few are highly specific and comprehensive; others are vague and incomplete, and several key social-service delivery systems have failed to develop
any formal guidelines for handling confidential data. While the National
Association of Social Workers has developed some suggested guidelines for
social work practice,[2] they relate primarily to the use of computerized data
systems and are not comprehensive enough to serve as a model that can be
adapted for all social-service settings.

This chapter will examine some of the issues pertaining to the release of
confidential information to persons, institutions, and systems other than
the consumer, and will suggest standards for handling the disclosure
process.

[1] *Confidentiality: A Report of the 1974 Conference on Confidentiality of Health Records,*
American Psychiatric Association (Washington, D.C.: 1975). Quoting Professor Arthur Miller
of the Harvard University Law School, who was attending the conference. See pp. 32–33.

[2] See Appendixes B-1 and B-2.

"Informed Consent"

"Informed consent" once meant securing permission from a patient before certain medical procedures could be performed. The medical literature is laced with articles exploring every ramification of this issue. However, the term "informed consent" is now being applied to confidentiality ethics as well. There has been general agreement with the principle that a consumer's consent should be obtained before confidential information is disclosed. Unfortunately, there have been some abuses and rather free interpretations of the term "consent." Thus, recent writings concerning confidentiality now tell of the need for consumers to give *informed* consent before disclosure of confidential data can occur.

The NASW "Policy on Information Utilization and Confidentiality" recommends:

> Information about an individual client [may] not be shared with any other individual or agency without that individual's express, *informed consent.*
>
> Case records and related files [must] not be transferred to another agency or individual without the express *informed consent* of the client or guardian, and then under rules that the receiving agency provide the same guarantee of confidentiality as the transferring agency.
>
> The client's *informed and express consent* should be a prerequisite to transmitting or requesting information from third parties [emphasis added].[3]

Unfortunately, NASW policy does not spell out the conditions that must be met before consent can be considered "informed."

What exactly, then, is "informed consent"? How can the social work practitioner be sure that his client's consent is truly informed?

The American National Red Cross is one social-service program that has addressed this issue:

> Signed consent from the client or the legal guardian is secured each time information is to be released outside the agency, stating the specific information to be given, to whom and for what purpose.
>
> Before the "release of confidential information" form is signed, the SMF worker must be assured that the client or responsible representative understands what information is to be given, to whom and for what purpose.[4]

It is argued that in order for a consumer to really understand just what information will be released, he himself must have access to it:

> "Informed consent," once simply the patient's consent to a medical procedure, has come to mean also his consent to the release of medical information to

[3] NASW, "Policy on Information Utilization and Confidentiality," policy adopted at the National Association of Social Workers 1975 Delegate Assembly, May 30–June 3, 1975, Washington, D.C., pp. 4–5. See Appendix B-1.

[4] "The American National Red Cross Guidelines for Service to Military Families: Confidentiality. For the Use of SMF in Applying the Principle of Confidentiality in Services to People," ARC 2049, October 1974 with two attachments: (1) "Establishment, Maintenance and Disposition of Case Records" and (2) "Release of Confidential Information" (form).

others and this has come to include his right to see his own medical record in order to assure its accuracy.[5]

If the ideas of a number of different authors, representing several disciplines, are combined, it is possible to arrive at ten conditions that should exist before a consumer's permission to release confidential information can be considered "informed consent":

1. The consumer must be told that there is a desire or a request to release certain data.

2. The consumer must understand exactly what information is to be disclosed. He cannot intelligently decide if he wants it revealed unless he knows exactly what material is in question.

3. In order for the consumer to know what is to be released, he should actually see the material and/or have it read to him and explained in terms he can understand.

4. The consumer must be told exactly to whom the information is being released—name, position, and affiliation.

5. The client must be told why the information is being requested and exactly how it will be used by the receiving party.

6. There must be a way for the consumer to correct or amend the information to insure its accuracy and completeness before it is released.

7. The consumer must understand whether or not the receiving party has the right to pass the information on to a third party. The consumer must have the right to specify that this not be done without his knowledge and consent.

8. The consumer should be fully informed of any repercussions that might occur should he (a) grant permission for the disclosure or (b) not give permission.

9. The consumer should be advised that his consent for release of information is time-limited and revocable. He should be advised how he can withdraw his consent and be given periodic opportunities for doing so.[6]

10. The consumer's consent for release of information must be in writing on a "Consent for Release of Information" form.

THE "CONSENT FOR RELEASE OF INFORMATION" FORM

This form exists in many versions in as many different settings. Very few agencies and practitioners use it appropriately, and abuses of consumer privacy rights occur almost daily. Social work is not the only profession con-

[5] *Confidentiality: A Report of the 1974 Conference on Confidentiality of Health Records, op. cit.*, p. 10.

[6] *Ibid.*, p. 35. This is suggested by the American Civil Liberties Union in its proposal as to how consent should be handled. It was one of many organizations represented at this 1974 conference on confidentiality.

cerned with this problem; in fact, the most vocal criticism of improper use of consent forms has come from the medical field.

Most settings realize the need to obtain written consent for release of information. However, many social-work settings, and those of other disciplines as well, have handled this process in such a way that its very purpose is effectively sabotaged. Consumers have tolerated the abuses in ignorant or deliberate silence, but this pattern should change with increasing consumer awareness of privacy rights. The following vignette, based on routine practice in many social work agencies, presents a typical instance of this profession's greatest misuse of consent forms. The scene is an intake interview in a program granting financial assistance. The applicant has a second-grade education:

> _Worker:_ OK, Mr. Jones. We will need to verify your disability and also your financial situation. Since you have a checking and savings account, we'll need to check with the bank, and we'll also be checking your medical records. If you'll sign this form, we'll be all set._ (Shoves five copies of a "Consent for Release of Information" form across the desk to the client) _Just sign right here. I'll fill in the blanks later when you get me the exact address of your physician and your bank account numbers._
>
> _Client:_ Sign here?_ (Pointing to the blank line for his signature)
>
> _Worker:_ Yes_
>
> (Client slowly and laboriously signs all five copies without reading the form.)
>
> _Worker:_ Thank you, Mr. Jones. You get me that information regarding your doctor's address and bank account number, and I'll let you know as soon as we have a decision on your application._
>
> (Client thanks the worker, expresses his hope for a quick decision and leaves.)

Variations of this theme occur daily in social work practice. Blank forms are signed, to be filled in later at the worker's convenience. The forms are so general that they cover any and all situations that might arise during the consumer's lifetime. Extra signed copies are kept in the file "so the client won't have to come in again should we need permission to get or release some information. Besides, I don't want to run the risk of him saying 'no.'"

What is wrong with this approach? A few well-chosen quotes provide some strong answers:

A consent form cannot be considered truly "informed" when it reads, "I hereby authorize the undersigned physician to release any information acquired in the course of examination or treatment." When a patient signs such forms— usually as a routine matter, and without considering probable consequences— they [sic] may be unlocking the key to a Pandora's box packed with privacy problems.[7]

[7] _Ibid.,_ p. 23.

"Informed consent" should apply to the disclosure of personal health information to third parties, like insurance companies, attorneys or estranged spouses. Too often, the patient's consent, obtained by small type at the bottom of the page, and anything but "informed," releases the most personal, private information to—who knows? According to one life insurance official, life insurance companies routinely ask applicants to sign such a "blanket" consent form, enabling the carrier to write to a host of people and institutions, friendly and unfriendly.

Most experts condemn such "blanket" forms and feel their demise would benefit both patient and providers. Hospital personnel especially are now caught in the bind of having to furnish information against their better judgment to the release of which patients have consented through blanket consent forms. Before patients give their consent to disclosures they should know what information they are disclosing, the exact use that will be made of it and the consequences of the release, so that they may be helped and not hurt thereby.[8]

An example of a blanket "Consent for Release of Information" form used by a private insurance carrier is provided in a report by the Governor's Commission on Privacy and Personal Data for the Commonwealth of Massachusetts:

I authorize all physicians, hospitals, clinics, dispensaries, sanitariums, druggists, employers, and all other agencies to disclose and release any information regarding the medical history, physical or mental condition of me or my dependents to _____. It is agreed that a copy of this authorization will have the same effect as the original.[9]

Consider the following blanket consent form in use in a large hospital:

This is authorization for [XYZ] Hospital to convey to _____ any and all information which you possess relative to my disability on _____ for which I was confined within and treated at your hospital. The question of privacy between your institution, my attending physician or physicians and myself is waived. This authority extends to the furnishing of copies of all or any desired parts of the hospital record. Information to be used: _____.

This form was originally developed for release of information to the Social Security Administration. However, it soon became standard for all releases of information and was utilized by the social-work department as well.

The American National Red Cross makes its position on this matter quite clear:

Before the "Release of Confidential Information" form is signed, the worker must be assured that the client or responsible representative understands what information is to be given, to whom, and for what purpose. A blanket release

[8] *Ibid.,* pp. 34–35.

[9] "Health and Privacy: Patient Records: A Report of Current Practices with Recommendations for Changes," The Commonwealth of Massachusetts, Governor's Commission on Privacy and Personal Data. Adopted November 22, 1974.

should never be requested. If the client is unable to be present, verbal consent should be obtained and noted in the record.[10]

The National Assembly for Social Policy and Development takes a similar stand:

> Information about an individual client may not be shared with any other individual or agency without his express consent. Consent is necessary even when verification of information given by the client is needed. Blanket consent, real, implied or assumed, is never acceptable for either gathering or giving information, whether factual or evaluative, or plans for the future.[11]

Even as early as 1947, the issue had been addressed by the American Association of Social Workers (the forerunner of NASW):

> Could a blanket consent be obtained to consult other persons and agencies as necessary? The answer to the last question must apparently be "no," as it is inconsistent with adequate discharge of the agency's responsibility for confidentiality.[12]

Several legal authorities also make it quite clear that a general consent-for-release-of-information form is useless and does not constitute consent. Consent for releasing information cannot be obtained in advance of the generation of the information. If at the time he signs the form the client does not know what information is being released and under what conditions, his consent is not informed and is therefore meaningless. Such consent forms would probably not hold up in court if legally challenged by the consumer.[13]

If consent is given for release of one kind of information to a certain party and the practitioner discloses additional or different data, or releases the information to a different party, he could be held liable. Consumers have already won several suits centering around this issue.[14]

If oral rather than written consent is obtained and the consumer brings legal action, the practitioner could be the loser. In one case, a couple consulted a psychiatrist for treatment. Ten years later, he published a book giving an "exact account of the Doe family therapeutic experience." When

---

[10] "The American National Red Cross Guidelines for Service to Military Families," p. 2.

[11] "A New Look at Confidentiality in Social Welfare Services," The National Assembly for Social Policy and Development, Inc. (New York: Cambridge Press, November 27, 1973), pamphlet, unpaged.

[12] *Principles of Confidentiality in Social Work* (Washington, D.C.: Committee on Records, District of Columbia Chapter, American Association of Social Workers, 1947), p. 20.

[13] See "Case Notes: *Roe v. Doe: A Remedy for Disclosure of Psychiatric Confidences*," *Rutgers Law Review*, Vol. 29 (Fall 1975), pp. 190–209. Also stated by A. Budd Cutler, Attorney and President of the Health Systems Agency of South Florida Inc., in a talk on "Legal Problems and Health Care" given at a meeting of the Florida Chapter of the Society for Hospital Social Work Directors, 11-12-76, Orlando, Florida.

[14] See "Case Notes: *Roe v. Doe.*" In one case described *(Feeney v. Young)* a doctor showed a film publicly of a patient in childbirth. The patient sued and won because she had consented only to exhibition of the film to medical societies—not the general public.

Mr. Doe sued, the court ordered distribution of the book stopped. The psychiatrist had disguised the family's name but did not adequately alter other identifying details. Furthermore, he had obtained oral rather than written consent to use the material.[15]

Thus, written consent-forms must be used, and these must be quite specific. In order to meet the criteria of "informed consent" outlined earlier and to avoid the ethical and legal difficulties inherent in blank consent forms, the following guidelines for the use and content of such forms are proposed. Appendix C contains an example of a model form that incorporates these ideas:

1. The consumer should sign a new "Consent for Release of Information" form whenever
   a. a disclosure is to be made;
   b. there is a change in the party to whom the information is being released *or* additional information is sought by the same party;
   c. a consent form already on file has expired;
   d. a previously signed consent form is revoked by the consumer and a new one is desired.
2. Conditions governing "informed consent" (see p. 57, no. 1–10) should be discussed with the consumer before he is asked to sign the consent form.
3. Copies of the signed consent form should be distributed to
   a. the agency/practitioner who obtained the consumer's signature;
   b. the consumer;
   c. the party to whom information is being disclosed or from whom information is being sought.
4. The form itself should contain the following items:
   a. the agency/department/practitioner seeking the consumer's signature;
   b. the date the form is signed;
   c. the exact name, address, position, and related identifying data regarding the party to whom the disclosure will be made;
   d. a description of the exact material to be released;
   e. the purpose for the disclosure—why the receiving agency wants the information and/or how it will be used;
   f. limitations imposed upon the receiving party as to how it may use the material, and whether it can be released to third parties and under what conditions, if any;
   g. a statement indicating the period of time for which the signed consent form will be valid (an expiration date should be given which corresponds with the estimated time when the transfer of information will be completed);

---

[15] *Ibid.*, p. 190.

> h. a statement that items mentioned in No. 2 above (governing "informed consent") have been reviewed prior to request for client's signature;
>
> i. a place for the client's signature. (His name should be printed or typed beneath his signature. If the consumer is illiterate, his "x" should be witnessed by two persons. It may be desirable to have one witness other than the social worker sign all consent forms. If a guardian or other legal representative is signing in the client's behalf, this should be clearly indicated.)
>
> j. an indication that carbon copies are going to certain places (see No. 3 above).

5. There should be no blank spaces on the form when it is presented to the consumer for his signature (except, of course, the space for his signature and the date).

6. If a practitioner/agency serves a population speaking several languages, copies of the form should be available in each language.

Consent forms can be used in several ways. An outside agency may contact a social worker asking for certain information from his files. If the person desiring the data has obtained written consent from the consumer, a copy of the signed consent form should be received and carefully reviewed by the record-holder before any information is released. If the form is of the "blanket consent" variety and otherwise fails to meet the standards for consent to be considered "informed," the record-holder should reject it; he should not release the information until a proper consent form has been executed.

In other situations, the record-holder may be the one requesting data from outside sources; this is especially common in settings where eligibility determinations are done. At other times an agency may make a referral and send information along as part of the referral process. If the practitioner is exploring possible resources to meet a consumer's need, certain identifying data may have to be disclosed before the resource can determine whether it can serve the client. If general information is shared ("I have a man who needs a wheelchair. . . . ") no consent is required. However, if client-identifying details must be disclosed, written consent is necessary.

SPECIAL CONSIDERATIONS

There are some special considerations and problem areas involved in releasing confidential information, even if fully informed consent has been obtained. One is the temptation to make disclosure a *requirement* for treatment or services. Certainly there are settings and situations in which a consumer cannot receive the services requested unless a certain amount of disclosure occurs. The applicant for financial assistance must be willing to have his resources verified; the applicant for disability benefits or vocational rehabilitation services must permit the agency access to pertinent medical and/or psychiatric records. However, such disclosures should be kept to the minimum information needed by the agency to provide its service—there should be no "consent-to-release-everything-and-anything-forms" as a prerequisite for services.

If we adhere to the policy that consumers must see the material in question before informed consent can be given for its release, some special problems arise. How would the consumer be affected by seeing the information? Has the person who generated the data asked that it be kept confidential as regards the client? These questions will be discussed in detail in Chapter 6. However, it is worth noting here that these questions have led some to advocate the dual record-keeping system (see pp. 49-52) as one way of designating certain information as "not sharable" with the consumer. Another suggested approach has been to create three "zones" in medical records accessible to different groups of data-users:

1. primary health-care or patient-care institutions such as physicians' offices, clinics, hospitals, and nursing homes
2. secondary support or ancillary services such as private and governmental third-party payers, professional and governmental quality care assurance, and in-house research
3. secondary users of medical data: credential-givers and evaluators, insurance company licensing boards, the judicial process, public health and media reporting, law enforcement and security investigations, social welfare and social rehabilitation programs, medical and social research[16]

Thus, persons representing these three zones could have access only to material pertinent to their needs. Consumers would have some kind of access to all three areas, and consent would be necessary for release of information in most instances.

Very little attention has been given to the issue of consumer withdrawal of consent (see p. 61, No. 1d). It may be assumed that if consent was given in writing, the withdrawal must also be written. It would be interesting to determine if state statutes regarding the granting and withdrawal of consent for the performance of medical procedures would also apply to consent for disclosure of confidential information. Agencies and settings where social work is practiced must be clear on this point. As more formalized consent procedures are developed, issues relating to consent revocation will have to be addressed.

It has been established in medicine that the individual who obtains the patient's consent for a procedure must be qualified to actually do the pro-

---

[16] *Confidentiality: A Report of the 1974 Conference on Confidentiality of Health Records, op. cit.,* pp. 14-16.

cedure.[17] Thus, secretaries cannot obtain the patient's signature in the physician's absence. One wonders if this same principle would apply to social-work consent-for-release-of-information forms. Ethically speaking, such a policy is indicated, as few secretaries would be in a position to meaningfully discuss with clients the ten points we recommend be reviewed before the consumer's consent is obtained (see pp. 57).

It is important that the proper person sign the consent form. If the consumer is a legally competent adult, no one should sign for him. If he has been legally adjudged mentally incompetent, his court-appointed guardian must sign all consent forms. Some competent adults may designate someone with the legal power-of-attorney to sign such forms, though this would be rather rare. Children, being minors, are usually considered incapable of understanding the various factors necessary to give informed consent, and thus their guardians and/or parents sign in their behalf. However, at least one pediatrician and one state legislature are seriously questioning this concept. [18]

The practitioner who releases information (after client consent has been obtained) must find some way to prevent the receiving party from passing it on to a third person without the client's permission. A special restrictive clause either on the consent form or stamped on the confidential material itself could set the desired limits. This precaution should become a matter of routine in view of the large number of individuals seeking information and rather freely disclosing it to many outsiders.

Finally, there are still some agencies and practitioners who seek confidential information by oral request. Often they simply want to verify that the information they need exists before going to the trouble of submitting a formal request. However, such requests are just as often *the* request—"I want the material and I need it as soon as possible." The response to such inquiries should be standard: "I'll be glad to consider your request if you'll submit it to me in writing accompanied by a signed consent-for-release-of-information form. If you like, I'll send you a copy of the form to fill out for the client's signature."

Release of Information without Client Consent

The general rule is that client consent must be obtained before information is released. However, there are a few exceptions to this. If a practitioner works in a state that treats communication between him and his clients as

[17] A. Budd Cutler, *op. cit.*

[18] See Adele D. Hofmann, "Confidentiality and the Health Care Records of Children and Youth," *Psychiatric Opinion,* Vol. 12, No. 1 (January 1975), pp. 20–28. Dr. Hofmann has written a number of articles outlining some of the special confidentiality problems associated with children's records.

privileged, state laws will specify the exceptions. If any other disclosure of confidential information occurs without client consent, the social worker could be held liable. For those individuals practicing without privileged-communication coverage, there are no legal guidelines regarding exceptions, except perhaps precedents from previous court cases or specific state and federal regulations. In such instances it would probably be safe to consider as exceptions the same kinds of situations excepted under most privileged-communication statutes (see Chapter 8), though this would not necessarily guarantee protection in the courts. In any event, there are a few situations in which it is commonly recognized that information can be disclosed without client consent.[19]

In a bona fide emergency in which the client's life appears to be at stake, information may be released as needed to protect the consumer. This concept could be expanded to include a need to protect others from harm as well.[20]

If the consumer is legally incompetent, information is usually released without his consent via the court-appointed guardian. This can become complicated, however, when an individual appears incompetent, is unable to understand what is taking place, and yet has no legal guardian. It can be tempting to go ahead and obtain his signature on a consent form. However, once he is found legally incompetent and a guardian is appointed, the latter individual could conceivably bring suit against the practitioner if he feels the consumer was damaged in any way by the disclosure that took place without his "informed" consent. On the other hand, it might be argued in a case like this that release of information with or without the individual's signed consent was necessary for his own protection. This position was adopted by the American Association of Social Workers in its 1947 publication on confidentiality:

> He [the client] may be so out of touch with reality, so upset emotionally, or so handicapped mentally that he is unable to understand the need for, or to pro-

---

In Illinois a "Mental Health and Developmental Disabilities Confidentiality Act" is under consideration. It would grant minors, age 12 or older, the right of access to their record(s). In order for disclosures to occur, "If the recipient is at least 12 but under 18, the recipient must join the parent or guardian in the consent. If, however, the recipient refuses to consent, there may be no disclosure unless the therapist finds that disclosure is in the best interests of the recipient." Some version of this Act may eventually be presented to all states for uniform adoption. *Confidentiality of Health & Social Service Records: Where Law, Ethics & Clinical Issues Meet,* Proceedings of the Second Midwest Regional Conference, December, 1976 (Chicago: University of Illinois at Chicago Circle, 1976), pp. 157-158. (This edition is undergoing revision and will soon be published in more polished form.)

[19] Exceptions discussed in Chapter 8 under privileged communication statutes will not be repeated here.

[20] For example, see "A New Look at Confidentiality in Social Welfare Services," *op. cit; Principles of Confidentiality in Social Work, op. cit.;* and "Legal Regulation of Social Work Practice" (New York: National Association of Social Workers, 1973), pp. 7-8. See also Chapter 7.

vide information even though he obviously needs service and could reasonably be expected to want it were he able to make a rational decision. His right to protection may supersede his right to confidentiality.[21]

The idea that it is permissible to release information without client consent "as long as we are acting in his best interests" is suggested rather boldly in a letter to the editor of the September 1964 *Social Service Review*:

> By confidentiality we simply mean that we agree not to reveal what the client has told us without his consent. But, as we all know, sometimes people are not able to give such consent. Then we must act for them. . . . [P]erhaps in those instances we have to use our God-given common sense, rather than policy, to make a decision.[22]

Such thinking brings us full circle back to the starting point, as if to say, "Let each practitioner decide for himself what is in the client's best interests. Let each social worker individually assess whether the client is able to give consent. Let's not be bothered by guidelines or rules that might guarantee client rights or add consistency to social work practice." Undoubtedly, there are times when common sense must prevail, but decisions to release information without client consent stand a much greater chance today than ever before of being challenged by the consumer, and the practitioner taking such action should be well prepared to defend himself with specifics and precedents based on law, social work practice, and the experiences of related helping professions.

There is much greater leniency regarding the release of information without client consent when the practitioner is acting to protect the best interests of a minor. Child abuse, crimes involving children, emergency medical treatment, and other specific situations have been repeatedly identified as instances when even parental consent is not mandatory.

The National Assembly for Social Policy and Development recently stipulated that release can occur without client consent "when a client so misrepresents the agency as to seriously damage its potential usefulness to the community."[23] The point is not explained in detail; however, it appears that such a policy is designed to allow the agency to defend itself. Presumably, the agency would use legal counsel to initiate action for libel or slander and would very likely need to disclose information without client permission. If the agency were to attempt to publicly correct the client's misconceptions and release confidential information without his permission in the process, it appears it could be treading on very shaky ground unless this action were done in connection with a suit against the client and/or under advice from the agency's attorney.

[21] *Principles of Confidentiality in Social Work, op. cit.*, p. 7.

[22] Rita Lindenfield, "Letter to the Editor," *Social Service Review*, Vol. 38 (September 1964), pp. 341–342.

[23] "A New Look at Confidentiality in Social Welfare Services," *op. cit.*

Finally, it is generally recognized that confidential information is often circulated within an agency among staff needing access to it in order to provide service delivery.[24] Client consent is not required each time this occurs. However, it is important that consumers be notified that records are being kept, and that certain types of information exchanges do occur without their express knowledge and permission. An explanation to this effect could be provided during the initial contact with the consumer. This might also be done in written form. For example, the Massachusetts Governor's Commission on Privacy and Personal Data recommended that the following statement be given to hospital patients, covering both internal and external information sharing:

> The hospital releases medical information about many of our patients for purposes of claims reimbursement for both privately insured and publicly funded patients, for reviews of quality of care and for other reasons. We will be pleased to discuss these obligations with you upon request. In addition, at your request, we will provide a list of the persons and organizations who have received information from your medical record.

The commission went on to offer the following explanatory comment:

> At the present time, few if any patients are aware of the numbers of institutions which not only have access to, but systematically collect information from, the medical record. Recommendation is not made that the patient automatically be given a list, even with explanation, of recipients. The reasons for acquisition are sufficiently diverse and complex that they deserve discussion. However, such information should be readily available; patients should in no way be discouraged from requesting access to it. To pay proper attention to this recommendation, hospitals will have to make a commitment which will include assigning personnel to this task.
>
> While it was not specifically included in the recommended wording of the above notice, some Commission members felt strongly that a statement recognizing that greater personal information is shared with government for publicly funded patients should be routinely brought to the attention of all patients.[25]

Common Sources of Requests for Information

The various places that ask for or need confidential information from consumer records are too numerous to list in their entirety. Consider for ex-

---

[24] For example, see *Principles of Confidentiality in Social Work, op. cit.,* Principle II, which states that "within the agency information regarding a client should be revealed only to those persons and to the extent necessary to provide service" p. 9. The explanation is given that everyone in the agency has confidentiality obligations, but should have access only to data needed to do their job. If the agency performs several different functions, it should not use information for a purpose other than it was collected for without client permission.

[25] "Health and Privacy: Patient Records: A Report of Current Practices with Recommendations for Changes," p. 78.

ample, the potential assault on medical records (many of which contain social work entries) listed here:

> Governmental and private health insurers, peer review organizations, medical audit committees, legislated drug abuse registries, communicable disease reporting centers, automated multistate health information systems, the courts, employers, social agencies and institutions, and research investigators. For children, add schools, colleges, camps, state departments of labor (working papers), private and governmental child welfare agencies, day care centers, Headstart programs, Job Corps, juvenile courts, detention centers, foster homes, residential centers.[26]

As social work moves into private practice with increasing fervor, and as we dutifully embrace the merits of peer review and third-party reimbursement, our records will also be prey to a wider variety of information-seekers than ever before. A few of the more common ones are worthy of discussion:

I got a phone call from a social worker in another agency asking for a copy of our entire social service file. That's ridiculous, as it covers five years and is over sixty pages long. She then asked if she could come to my office and read the record. I told her "no" and she got rather upset at the inconvenience I was causing her. Now I'm wondering if I made the right decision — did I?

---

1. STAFF IN THE SAME AGENCY

As previously mentioned, many of these individuals already have a legitimate right of access to confidential client-data. However, there are those who do not. Thus, personnel having no professional reason for perusing confidential records should be identified and denied access.

2. FAMILY AND FRIENDS OF THE CLIENT

It is easy to assume that family and friends always have the client's best interests in mind and should therefore be given whatever information they want. However, several factors must be considered: What information is being requested? By whom and for what purpose? Would the client want information released to them? Most of these inquiries come by phone or personal contact, and one can never be certain of a telephone caller's identity, and the practitioner receiving the inquiry may feel pressured to respond with the desired information "right now." A standard response should be "I'm sorry, but I cannot give you that information. If you like, I'll contact

---

[26] Adele D. Hofmann, "Is Confidentiality in Health Care Records a Pediatric Concern?," *Pediatrics,* Vol. 57 (1976), p. 170.

the client, and if he gives me permission I will get back in touch with you. Or, I can have him contact you directly." The caller may respond that he has already talked with the client who "told me it's OK." This is still inadequate—formal written consent should be obtained except in unusual circumstances.

It is possible for a social worker to be aware of some significant information that *should* be released to significant others but which the client refuses to disclose or is perhaps unaware of himself. Most medical social workers have experienced this at one time or another, as, for example, when a dying patient insists that his family not be told his prognosis, or the family and physician know the prognosis and do not want the patient informed. The person who is "not supposed" to have the information in question may look the social worker directly in the eye and ask, "Tell me, am I going to die?" or "My father is going downhill—I can see it—is he dying?" The practitioner will need to carefully evaluate the pros and cons of revealing the information; perhaps he should establish a casework goal of preparing the individual to look more completely at the possible repercussions of his sharing or not sharing certain information. As members of other disciplines are often involved in this particular situation, they would need to assist in this process as well.

Rather awkward situations can sometimes develop. In one instance, a medical social worker received a phone call asking what nursing home "Mrs. Smith" had been discharged to from the hospital. The caller sounded like an elderly woman and she identified herself as a friend of the patient's who had not seen her in some time and wanted to visit her in the nursing home. When the social worker asked for her phone number so she could check into the matter and call her back, the woman indicated that she was from out of town and was at a pay phone. The worker had the caller wait while she checked the records. To her dismay, they showed that the patient had not been discharged to a nursing home, but had died the day before. Something had to be said to the person on the phone, whose relationship to the patient (as well as her probable reaction to news of the patient's death), was unknown. Fortunately, the hospital had a "public relations" department designed to handle these sorts of problems; the worker used another phone to alert them to the incident, and then transferred the call. They then verified that the patient had indeed expired, checked hospital records to make certain that all next of kin had been notified, and told the caller of Mrs. Smith's death.

If one is in doubt about whether to release information, the consumer should always be consulted. He might be notified simply that "Mrs. Jones was asking about you," and then permitted to decide for himself if he wants to contact her.

If a therapist is treating several members of a family unit, some negotiation should take place during the initial contract-setting phase to establish ground rules regarding the sharing of information and confidentiality rights of all concerned.

Release of information to parents of minors presents a special problem. Parents have a right to know what is being done with their children, and in public school systems they have a legal right to read their school records. However, it has been suggested that some information not be revealed to parents because it would be too upsetting to them or would damage the child-parent relationship because the child does not want his parents to know certain things. At least one author has suggested that the service provider, parents, and child may all have information in a record that should be kept confidential from parent or child.[27] It has been argued that minors are individuals in their own right and thus should have the option of keeping certain data confidential if they wish. Recent state laws are now guaranteeing minors the right to treatment for venereal disease and service for pregnancy under promise of confidentiality regarding their parents. Family-planning services and general health care also come under this mandate in some states.[28] On the other hand, parents' confidentiality is also protected; in most states adopted minors, even after they become adults, are prohibited by law from learning the identity of their biological parents. Thus, the sharing of information with family members of minors should be done not automatically but with some caution.

3. THE GENERAL PUBLIC

These inquiries are quite often for general, rather than specific, information. "How many clients does your agency serve?" or "How would I go about applying for services through your office?" or "Do you charge much?" and so on. If a person with no apparent relationship to a consumer should ask for specific information about that person, the standard reply should be, "I'm sorry, but we cannot give out that information." If the individual persists, a brief explanation of the rules of confidentiality usually suffices. Some settings have a public relations department or a designated individual to handle inquiries about the agency and its clients. If not, there is usually one supervisor or administrator to whom these questions are routinely referred. It is important that staff and student know where to direct inquiries before the need to do so arises.

4. OTHER AGENCIES AND MEMBERS OF OTHER DISCIPLINES

This is perhaps the most common source of requests for information. As previously indicated, the client must give informed consent for the

[27] *Ibid.*

[28] For example, see *ibid.*

disclosure to occur. It is important that (a) the request be in writing, (b) it state specifically what data is being sought and for what purpose, (c) the client be informed of the request and his written permission obtained for disclosure, and (d) the agency releasing the information include a statement of rules for the receiving party to follow in order to maintain confidentiality of the material. When requests are received, the record-keeper must determine just what information is needed; he should supply nothing further.

> Such selectiveness automatically rules out all those forms which say, "We note your clearing. . . ; please send us a summary of your contact"—which is to say, "Send along whatever you've got. Maybe somehow, sometime, it will prove useful." It calls for an end to the practice of automatically sending out copies of letters once written for a specific purpose and now used as the carbon copy response to all inquiries whether they come from a home for the aged or a well-baby clinic. The thoughtful selection of what to send to whom and whom to ask for what will, in brief, serve as one means of guarding against useless or irresponsible exchange of information.[29]

It is more time-consuming to selectively photocopy pages (perhaps blanking out irrelevant sections), or to prepare a special summary for the agency requesting the information, but this must be done if confidentiality is to be preserved and legal and ethical requirements met.

A setting may work so closely with another agency that a special arrangement is made for the automatic sharing of certain kinds of information without consumer permission. If this is the case, clients should be notified that such a data-exchange process occurs and told of its purpose.

5. THIRD-PARTY PAYERS

State and federal insurance programs, private insurers, sources of grant monies, and program fiscal supporters require a certain amount of data regarding individual clients served, in order for them to determine that the service for which they are being billed actually occurred and that it warrants the amount of payment requested. Thus, information is usually released with some client identification. There seem to be few practical ways to avoid this. However, safeguards can be taken. Since data is being released which fully identifies the client, his permission should be obtained. Only that information which the third-party payer needs in order to process its payment should be sent. There should be appropriate restrictions prohibiting the third party from releasing the data to anyone else or using it for any purpose other than the processing of the claimed fee.

Much criticism has been made of insurance carriers for allegedly mishandling confidential information. If this is indeed a problem, its ramifi-

---

[29] Helen Harris Perlman, "The Caseworker's Use of Collateral Information," *The Social Welfare Forum, 1951.* 78th Annual Meeting, Atlantic City, New Jersey, May 13–18, 1951 (New York: Columbia University Press, 1951), pp. 202–203.

cations are so widespread as to be almost unimaginable. For example, the Medical Information Bureau (MIB) is a private firm serving over 700 life- and health-insurance companies. It provides for insurance carriers com- puterized data about any of the twelve million individuals in its files.[30] The picture is not totally bleak, however; insurance companies are aware of con- fidentiality issues, and they are developing confidentiality guidelines and helping to draft new legislation.[31] So far, these efforts are directed primarily toward medical records and policies are often developed in cooperation with the American Medical Association and related groups. It is thus easy to respond with, "Oh well, that doesn't concern me—I'm a social worker." There was a time when this avoidance tactic would have been appropriate. However, the situation is rapidly changing. Social workers in private prac- tice are actively seeking recognition as professionals whose services should be reimbursable under various insurance programs. Interdisciplinary set- tings are beginning to seek direct reimbursement for services provided by social workers as well as physicians, psychiatrists, and others. The problem of release of information to third-party payers is not going to go away—it is intensifying. Psychiatry has been grappling with this problem much longer than has social work, and its experience should be utilized to assist in developing strong social-work position statements on the matter. Further- more, representatives of key social-work professional groups should be working hand-in-hand with those insurance groups that are developing policies, providing input into legislation so that social-work thinking can be taken into consideration.

6. PROFESSIONAL STANDARDS REVIEW ORGANIZATIONS (PSROs)

Federal law has made it mandatory that health-care services provided under Medicare, Medicaid, and maternal and child-health programs be reviewed for appropriateness and quality of care. In practice, selected medical records are "pulled" and reviewed by a team of physicians to deter- mine whether certain standards are being met. In interdisciplinary settings, social-work entries can be found in many of the records being reviewed. If social work discharge activities have affected or delayed in any way the pro- vision of health-care services, for example, the social worker's entries could become part of the review process itself. As social workers (and institutions within which they practice) seek reimbursement for services from these governmental providers, they will also be required to participate in some

[30] Adele Hofmann, "Is Confidentiality in Health Care Records a Pediatric Concern?," *op. cit.*

[31] Jeffrey J. Lampos, "Third-Party Access: Blue Cross and Blue Shield Plan Practice As An Example," Chapter 2 in *Confidentiality of Health & Social Service Records: Where Law, Ethics & Clinical Issues Meet,* pp. 53–78.

form of peer review. Indeed, many agencies have already developed or are in the process of setting up a peer-review mechanism in anticipation of the day when this will be a requirement. Thus, social work as a profession must now deal with confidentiality issues related to the release of information to these "professional standards review organizations" ("PSROs").

The Department of Health, Education, and Welfare is developing federal regulations which will set policies for confidentiality of PSRO data. In the interim, several HEW documents exist which set forth confidentiality policies which can be followed until the federal regulations take effect, which is not anticipated until sometime in 1978.[32] The following paragraphs from the "Transmittal Memo" accompanying the "Specifications for Confidentiality Policy on PSRO Data and Information" describe the policies and how they are to be used:

> The enclosed policy statements governing confidentiality of PSRO data and information have been approved by the Secretary as specifications for the development of regulations. Although the policies are not regulations and are subject to change as a result of the public rule-making process, PSROs will be expected to adhere to the policies pending publication of regulations.
>
> The following areas are addressed in the policy: (1) limitation on data acquisition, (2) responsibility for maintaining confidentiality, (3) public knowledge of the data system, (4) access to one's own records, (5) access to information by those within the PSRO review system, and (6) rules governing disclosure outside the PSRO review system. The definitions accompanying the policy statements should be read carefully so that key terminology is fully understood. Of special importance is the definition of "privileged information" which underlies the policies on what information may be disclosed outside the PSRO review system.[33]

PSROs are required to make their existence known to the general public, including consumers and providers of health-care services. The following excerpt from the Dade-Monroe PSRO's "Confidentiality Policy" illustrates how its basic confidentiality policies are explained to patients (a similar notice is supplied to health-care providers):

> Dear Medicare, Medicaid, or Maternal and Child Health Enrollee:
>
> Under Federal Law, health care services which may be paid for under the Medicare, Medicaid, and Maternal and Child Health programs are subject to review by authorized physician organizations to determine if the services are

[32] Three documents defining current PSRO confidentiality policies are: (1) PSRO Transmittal #16 dated February 14, 1975, entitled "Specifications for Confidentiality Policy on PSRO Data and Information." It defines the original policies on confidentiality of PSRO data and information; (2) PSRO Transmittal #41 dated October 6, 1976, entitled "Revisions and Addenda to Transmittal No. 16—Effective Upon Issuance;" and (3) "Specifications for Confidentiality Policy on PSRO Data and Information," a Notice of Proposed Rulemaking for interim regulations on confidentiality and disclosure of PSRO data and information. All originate from the Department of HEW, Public Health Service, Health Services Administration, Bureau of Quality Assurance, Rockville, Md. Item number (3) is undergoing revision.

[33] PSRO Transmittal Memo #16.

medically necessary, of a quality which meets professionally recognized standards of health care, and are appropriately furnished in a hospital or other health care institution. The Dade-Monroe PSRO has been designated as the Professional Standards Review Organization responsible for this review activity in this hospital. For review purposes, certain minimal information about your stay will be collected and analyzed. Federal law requires that information acquired for review purposes shall remain confidential and unauthorized disclosure is punishable by criminal penalties. Under policies of the Dade-Monroe PSRO governing confidentiality of information, medical information identifiable to individual patients may not be disclosed for other than review purposes. Procedures are provided for you or your representative to examine information about you maintained by the Dade-Monroe PSRO if you wish to verify its accuracy. For further information about these procedures or our policies governing confidentiality, please contact. . . .[34]

In summary form, PSRO confidentiality policies provide that:

1. Only specifically identified professional reviewers and staff will be authorized to review medical data.

2. All confidential records (including copies of printouts, analyses, encounter forms, etc.) will be disposed of in a manner which will render them useless when they are no longer needed.

3. All persons to whom an offer of employment is tendered will be informed prior to employment of the confidentiality of data and the rules and regulations governing that data.

4. All employees of the local PSRO will reaffirm their awareness and agreement with the local PSRO regulations regarding the confidentiality of data at least every six months.

5. Any employee of PSRO will be subject to immediate termination for violation of the PSRO policies regarding confidentiality. (They will, in addition, be subject to federal regulation and law which includes fines and/or imprisonment.)

6. Computer data files will be purged of all personal identifiers as soon as such identifiers are no longer required for purposes of review appeals, program monitoring, and program evaluation.[35]

Health-care providers are allowed access to their own PSRO files, and may receive copies. Patients can also gain access; however, the physician of record is notified at least ten days before patient access occurs even though he cannot prevent it. He may, however, object to the release of the information without clarification and may be present at the time of the consumer's access to make the desired clarification. Patient identifying data is kept in coded form. Computer files can be maintained "indefinitely"; however, personal identifying information must be removed when it is no longer

---

[34] Dade-Monroe Professional Standards Review Organization Inc., "Confidentiality Policy," Miami, Fla., November 1976, pp. 2-3.

[35] *Ibid.,* Section II.

needed. All disclosures are recorded; PSRO records and deliberations are considered privileged information and cannot be subpoenaed in civil litigation. However, certain governmental regulatory bodies can gain access to various types of PSRO data under certain circumstances.

A certain individual in each local PSRO group is designated as being responsible for monitoring confidentiality provisions. All employees are appraised of their confidentiality responsibilities, and must complete a training program before being allowed to handle confidential PSRO data. Furthermore, the employee must sign a statement acknowledging his responsibility to maintain confidentiality of PSRO data and his awareness of legal penalties for violations.[36]

In spite of all these elaborate precautions, there is still much concern about confidentiality of PSRO data. Massive amounts of information on hundreds of thousands of Americans are being collected and perused, and it is conceivable that one day virtually every U.S. resident will be found amongst the PSRO files. If this mountain of data is not handled appropriately, the results could be disastrous. Time and experience will tell if the system's safeguards are adequate and if they can be successfully implemented without abuses.

7. COMPUTERIZED DATA-BANK SYSTEMS

Much data ends up in computerized data banks, regardless of the party receiving the information. Several of the common sources of requests for information which we have already discussed store their data in computers. The confidentiality hazards associated with computerized data systems have been discussed in Chapter 4 and need not be repeated here.

8. RESEARCHERS

Persons desiring access to confidential information for research purposes may come from within or without the setting. A graduate student may be working on a dissertation and need access to a particular client-group or the internal workings of the agency; a business that solicits a certain consumer group may want to study the purchasing habits of those serviced by a given program; a governmental representative may be studying costs in relation to delivered services as preparation for recommending changes, and so on *ad infinitum*. Most settings require all researchers, including employees, to submit a written proposal outlining the purposes of the study and the specific information desired to an administrator or a screening committee for

---

[36] "Specifications for Confidentiality Policy on PSRO Data and Information," "Policy Statements," *op. cit.*

official authorization. Publicly funded settings often have a more formalized mechanism for this process than do small, private programs.

The Federal Privacy Act of 1974 specifies that federal records can be released to a researcher without the consumer's permission if the researcher has "provided the agency with advance adequate written assurance that the record will be used solely as a statistical research or reporting record, and the record is to be transferred in a form that is not individually identifiable."[37] The federal provisions for handling alcholol- and drug-abuse records are even more specific:

> . . . The content of records pertaining to any patient which are maintained in connection with the performance of a function subject to this part may be disclosed, whether or not the patient gives consent, to qualified personnel for the purpose of conducting scientific research, management audits, financial audits, or program evaluation, but such personnel may not identify, directly or indirectly, any individual patient in any report of such research, audit or evaluation or otherwise disclose patient identification in any manner.[38]

Thus, these regulations suggest that information might be released with identifying data intact, but the report produced by the researcher must disguise the data so that no individual is identifiable. The American Psychiatric Association in its "Position Statement on the Confidentiality of Medical Research Records" establishes even stricter controls:

1. Every investigator and agency has the ethical responsibility to preserve confidentiality of records.
2. Professionals of the agency may release research data only to professionally qualified and responsible investigators and only if such data are essential. Identifying data should never be released without having consent of the patient, his guardian, or his survivor.
3. The investigator should explain to the patient the extent of confidentiality of the information furnished.
4. Information should not be released to other researchers unless there is written assurance that they will follow the same principles regarding confidentiality.
5. The investigator has primary responsibility for the confidentiality of research records using data processing systems or any other methods of record storage.
6. Federal and state laws should be enacted to implement these principles.[39]

This statement of principle specifies that when identifying data is to be released, the client's permission must be obtained. Furthermore, the responsibility for maintaining the confidentiality of the material, once

---

[37] Federal Privacy Act of 1974. Public Law 93–579, December 31, 1974 (effective 9-27-75), Section 552a(b)(5).

[38] "Department of Health, Education and Welfare, Public Health Service: Confidentiality of Alcohol and Drug Abuse Patient Records—General Provisions." Found in the *Federal Register,* Vol. 40, No. 127 (July 1, 1975), Part IV, p. 27815, §2.52(a).

[39] "American Psychiatric Association Position Statement on the Confidentiality of Medical Research Records," *American Journal of Psychiatry,* Vol. 130, No. 6 (June 1973), p. 739.

released, clearly rests with the researcher. Other researchers may request the initial raw data in order to run a new analysis either to verify the results of the study or to extract the data in a different form. It would appear then that the initial researcher must transmit his raw data in a fully disguised form. Otherwise, he would need to obtain specific permission from each client involved before he could ethically release the information in identifiable form to a third party.

An interesting study by Nelson and Grunebaum[40] points up some of the difficulties that can be encountered in doing follow-up studies. They wished to determine what happened to several patients who had been hospitalized several years earlier for attempted suicide. The researchers started with the hospital records and were rather surprised to find that most record custodians readily gave them access as soon as they had identified themselves as psychiatrists. This disclosure occurred without the patients' knowledge or consent. "Fourteen out of fifteen professionals agreed to give information, taking the interviewer's word that he was a psychiatrist pursuing a research study." Problems began to surface, however, as the researchers started contacting the patients. Many had moved, and friends and relatives often had to be approached about their whereabouts. Yet, the psychiatrists could not reveal to them why they wanted to contact the former patient. During the course of the study, several patients became quite upset over the researchers' efforts to reach them, and resented having something from their past "dug up" without their knowledge or permission.

A strong argument in favor of the requirement that settings should release data to researchers in unidentifiable form is the fact that persons conducting research have been subpoenaed and forced to reveal names of individuals and research findings. Obviously, if a researcher does not know the identity or identifying numbers of any individual contained in his raw data, it would be much more difficult for the courts to get at this information. The federal provisions for handling the records of substance abusers contain a rather specific clause designed to prevent researchers from being forced to disclose data:

> Where the content of patient records has been disclosed pursuant to this subpart for the purpose of conducting scientific research, management audits, financial audits, or program evaluation, information contained therein which would directly or indirectly identify any patient may not be disclosed by the recipient thereof either voluntarily or in response to any legal process whether Federal or State.[41]

However, Nejelski and Finsterbusch[42] give several examples of instances

[40] Scott H. Nelson and Henry Grunebaum, "Ethical Issues in Psychiatric Follow-up Studies," *American Journal of Psychiatry*, Vol. 128, No. 11 (November 1972), pp. 1358–1362.

[41] Confidentiality of Alcohol and Drug Abuse Patient Records, p. 27819, §2.56.

[42] Paul Nejelski and Kurt Finsterbusch, "The Prosecutor and the Researcher: Present and Prospective Variations on the Supreme Court's *Branzburg* Decision," *Social Service Review*, Vol. 21, No. 1 (Summer 1973), pp. 3–21.

where researchers have been subpoenaed. They also report that researchers have been required to violate confidentiality if they have learned of a serious crime while doing research. Furthermore, in the *Branzburg* case reported by the authors, a reporter studying drug usage was subpoenaed and asked to reveal the sources of his information. He refused. The Supreme Court "held that a reporter does not have to identify sources of knowledge told to him, but he cannot refuse to testify regarding things he has seen himself."[43]

Researchers are gaining the right of privileged communication in some states, thus increasing the chances that information released to them will remain confidential. James D. Carroll and Charles R. Knerr have conducted an extensive research project in which they have collected and studied examples of confidentiality problems encountered by researchers from various disciplines.[44] Approximately 250 incidents were reported. Only one case was identified in which a researcher was actually imprisoned for refusing to disclose confidential information, that of Samuel Popkin in 1972. The problems encountered in keeping research data confidential are identified rather specifically and supported by case examples:

> . . . [The] data gathered suggests a problem of serious magnitude. Some two dozen scholars have been subpoenaed in recent years, or indirectly threatened with a subpoena, in efforts to obtain research data. Instances of data theft have been isolated. Instances of suspected wiretapping and mail covers have been identified. Numerous scholars have reported direct pressure and intimidation exerted by governmental or other actors seeking raw data. A number of other confidentiality difficulties have also been reported: unanticipated discovery of criminal activities of subjects; denial of access to sources of data based on claims of privacy or condfidentiality; organized subject or community reluctance or refusal to participate in research; and legal processes initiated by subjects oriented toward terminating research or preventing the publication of research findings.[45]

Thus, there is no guarantee that information released to researchers can be kept confidential. Social work programs and practitioners disclosing data to them should thus do so only with client permission and/or all identifying details thoroughly disguised.

9. THE NEWS MEDIA

Certain settings seem to find themselves approached by newspeople more than others. Agencies serving the victims or perpetrators of crimes,

---

[43] *Ibid.*, p. 5n.

[44] James D. Carroll and Charles R. Knerr, "The APSA Confidentiality in Social Science Research Project: A Final Report," *PS* (Fall 1976), p. 417, footnote 5.

[45] James D. Carroll and Charles R. Knerr, "A Report of APSA Confidentiality in Social Science Research Data Project," *PS* (Summer 1975), p. 259. See also "The APSA Confidentiality in Social Science Research Project: A Final Report," *op. cit.* An additional report is forthcoming from these authors in the near future.

settings involved with child abuse, and welfare and publicly funded programs often find themselves (or the clients they serve) of interest to the news media. Reporters may be evaluating the quality of a program, perhaps even noting consumer perceptions of the effectiveness of the service-delivery system. A client or an employee may initiate a contact with the news media in order to ventilate a concern or trigger an investigation. Reporters respect the confidence of the person contacting them and will not usually reveal to agency staff the full information which prompted their contact. When a news article is being prepared for publication, agency staff often cannot accurately predict just what it will say or in what light the agency will be presented until it has actually come out. Thus, the agency must try to assure the accuracy of public representation of the service-delivery system, while protecting from unauthorized publicity material which is condifential either in respect to its clientele or its internal workings. Therefore, individual social workers are often discouraged from talking directly with reporters. Instead, the contact is reported to a supervisory-administrative person, and the newsman is referred to him with a simple, "I'm sorry, but I am not authorized to give you that information." If the reporter knows that the social worker has the information he needs, pressure may be subtly or directly applied, but the worker's response must remain unchanged. The public relations office or a designated administrator will usually decide what information is to be released, if any, and in what manner. The administrator may in fact authorize the social worker to engage in a formal interview with the reporter, but it would be with definite guidance as to how the information should be presented. Very often it is in the agency's best interest to release some data so that all aspects of the subject under investigation can be represented. Administrators may consult with agency attorneys if in doubt about how to handle disclosures to the news media.

When it comes to contacts concerning individual clients, strict policies must apply. Most settings require the consumer's written permission before any identifying data about him can be released in any form. Again, releasing the information may be in the client's and the agency's best interests, but consent for the disclosure is still necessary. Specific signed releases must be obtained if any photographs are to be taken. Several suits have been brought and won by patients who were photographed while unconscious or whose pictures were published in a medical journal to illustrate a procedure—all without their permission. The agency personnel allowing the unauthorized photographs were the ones held responsible.[46] However, there are situations where patient photographs without formal consent might be permissible. For example, if an individual is brought into a hospital emergency room unconscious, confused, or amnesic, it may be necessary to publicize his photograph with all known data in an effort to determine his identity and locate friends and relatives. Such action would clearly be in the best

[46] Arthur H. Bernstein, "Unauthorized Disclosure of Confidential Information," *Hospitals,* Vol. 48 (November 1, 1974), p. 126.

interests of a consumer obviously unable to act in his own behalf, and who probably has no legal guardian.

Occasionally a client will initiate the news media contact. This is his prerogative, of course, and in so doing he is automatically authorizing release of whatever information he gives the media. If the agency is then approached by a reporter seeking additional details, it would be important to ascertain whether the consumer has given specific permission for release of the additional information.

Employees wishing to initiate contacts with the media should obtain clearance from their administrators before doing so. If the agency will not grant permission, the social worker should weigh the importance of the goal he is seeking to accomplish against the probable effect of such contact upon his continued employment.

10. CONSUMER-IDENTIFYING INFORMATION IN PUBLISHED REPORTS

Professionals are encouraged to publish the results of their research and academic activities. Those involved in direct consumer contact often feel a need to illustrate their writings with case examples. As discussed previously, the client's consent must be obtained in writing if identifying details are to be used. There has been at least one case in which distribution of a psychiatric text was halted because of failure to comply with this guideline.[47] In a somewhat similar action, a man involved in a crime published an account of what had happened eleven years earlier. As part of his story, he mentioned the name of another person also involved at that time. This individual sued because most people did not know of his past activities and the article created some significant problems for him. The Supreme Court overturned the decision of a lower court when it ruled that, although the facts of a criminal act are newsworthy, the name of an individual is not, and therefore cannot be published without consent.[48] In an effort to avoid these kinds of difficulties, the American Psychiatric Association has adopted the stance that "if a case study is ever to be published without consent, there must be no reasonable likelihood that the subject can be identified."[49]

11. ATTORNEYS

There seems to be a tendency, especially among beginning practitioners and students, to discard all the usual principles of confidentiality when a

[47] "Case Notes: *Roe v. Doe:* A Remedy for Disclosure of Psychiatric Confidences," *Rutgers Law Review,* Vol. 29 (Fall 1975).

[48] "Invasion of Privacy—Former Criminal's Name Entitled to Protection," *Briscoe v. Reader's Digest Assoc. Inc.,* Supreme Court of California, 4-2-71. Found in the *Social Welfare Court Digest* Vol. 16, No. 6 (June, 1971), p. 1.

[49] "Case Notes: *Roe v. Doe,*" *op. cit.,* p. 196.

voice on the telephone says, "This is John Henry Higgenbotham III, attorney-at-law. I need to know. . . . " Often it is a very simple, seemingly innocuous question such as, "My records show Jerry Akins' address as 81 North Blossom Drive—does that agree with your files?" However, even a simple "yes" or "no" could be a violation of confidentiality. Unless the social worker, or his records, has been subpoenaed, release of information to an attorney is handled in basically the same way as disclosure to any other person. The practitioner being asked the "simple" question here does not know if Mr. Akins has given permission for the data to be released to Mr. Higgenbotham. Mr. Higgenbotham may be the attorney for the prosecution rather than for the client, and the social worker has no way of knowing exactly how he intends to use the desired information. Thus, unless the service provider has specific permission from the client to release the information, the standard reply should be, "I'm sorry, but I cannot give you that information." Most attorneys realize that settings in which social work is practiced consider their records confidential, and therefore they expect to receive an "I'm sorry" in response to their inquiries. One wonders, however, how many attorneys call anyway, hoping to catch a secretary, inexperienced employee, or student off guard. If the lawyer is lucky and the requested unauthorized release of information occurs, it can save him the trouble and expense of getting a subpoena. However, in states where social workers are covered by privileged-communication statutes, the attorney may still get an "I'm sorry—I can't release that" even in response to his subpoena. Without this protection, agency materials are, of course, much more accessible to the courts.

12. POLICE

This situation is similar to that involving release of information to attorneys. The mere fact that a policeman or a law enforcement agency requests information does not automatically mean that it should or must be released. However, police departments do have routine access to the records of certain settings; this should be ascertained for the specific state in which the social worker is practicing.[50]

The Federal Privacy Act of 1974 states that records can be released to law enforcement personnel without the individual's consent under certain conditions:

> [When] the agency or an instrumentality of any governmental jurisdiction [is] within or under the control of the United States for a civil or criminal law enforcement activity, [the record can be released] if the activity is authorized by

---

[50] Alan Sussman, writing on "The Confidentiality of Family Court Records," *Social Service Review* (December 1971), pp. 455–481, reports that in New York State in 1971, despite laws governing confidentiality of juvenile court records, the police department was one of several agencies having routine access with or without the child's or his legal guardian's consent.

law, and if the head of the agency or instrumentality has made a written request to the agency which maintains the record specifying the particular portion desired and the law enforcement activity for which the record is sought.[51]

The federal provisions for substance-abuse records are more complex, but do provide for release of information to law enforcement officials under certain circumstances. They also specifically prohibit any law enforcement person from enrolling in a drug treatment program as an "informer" in an attempt to get inside information.

In summary, when law enforcement officials request information from an agency's files, it is essential to determine whether they are acting as the result of a court order; this information will then help to determine what action the agency should take.

13. THE COURTS

An attorney or law enforcement representative may obtain a subpoena or a court order requesting that case record-material, agency personnel, and/or clients appear in court. The request is usually quite specific as to what information is desired. If it is not, every effort should be made to determine exactly what issue is being investigated and what, specifically, the court wants the agency to provide. The custodian of the records (or the unrecorded data) should carefully evaluate what information is relevant to the court's request and what is not. If material for which the court is asking appears to have no direct bearing on the issue at hand, the agency should try to avoid having to produce it. If the social worker receiving the subpoena functions in a state where laws grant the right of privileged communication, he may be able to resist compliance with the subpoena. There are a number of exceptions, however. If the practitioner is in a state granting privileged communication but is *not* licensed by that state, he may be forced to produce the records, since most state privileged-communication statutes grant it only to licensed members of the professions so covered. If a social worker is totally without this protection, he has no legal recourse and must comply with the subpoena or be held in contempt of court. There have been situations, however, when attorneys for the social worker have been able to convince the courts that the information should not be released. Privileged communication and requests for information from the courts are discussed in detail in Chapters 7 through 9.

---

[51] Federal Privacy Act of 1974, Section 552a(b)(7).

6. Consumer Access to Record Materials

What stands out is the extent to which the client is not involved in the process. He plays almost no part in writing the record and almost certainly never reads it. Even if the client is aware that supervision, psychiatric consultation, or interagency conferences occur, he seldom learns the results. Certainly these activities are essential to treatment. Why is the client not involved more?[1]

Harris Chaiklin

ONLY A FEW SHORT YEARS AGO, the social work profession simply assumed that a record was the private property of the professional or the agency, and that was that. A few therapists occasionally advocated client participation in recording as part of the therapeutic process, and others began using the video-recorded interview as a means of allowing the individual to study how he communicates and to provide feedback regarding the therapist's effectiveness. However, such procedures were considered experimental rather than routine.

The medical profession was one of the first to have open files. The American Hospital Association's "Patient Bill of Rights" recognizes the importance to patients of having knowledge of their illness, treatment procedures, and related matters, and advises that this be conveyed to them in terms they can understand. Earl Rose, in an article discussing the availability of information on pathology and autopsy, reports that various court decisions have ruled that the physician and the hospital own the medical chart, although the patient can order that the record not be destroyed.[2] The patient also has the right of access to his record. If he dies, his next of kin have the same right to medical and lab reports as did the patient when he was

[1] Harris Chaiklin, "Honesty in Casework Treatment," *The Social Welfare Forum, 1973.* NCSW, Atlantic City, May 27–31, 1973 (New York: Columbia University Press, 1974), pp. 266–267.

[2] Earl F. Rose, "Pathology Reports and Autopsy Protocols: Confidentiality, Privilege, and Accessibility," *American Journal of Clinical Pathology,* Vol. 57, No. 2 (February 1972), pp. 144–155.

alive. In a recent issue of *Nursing Outlook,* it was reported that as of January 1976 nine states had laws on the books granting patients the right of access to their medical records. In six of these states (Massachusetts, Wisconsin, New Jersey, Louisiana, Mississippi, and Connecticut) the patient can have direct access, and in the remaining three (Utah, California, and Illinois) access can be achieved through an attorney.[3]

Comparatively few persons seek access to their records; however, with increasing awareness of consumer rights, this can be expected to change. With the advent of the Federal Privacy Act of 1974, a new era has begun. Not only must the consumer being served by a federal agency have access to his files, but he must be permitted in inspecting his file to bring someone with him if he wishes and be given copies of his file if desired. Furthermore, a detailed procedure is prescribed permitting the consumer to amend or correct his records. There is also a mandate to publicize these rights so that consumers are aware of them.

Federal agencies must

permit an individual to gain access to information pertaining to him in Federal agency records, to have a copy made of all or any portion thereof, and to correct or amend such records;

upon request by any individual to gain access to his record or to any information pertaining to him which is contained in the system, permit him and upon his request, a person of his own choosing to accompany him, to review the record and have a copy made of all or any portion thereof in a form comprehensible to him, except that the agency may require the individual to furnish a written statement authorizing discussion of that individual's record in the accompanying person's presence;

permit the individual to request amendment of a record pertaining to him. . . .[4]

As a result of this legislation, all patients receiving medical care under the federally administered Medicare program, all patients in Veteran's Administration Hospitals, and recipients of Social Security or SSI (Supplemental Security Income) benefits under the Social Security Administration have access to their records. Social work recording of some type finds its way into many of these and other federal records.

Non-federally funded and administered social-work settings are not currently required to grant consumer access to their files. However, settings receiving federal funds for services to certain types of clients are required to abide by certain federal regulations.[5]

[3] Lucie Young Kelly, "The Patient's Right to Know," *Nursing Outlook,* Vol. 24, No. 1 (January 1976), p. 30.

[4] Federal Privacy Act of 1974, Section 2(b)(3) and Section 552a(d)(1) + (2).

[5] See, for example, "Confidentiality of Alcohol and Drug Abuse Patient Records—General Provisions." U.S. Department of Health, Education and Welfare, Public Health Service. Found in the *Federal Register,* Vol. 40, No. 127 (July 1, 1975), Part IV, page 27805, Section 2.11(o).

Although the majority of social work agencies and practitioners are not affected by federal privacy laws and regulations, as consumers of federal services become aware of their rights and begin exercising them in these settings, they can be expected to come to the private agency seeking the same basic privileges. Thus, there will be increasing pressure from consumers (and also as a result of the ethical philosophy of the social work profession) for all settings to be more open in sharing record materials with clients.

Even one of the oldest and most traditional strongholds of secrecy is beginning to give way under the pressure of consumer groups—the sealed records of adoptions. More and more adoptees upon reaching adulthood are demanding access to their birth records and the identity of their natural parents; they feel strongly that this is their right. As of 1974, only three states (Alabama, South Dakota, and Virginia) did *not* keep adoption records completely sealed; the courts have traditionally refused to reveal the identity of the natural parents to adult adoptees (and vice versa) except in situations involving unusual health and legal issues. Several groups of adult adoptees have formed and are experiencing some success in helping members and others to identify and locate their biological parents.[6]

The NASW official policy statement on confidentiality is quite general and does not specify the type of client access it recommends.

> Clients should be apprised of the kind of record(s) maintained by the worker and/or the agency and should have the right to personally verify its accuracy.[7]

Many agencies not directly affected by legislation or other mandates simply have no policies regarding openness of their records to clients because they have never been faced with a request. These settings should develop a policy which (1) states whether consumers do or do not have access to the various files maintained by the agency, (2) gives procedures by which clients may gain access, (3) provides a specific method by which the information will be shared (i.e., by discussing it orally, allowing the consumer to actually read his file, permitting him to duplicate it, or releasing contents only to the client's legal representative, among other procedures). Such a policy could prevent an agency from making a hasty decision when faced with an unexpected request. Such hasty decisions often set precedents that are very difficult to alter later when there is more time to carefully develop the desired policy.

Serious consideration is now being given to extending the Federal Privacy Act to local governmental and private programs. The act established the Privacy Protection Study Commission, which, among other tasks, was charged with the responsibility of studying private programs and

[6] Annette Baran, Reuben Pannor, and Arthur D. Sorosky, "Adoptive Parents and the Sealed Record Controversy," *Social Casework,* Vol. 55, No. 9 (November 1974), p. 532.

[7] NASW "Policy on Information Utilization and Confidentiality Policy adopted at the National Association of Social Workers 1975 Delegate Assembly, May 30–June 3, 1975, Washington, D.C., p. 5.

determining the need for federal legislation to protect consumers of these services as well. Hearings have been held before the commission on this topic. Several groups which testified opposed the extension of this act to their respective areas, on the basis that it would be unnecessary or would create an unmanageable accountability burden hampering service-delivery to consumers.

Why then is the government even examining the practices of private settings? Obviously there is federal concern about record-keeping practices and openness with consumers. As many social-work settings have failed to develop official guidelines of their own, this concern is justified to a certain extent. One cannot help but speculate that if various professions had paid more attention to confidentiality matters in earlier years, there would be little need now for federal intervention.

The openness of case record-material, whether voluntary or required by law, arouses considerable controversy, raising a host of questions and concerns. Other disciplines have already grappled with many of the key issues. Their experiences can be useful to the social work profession.

Arguments for Restricting Client Access to Records

Most social workers are strongly opposed to total openness of records, maintaining that if this practice becomes mandatory they will keep only "clean" and "fully sanitized" records. Such files would contain minimal diagnostic material and little else that would be meaningful. Many practitioners argue that the social worker *must* have control over what is shared and what is not shared if treatment is to be effective. Arguments against total sharing of record material are often quite caustic and to-the-point: "If I have to get all bogged down in having to document every time I breathe, and record every disclosure of information and every request for client access, that's all I'll be doing—forget social-work services—there won't be time for any of that."

The literature of various professions clearly expresses a number of reasons why consumers should not have full access to their records. Some concerns seem motivated by a desire to protect the consumer, while others address themselves more to the needs of the professional. But even when consumer access is recommended, repercussions are often mentioned along with cautionary comments.

1. PSYCHOLOGICAL DAMAGE TO CLIENT

Does the record show that the recorder respects the consumer as a person with dignity and privacy rights, or does it contain judgmental, unprofessional, careless, irrelevant, and perhaps downright negative remarks that speak so loudly they overshadow the social worker's verbalized allegiance to professionalism? What effect would such remarks have on the client who reads them?

I once conducted a review of intake recordings in a public-welfare setting employing persons with a bachelor's degree not trained in social work. They were learning the rudiments of diagnostic thinking. Among the officially recorded and typewritten entries was this remark, included under the heading "Worker's Impression":

> Mrs. A. had long, stringy hair hanging down over her face. Her skin was very wrinkled and her clothes quite messy-looking. She was all stooped over. I hate to say it, but to describe this woman I would have to say that she looked like a witch out of a horror movie.

When records contain this kind of recording, the client would obviously be damaged by what he sees. Furthermore, he might have a basis for legal action against the worker for slander or libel if he felt and could prove the material was unprofessional and had been harmful. Adherence to proper recording techniques along with maintenance of full respect for the consumer will greatly reduce possible harm to consumers from viewing their record material.

2. ADVERSE CLIENT REACTION TO PROFESSIONAL DIAGNOSTIC MATERIAL

The professionally trained therapist diagnostically assesses the counselee's adjustment, his coping mechanisms, and overt and covert feelings and behaviors. This is obviously essential to the treatment process. However, it is equally obvious that it is not always appropriate or desirable for the client to achieve the same depth of diagnostic awareness as does the counselor. While one of the goals of the therapeutic relationship may be to help the individual gain insight himself, it should be done gradually and with appropriate reinforcement. If the client has continuous open access to his file, the counselor has no choice but to omit some of his diagnostic thinking from the record to prevent a premature (and possibly damaging) awareness in the client deleterious to him and the therapeutic process. The therapist might occasionally make an entry designed to confront the patient with something he has had difficulty recognizing in himself, but it would be made selectively and used primarily as a therapeutic tool.

Thus, if records are to be openly shared with counselees, it appears that the format of social work recording will need to undergo some changes. Simply to make skimpier entries is obviously not a lasting solution, and overreactions in this direction could lead to some of the problems we have discussed earlier, in Chapter 4. On the other hand, with more selective recording the omission of some highly sensitive material that may have been recorded in the past reduces the risks of unauthorized disclosures and other confidentiality violations.

A rather important question which affects basic casework technique must be faced: What, if anything, is wrong with sharing with the client a great deal more than we have traditionally shared regarding treatment approach and our assessment of his condition? What exactly *would* happen if we were more open in our approach to the treatment process? Although withholding of all diagnostic material from social-service records is becoming standard in some settings, it does carry its risks, as we have already pointed out. Perhaps the social work profession needs to give serious consideration to the suggestion of the American Hospital Association's "Patient's Bill of Rights," which states:

> The patient has the right to obtain from his physician *complete* current information concerning *his diagnosis, treatment, and prognosis* in terms the patient can be reasonably expected to understand. *When it is not medically advisable to give such information to the patient, the information should be made available to an appropriate person in his behalf.* [Emphasis added.]

It may be necessary to develop some definitions of just what kinds of diagnoses would be "inadvisable to give to the patient" and build in appropriate safeguards rather than eliminate pertinent professional observations entirely. It is conceivable that these definitions might well vary from one setting to another, and that each agency would want to set up its own mechanism for handling record sharing.

Another approach that has been suggested is to define who owns the information contained in records. The Joint Task Force on Confidentiality of Computerized Medical Records decided that

> the patient should be the owner of the information provided by him during medical care, and of his clinical data. . . [and] the physician shall be the owner of the information generated by him during medical care.[8]

Thus, the consumer owns the information he provides, and diagnostic, prognostic data generated by the professional belongs to him; he, in turn, controls its release. The Joint Task Force further recommends that "other health professionals, such as dentists, social workers, nurses, and other members of the health team may also wish to place similar restrictions on their part of the medical record."[9] Unfortunately, such recommendations would result in a dual record-keeping system, unacceptable under the current provisions of the Federal Privacy Act, which opposes "secret" files.

[8] "Ethical Guidelines for Data Centers Handling Medical Records," Joint Task Group on Confidentiality of Computerized Medical Records, E.R. Gabriel, Chairman. Adopted by the House of Delegates of the Medical Society of the State of New York, March 1975; adopted by the Board of Directors of the Society for Computer Medicine, November 1975. Also a position statement of the National Association of Blue Shield Plans. p. 3.

[9] *Ibid.,* p. 4.

3. MATERIAL FROM OUTSIDE SOURCES UNSUITABLE FOR CLIENT'S PERUSAL

Once an agency opens its files, it is relatively easy to prevent the accumulation of new material of this nature. Agencies and members of other disciplines submitting material can be advised that records are open to inspection by clientele, including reports coming from outside sources. Should something come in that is obviously not appropriate for the consumer to view, it might be shared with his representative instead. Another less desirable alternative would be to abstract pertinent facts from the report for the record and then destroy the original. It might be tempting to set up a special file for these kinds of reports; however, this would clearly be in opposition to current legislation affecting federal programs.

All this does not solve the problem of what should be done with material from outside sources already in the record at the time the open-sharing policy is implemented. The Federal Privacy Act includes a clause that exempts a federal agency from having to disclose information to the client if

> disclosure of such material would reveal the identity of a source who furnished information to the Government under an express promise that the identity of the source would be held in confidence, or, prior to the effective date of this section, under an implied promise that the identity of the source would be held in confidence. (§552a[k] [2].)

This does not apply to all types of information, and it is important to note that it concerns the identity of the source of the data furnished rather than the content. However, these guidelines do suggest some concepts that could well be implemented in private settings.

An article in the *Journal of the Kansas Medical Society* (November 1975) describes an approach used by the Social Security Administration when medical reports are received in processing disability claims. It is stated there that Social Security expects to get requests for release of medical records to recipients under the Federal Privacy Act and anticipates some situations in which "direct access to a medical report may have an adverse effect on the individual. Procedures, therefore, call for a screening of medical reports to identify these cases. In such cases, the report will be released only to an authorized representative designated by the individual."[10] It can be expected that other settings will adopt their own versions of this practice.

4. CLIENT LAWSUIT AGAINST THE SOCIAL WORKER

Consumers are certainly more lawsuit-conscious today than ever before. Anyone can institute a suit over anything, no matter how absurd the

[10] "Federal Privacy Act: Disclosure of Medical Reports in Social Security Disability Claims" (no author), *Journal of the Kansas Medical Society*, Vol. 76, No. 11 (November 1975), p. 282.

charges. The practitioner's concern should be whether the individual has any basis for winning the claim and collecting damages or other court-awarded settlements.

If a record contains the kind of irresponsible entry illustrated on page 87, the worker has reason to fear legal action. But suppose a professional recording happens to use diagnostic labels such as "displays paranoid ideation," or "reality testing is still poor," or "manipulative tendencies were quite evident in today's session," or "client is functionally illiterate and has been classified as an educable retardate"? It is conceivable that a consumer could take issue with some of these terms, particularly those that appear negative to him. Such a suit would probably claim damages for libel or slander.

Webster's New Collegiate Dictionary gives the following basic definition of "libel":

> Any statement or representation, published without just cause or excuse, or by pictures, effigies, or other signs, tending to expose another to public hatred, contempt, or ridicule; also, the act, tort, or crime of publishing this.[11]

"Slander," on the other hand, refers primarily to spoken words:

> [n] A false report maliciously uttered and tending to injure the reputation of another. . . . [vb.] To utter slander against; to defame.[12]

To "defame" means

> to harm or destroy the good fame of. To cast aspersion on the good name or reputation of; to slander. . .[13]

The key words in all these definitions are "false" and "malicious." As long as what is stated in the record is true and accurate, the social worker has little to fear. Furthermore, the remark must be damaging to the individual in some manner. A review of the literature reveals situations where consumers have sued, claiming damages for libel because of the use of a diagnostic term in a case record. Perhaps the most often quoted is *Iverson v. Frandsen* (1956). A student was referred to as a "high-grade moron" in a report sent to a public school by a psychologist. The parent reading the record objected to the use of the term and sued, but the courts ruled in favor of the school and the psychologist. Diagnostic labels do not constitute slander or libel if they represent the professional's best judgment and are free from malice.[14] It would be interesting to speculate what might happen should a person without professional training in the psychodynamics of

[11] *Webster's New Collegiate Dictionary* (Springfield, Mass.: G. & C. Merriam Co., 1961), p. 484.

[12] *Ibid.,* p. 795.

[13] *Ibid.,* p. 216.

[14] *Iverson v. Frandsen,* 237 F2d 898 (Utah Court of Appeals, 1956), discussed in Robert E. Boyd and Richard D. Heinsen, "Problems in Privileged Communication," *Personnel and Guidance Journal* Vol. 50, No. 4 (December 1971), pp. 276–279.

human behavior attempt the use of diagnostic terms. Would the courts feel that such a person used "professional judgment" in applying the label? Would the individual who calls himself a "social worker" but who does not have professional social-work training be held liable in such a situation?

This also raises an interesting point in favor of *not* doing away with records: Were a consumer to bring suit claiming that a certain diagnostic label was false, the social worker might find himself desperately in need of earlier documentation in the record to support his diagnostic assessment.

Finally, it has been pointed out that

[providing] it is assumed that a patient is competent, and not too young to exercise judgment, if such a patient asks to see [his] record, presumably he has considered the possibility that it may contain distressing information.[15]

Thus, consumers must be willing to assume some responsibility for the outcome when they ask to see confidential record materials. This concept should be quite compatible with social work's adherence to the principle of the "right of self-determination."

5. "PRACTITIONERS KNOW BEST"

This argument is sometimes presented as a reason for not allowing consumers to view their files.[16] "We would not want the consumer to interject his thinking when he obviously doesn't know as much as we do, and besides this would simply confuse the issue when we professionals have already reached a decision."

6. SECRECY OF RECORDS "ESSENTIAL TO PROFESSIONAL EFFECTIVENESS"

This rationale[17] would have us believe that therapists have become so dependent on the record's "safety" from clients that they could not function effectively in a more open atmosphere.

7. AVAILABILITY OF UNSUITABLE MATERIAL TO SIGNIFICANT OTHERS

The record may contain statements by the client concerning significant others in his life who may also have access to the file. For example, public

[15] Barbara L. Kaiser, "Patients' Rights of Access to their Own Medical Records: The Need for New Law," *Buffalo Law Review,* Vol. 24 (Winter 1975), p. 325.

[16] Stanley L. Brodsky, "Shared Results and Open Files with Client," *Professional Psychology* (Fall 1972), pp. 362–364.

[17] *Ibid.*

school records are now open to students and their parents. If a guidance counselor or school social worker involved in a helping relationship with a student had recorded that the individual had less-than-positive feelings toward his parents, problems could result if the parents see the file. This delicate situation can arise when persons other than the primary client have legal access to the record; it happens most frequently with minors, persons declared legally mentally incompetent, and, in some situations, with spouses. In reality, many professionals will probably cope with this problem by simply not recording potentially troublesome remarks, doing so strictly as a therapeutic tool or only after the family member has become aware of the client's feelings. The fact that other persons will have access to the record and how the social worker will handle this should be discussed with the consumer early in the relationship.

8. ADDITIONAL ADMINISTRATIVE RESPONSIBILITY

Openness of client records will certainly add to administrative responsibility. As no one relishes additional paperwork, this may cause some resistance to the open-file concept.

9. MANIPULATION OF INFORMATION BY CLIENT

It is possible that consumers could use the data in manipulative, damaging ways to promote what they see as their own interests. A client might maintain an inappropriate pattern of dependency by announcing to those who place undesired expectations on him, "But I am suffering from a depressive reaction, and therefore. . . ." Disability claims might be juggled and family members manipulated to gain sympathy. Crimes might even be committed with the excuse, "They'll never find me guilty—I'm a 'paranoid schizophrenic with overt psychosis'!"

10. REDUCED RECORDING AS RESULT OF CLIENT ACCESS

Social work records, according to some, need to be *more,* not *less,* detailed. Practitioners feeling this way do not welcome consumer access. Unfortunately, reduced recording is already occurring in some settings. The hazards associated with this action have already been pointed out (pp. 47–54) and will not be repeated here.

11. OUTSIDERS TAKING ADVANTAGE OF CLIENT ACCESS

It is conceivable that some persons might use a client's right of access to get information the agency refuses to release to them directly. For example, an unethical employer, suspecting that an individual has a history of treatment for an emotional problem, may make it a condition of employment that the employee gain access to his file and supply the employer with certain confidential data. This is not so improbable when one recalls how many employment applications, both governmental and private, ask the question: "Have you ever suffered from a nervous or mental disorder?"

12. ENFORCEMENT MECHANISMS REQUIRED

To ensure that consumers really do obtain access, and to prevent record-keepers from engaging in manipulative, delaying, and avoidance tactics to prevent full disclosure, new enforcement procedures and personnel will be needed.

13. ABUSES DUE TO CLIENT'S POSSESSION OF RECORD-COPY

It has been argued that even if access is granted, the consumer should never be given a copy of his record. Gordon and Barnard present a rather frightening list of possible consequences:[18]

1. The patient might misuse the reports by keeping some and disposing of others to bring them forth selectively, depending on how he wants to present himself.

2. Relatives searching through the belongings of a deceased patient may come across copies of psychiatric reports revealing diagnoses and treatment of which they were unaware. One does not need much imagination to consider the problems this could create.

3. Heirs may use the reports to overturn a will: "See, this proves my brother was not competent mentally when he wrote his will and failed to leave me a share of his estate," and so on.

4. Relatives or others may get hold of copies of the reports and use them to manipulate, blackmail, or control the patient in some manner.

5. Some patients might dwell on the contents of the reports and thus exacerbate their symptoms.

Arguments Favoring Client Access to Records

There is increasing commitment to the concept of open records, and recent position statements and professional writings illustrate this trend. The trend

---

[18] Richard E. Gordon and George W. Barnard, "Why a Patient Should Never Get a Copy of His Psychiatric Report," *Consultant,* Vol. 14, No. 12 (December 1974), pp. 110–111.

and its supporting arguments are quite powerful and cannot be passed over lightly:

1. Federal law requires that consumers have access to their records in federal settings and in some private settings receiving federal funds. There is a possibility that this law, or some version of it, will soon require open records in all private agencies.

2. The NASW "Policy on Information Utilization and Confidentiality" clearly indicates that social work clients should have access to record material, though specific guidelines and cautions regarding the implementation of this principle are not spelled out.[19]

3. The consumer will be able to give fully "informed consent" when requests come for release of information from his file, because he will have seen the material in question and will know exactly what is being released.

4. The consumer will have greater opportunity to amend or correct his file. It has even been suggested that every individual "be allotted a section at the conclusion of the evaluation or diagnostic reports for a narrative personal self-evaluation and comments on the rest of the report."[20]

5. The client will be a genuinely active participant in the definition and shaping of his treatment. This can be therapeutic in and of itself. While this can be achieved without full sharing of record material, it is much more difficult.

6. The knowledge that the client has access will act as a quality-control mechanism as professionals become more aware of what they record and the way in which they do so.

7. There will be greater reliance on the client as the primary source of information. This will enable him to participate more actively in the information-gathering and treatment process. He will also be assured that the practitioner has heard his version of any data being sought from outside.

8. Without client awareness of record content, the file might come to rigidly reinforce a definition of what the client is or should be, making it virtually impossible for him to change or become anything different from what his record dictates. This tendency is often reinforced as other professionals with legitimate access to the file simply incorporate this definition without evaluating for themselves whether it is current and accurate.

9. The professional's own growth would be facilitated if the client were free to challenge his assessments. Counselors might not cling so rigidly to conclusions that perhaps should be highly tenuous and flexible instead.

10. The language used in recording would probably become less cloaked in the technical jargon peculiar to the profession.

11. Highly sensitive, possibly incriminating, material would simply not

[19] NASW "Policy on Information Utilization and Confidentiality," *op. cit.*
[20] Brodsky, *op. cit.*, p. 363.

be recorded. This could be beneficial in some situations and problematic in others (see Chapter 8).

12. Suspicion and discomfort on the part of the consumer will be reduced as he no longer needs to wonder, "What kinds of records are they keeping on me here?" and "What do they do with all this stuff I tell them?"

It seems highly probable that as more experience is gained with the open-file concept, and as more consumers exercise their right of access, additional areas of concern and of benefit for both consumers and the social work profession will emerge.

Some Conclusions and Recommendations

It is obvious that consumers of social-work services must be informed that records are kept, must have a mechanism for finding out what is in them, and must be able to correct or amend their records as needed. It appears that policies to this effect must be developed by all individuals and settings providing social-work services; otherwise, the federal government will do this job for us. Clearly defined policies must be established by social workers at a national level and uniformly adopted. Furthermore, these ideas must be conveyed to the appropriate legislative bodies so that laws reflect the thinking of social workers rather than imposing unrealistic, unworkable requirements.

The following concepts, based on an extensive review of the pros and cons of consumer access, are suggested for consideration:

1. Consumers should have a right of access to social work records.

2. The consumer who seeks access must realize that he may find some material upsetting and should be prepared to assume some responsibility for the repercussions. Situations that could generate a valid complaint against the professional must be identified and differentiated from those recorded entries for which he cannot be held liable; these distinctions should be made known to the consumer and incorporated into any policies granting consumer access to confidential records.

3. There must be a process whereby certain information can be kept from the consumer when necessary. Student process recordings; preliminary, tentative diagnostic assessments; and similar data must sometimes be put into writing, especially by students. Such material would merely confuse or mislead the consumer, and it would therefore not be in his best interest for him to have full access. Student education in social work practice would be seriously impaired if every tentative, experimental thought either had to be shared or could not be put into writing at all.

4. If information is being kept from the consumer, he must be advised that this is occurring. The general nature of the material should be shared.

If its existence should prove upsetting or anxiety-provoking to the consumer to the point that his treatment is hampered, the material would have to be destroyed.

5. When information is being shared with a consumer, the social worker who provided the services and recorded the material must be present to answer any questions, deal with anxieties, if any, and generally help the consumer digest what he is reading or hearing. If this social worker cannot be present personally, the responsibility should be delegated to another social worker qualified to provide similar treatment.

6. If there is concern regarding consumer reaction to selected material, a mechanism can be developed for sharing such information with the client's representative rather than disclosing it to him directly. However, the types of information fitting this definition must be clearly specified in the policy, and preventive measures must be taken to insure that all record material does not suddenly get assigned to this category.

7. The current trend toward doing away with all records should be reversed. Record-keeping practices must be altered rather than abolished. Entries in formal records should be made with the idea in mind that if they are written, they will be shared.

8. More open sharing with consumers regarding the treatment process and professional assessments must take place during the therapeutic process itself. This practice would decrease the secrecy of recordings, and client access would not seem as threatening to the professional or the consumer.

There is a final question that will undoubtedly concern some practitioners: Is it possible to provide effective and timely social-work services if consumers are granted full access to all records? Is it possible to build in so many safeguards to protect the client that he will suffer as a result? Instead of getting caught up in the issue of "which is more important—consumer rights or the ability of a service delivery system to meet consumer needs?" the social work profession needs to make necessary internal changes so that both priorities can be accommodated.

7. Privileged Communication: What It Is and Who Is Covered

It has been demonstrated that many, probably most, social workers are only dimly aware of their rights and duties with regard to confidentiality and tend to overestimate the extent to which their communications are privileged.[1]

Robert Plank

SOCIAL WORKERS' ADHERENCE TO the principle of confidentiality is based on a professional ethic—a moral code—and not necessarily on a legal obligation. As one author has put it, "The duty to keep matters confidential is governed by ethics. The right to refuse to disclose them is governed by law."[2] That a social worker recognizes the need to keep something confidential does not mean that he will be able to do so, especially in the face of a court subpoena. It has been pointed out repeatedly that "confidentiality has no legal status; in a courtroom the lack of a privilege does indeed mean a lack of confidentiality."[3]

Unfortunately, some writings in the social-work literature have led members of the profession to believe that all they have to do is say no to an attorney if they do not want something to be disclosed. But without privileged-communication coverage, there is no legal backing to enable a social worker to carry out his professional obligation to maintain confidentiality of client information.[4] A recent article by an attorney in the *Social Casework Journal* indicated this rather firmly:

[1] Robert Plank, "Our Underprivileged Communications," *Social Casework,* Vol. 46, No. 7 (July 1965), p. 431.

[2] "NOTE: The Social Worker-Client Relationship and Privileged Communications," *Washington University Law Quarterly,* Vol. 1965 (1965), p. 382.

[3] "Privileged Communications: A Case by Case Approach," *Maine Law Review,* Vol. 23 (1971), p. 447.

[4] For example, see *Confidentiality in Social Services to Individuals,* National Social Welfare Assembly, New York, April 1958, p. 33, regarding "The Legal Profession." The uninformed reader could easily assume that no attorney would dare challenge a social worker's simple refusal to release confidential information to him.

Social workers are not granted any privilege from testimony in court. They can be subpoenaed by any party to a court action, either by subpoena for testimony or by a subpoena *duces tecum* which demands that the social worker appear with all relevant records specified in the subpoena at a certain time and in a certain court. The court can compel the social worker to give testimony either on behalf of the social worker's client or on behalf of the opposing party issuing the subpoena. Either plaintiff or defendant can compel the social worker to appear, and he can be forced to testify fully and under oath about all that transpired between the client and the social worker.

Although considered necessary in order to obtain the truth in the profound and legal meaning of the word, a court appearance can be detrimental to the mental health, well-being and future therapy of the client. Yet, should the social worker fail to honor a lawfully issued court process, he could be found in contempt of court by the judge. Because the penalty for contempt can be a fine or jail or both, and the witness can be held in jail until he purges himself of such contempt, the question is: How can a social worker prepare and protect himself while honoring professional ethics and standards?[5]

Thus, social workers are now fighting for the right of privileged communication in an effort to avoid forced disclosures of confidential information. In order to have this legal protection, a social worker must be licensed to practice in a state which has a statute on its books declaring that communications between social workers and their clients are privileged. His practice must be located in the state in which he is so covered. The social worker, acting on instructions from his client, can then legally refuse to release certain information in response to a subpoena. There are many exceptions to this, and many situations in which the courts have determined that the privilege should not apply; also, the rights and limitations of privileged communication vary from state to state. Only the more common definitions, exceptions and issues are presented in this chapter and in Chapters 8 and 9.

Various definitions of privileged communication have been offered:

In states where certain professional groups are granted privileged communication, the client or his attorney has the privilege of preventing the professional from answering questions about their communication when called as a witness in court.[6]

Privileged testimonial communication permits the patient or client to prevent his physician, psychologist [or other professional] from disclosing confidential communications in court [or] in other legal proceedings.[7]

Privileged communication is a legal right which exists either by statute or common law (non-statutory law) that protects the client from having his confidences

[5] Barton E. Bernstein, "The Social Worker as a Courtroom Witness," *Social Casework,* Vol. 56, No. 9 (November 1975), pp. 521.

[6] Mildred M. Reynolds, "Threats to Confidentiality," *Social Work,* Vol. 21, No. 2 (March 1976), p. 109.

[7] A. Louis McGarry and Honora A. Kaplan, "Overview: Current Trends in Mental Health Law," *American Journal of Psychiatry,* Vol. 130, No. 6 (June 1973), p. 628.

revealed publicly from the witness stand during legal proceedings. It means that certain professionals cannot be legally compelled to testify to the content of the confidential relation they entered into with their client. The privilege protects the client, and the right to exercise the privilege, i.e., the "ownership" of it, belongs to the client or lay person, not to the professional.[8]

The legal duty of professional confidentiality or secrecy refers to the obligation not to release information about a client or patient without his permission, except when divulgence is required by law. The concept of privileged communication involves the right to withhold information in a legal proceeding.[9]

What these definitions have in common is the assertion that privileged communication permits the professional to legally refuse to disclose certain data, even when asked to do so by a subpoena. In order for a profession, as a group, to ask that its client communications be considered privileged, certain conditions must be met. The profession must have clearly defined the requirements to be a member of that profession and described the functions of a practitioner. The proclaimed professional must meet these requirements and must also be licensed or certified to practice in the state of jurisdiction.[10] There are four additional conditions generally accepted as being necessary for a communication to be considered privileged:

1. The communication must originate in a confidence that it will not be disclosed.
2. This element of confidentiality must be essential to the full and satisfactory maintenance of the relationship between the parties.
3. The relation must be one which in the opinion of the community ought to be sedulously fostered.
4. The injury that would inure to the relation by the disclosure of the communication must be greater than the benefit thereby gained for the correct disposal of litigation.[11]

State law-making bodies study the nature of a profession's communications with its clients to determine whether these criteria have been met. Even if there is satisfaction on all four points, a given state may not see fit to grant the right of privileged communication to the profession seeking it. On the other hand, even where such statutes do exist, the court may determine on its own that a particular communication does not meet all four criteria

[8] Robert L. Geiser and Paul D. Rheingold, "Psychology and the Legal Process: Testimonial Privileged Communications," *American Psychologist,* Vol. 19, No. 11 (November 1964), p. 831.

[9] Ralph Slovenko, *Psychiatry and Law* (Boston: Little, Brown and Co., 1973), p. 434.

[10] Margaret Elizabeth Fearqueron, "A Study of Selected Aspects of Privileged Communication as Related to School Counselors, with Particular Reference to Florida," unpublished doctoral dissertation, Florida State University, Tallahassee, December 1973, p. 43. Also see the "Model Licensing Act for Social Workers" (Washington, D.C.: NASW, 1973) in Appendix B–2. It sets up the licensing criteria for social workers and attempts to define social work practice.

[11] John H. Wigmore, *Evidence in Trials at Common Law,* Vol. 8 (rev. by J. T. McNaughton) (Boston: Little Brown, 1961), p. 52.

and must therefore be disclosed. The fourth criterion is especially difficult to satisfy and its presence is responsible for many forced disclosures.[12] Thus, while state statutes may define the right of privileged communication generally for various professional groups, the courts are constantly interpreting the concept as applied to specific case-situations. As we shall see, these decisions often require the disclosure of the disputed information, thus rendering the privileged communication statutes meaningless.

Who Usually Has the Right of Privileged Communication?

Under English common law, no gentleman could be required to testify against another in a court of law; thus, they had the right of privileged communication. However, this is no longer the case in England or the United States; only communications between certain specific categories of individuals are so protected.

At first, only attorney-client communications were covered by privilege. Other disciplines soon examined the nature of their client communications and began arguing that they should have the same protection as attorneys. Early proponents of privileged communication thus advocated adoption of statutes patterned after the common-law attorney-client privilege for psychiatrists, psychotherapists, and other helping professionals.[13] Soon a wide range of disciplines began clamoring for the right of privileged communication. Some were successful in their bid for legal protection of confidentiality; others were not. A flurry of controversy resulted as opponents argued that "all this privileged communication makes it impossible for the courts to get the facts needed to render a just decision,"[14] while others maintained

[12] For example, see the Case of *Humphrey v. Norden,* 359 N.Y.S. 2d 733 (S. Court 1974) in which a social worker, covered by the right of privileged communication in New York State, was nevertheless required to testify in a paternity suit because the court ruled that "disclosure of evidence relevant to a correct determination of paternity was of greater importance than any injury which might inure to relationship between social worker and his clients if such admission was disclosed." See also Slovenko, *Psychiatry and Law* (1973), Chapter 4, for further discussion of this problem.

[13] One such group is the Group for the Advancement of Psychiatry (GAP). See *Confidentiality and Privileged Communication in the Practice of Psychiatry,* Group for the Advancement of Psychiatry, Report No. 45 (New York: Group for the Advancement of Psychiatry, June 1960), pp. 89–112. It is important to note, however, that they later revised their stand, concluding that helping professionals had some specialized needs regarding protection of the confidentiality of client communications. See also Abraham Goldstein and Jay Katz, "Psychiatrist-Patient Privilege: The GAP Proposal and the Connecticut Statute," *Connecticut Bar Journal,* Vol. 36 (1962), pp. 175–189.

[14] For example, see the case of *State v. Driscoll* 193 N.W.2d 851 (Wisconsin 1972), where a social worker tried to avoid testifying in a legal action, maintaining that his information was confidential. The court was asked to "create by case law a privileged confidential relationship for private and governmental social workers" but refused to do so and forced the social worker to testify. Obviously the court considered the availability of information crucial to its decision and was not in a mood to extend privileged communication to social workers.

that the various helping professions handle highly confidential material and therefore must be covered by the privilege.[15] Still others expressed the opinion that "It's not fair to give privileged communication to some professions and not others, so let's have one master privileged communication statute giving the right to the clients, regardless of who serves them, and do away with privilege statutes for specific professions."[16] One law professor, Ralph Slovenko, has even become quite outspoken in expressing his opinion that privileged-communication statutes are so full of loopholes that they cannot be depended upon to protect confidentiality.[17]

In spite of these various opinions, accountants, guidance counselors, clergymen, marriage counselors, nurses, physicians, psychiatrists, psychologists, and others have now been granted privileged communication in various states. Let us briefly review the nature of the privilege granted to these groups in order to compare it with that now beginning to be provided for social workers.[18]

ATTORNEYS

Lawyers had the right of privileged communication under British common law, the basis of American jurisprudence, and thus became the first group to acquire the privilege in the United States. Because attorneys have this right by common law, it is not necessary for individual states to enact

[15] For example, see "Underprivileged Communications: Extension of the Psychotherapist-Patient Privilege to Patients of Psychiatric Social Workers," *California Law Review,* Vol. 61 (June 1973), pp. 1050–1071; Robert M. Fisher, "The Psychotherapeutic Professions and the Law of Privileged Communication," *Wayne Law Review,* Vol. 10 (1963–1964), pp. 609–654; "NOTE: Social Worker-Client Relationship and Privileged Communications," *Washington University Law Quarterly,* Vol. 1965 (1965), pp. 362–395; Rev. Anthony F. Logatto, "Privileged Communication and the Social Worker," *Catholic Lawyer,* Vol. 8, No. 5 (Winter 1962), pp. 5–19; and Robert Plank, "Our Underprivileged Communications," *op. cit.,* pp. 430–434. See also "A Suggested Privilege for Confidential Communications with Marriage Counselors," *University of Pennsylvania Law Review,* Vol. 106, No. 2 (December 1957), pp. 266–278.

[16] For example, see "Privileged Communications: A Case by Case Approach," *op. cit.,* pp. 443–462, and Sandra G. Nye, "Privilege," Chapter 3 in *Confidentiality of Health and Social Service Records: Where Law, Ethics and Clinical Issues Meet* (Chicago: University of Illinois at Chicago Circle, December 1976), pp. 80–99. Also see Geiser and Rheingold, "Psychology and the Legal Process: Testimonial Privileged Communications," *op. cit.*

[17] Ralph Slovenko, "Psychiatrist-Patient Testimonial Privilege: A Picture of Misguided Hope," *Catholic University Law Review,* Vol. 23 (1974), pp. 649–673; and *Psychiatry and Law, op. cit.,* Chap. 4. These writings reflect a reversal of his earlier commitment to privileged communication for psychiatrists when he had argued that "a special statute is needed for the psychiatrist-patient relationship in states that do not have a medical statute as well as in those that do." "Psychiatry and a Second Look at Medical Privilege," *Wayne Law Review,* Vol. 6, No. 2 (Spring 1960), p. 184.

[18] For a detailed history of the development and extent of privileged communication for attorneys, physicians, clergymen, psychotherapists and marriage counselors, see Joseph Alves, *Confidentiality in Social Work* (Washington, D.C., Catholic University of America Press, 1959). This doctoral dissertation is available through University Microfilms, Ann Arbor, Mich.

legislation granting them the privilege, as is required for all other professions. The attorney's strong commitment to the necessity for preserving confidentiality is reflected in the profession's *Code of Professional Ethics,* which clearly distinguishes between the ethical and the legal obligations to protect client confidences.[19] The attorney's right of privileged communication is considered absolute and is not subject to the many exceptions found in state statutes for other professions. Furthermore, it is so widely accepted that it is rarely challenged. In law, unlike other professions, communications *to* the client as well as those *from* the client are privileged.[20]

PHYSICIANS

Physicians were the first group to attain the right of privileged communication by means of state law. This occurred in 1828 in New York. As of 1971, there were only twelve states that did not grant the privilege to physician-patient communications.[21] However, the term "physician" is not all-inclusive—medical students, chiropractors, pharmacists, veterinarians, psychologists, dentists, and Christian Science practitioners are usually excluded from the physician's right of privilege.[22] Since psychiatrists may or may not be included under physician privileged-communication statutes, it has been argued that they need separate coverage to meet their special needs.[23]

At one time, physicians were not obligated to maintain confidentiality, and they rather freely discussed patient confidences. In recent history, doctors enjoyed a period when they were revered as the "great healers"—saviors of mankind from many terrible and diverse diseases. However, "during the last century, as in the case of the sovereign king, the physician is no longer regarded as deriving his power from God,"[24] and courts have pursued his confidential information more freely and aggressively. As a result, physician privilege statutes have lost their power. States and courts have required doctors to report contagious and infectious diseases, to file birth and death certificates, and to report criminal activity and treatment of injuries that could have been the result of a crime (e.g., gunshot and stab wounds). Child abuse and neglect must generally be reported. Some states now require inspection of medical records if certain drugs are prescribed;

[19] See "Canon Four: A Lawyer Shall Preserve the Confidences and Secrets of a Client," *Code of Professional Ethics* (Chicago: American Bar Association, 1975), pp. 21c–23c.

[20] Alves, *Confidentiality in Social Work, op. cit.,* supra note 22, p. 58.

[21] "Privileged Communications: A Case by Case Approach," *op. cit.,* p. 448. The twelve states are Alabama, Connecticut, Delaware, Florida, Georgia, Maryland, Massachusetts, Rhode Island, South Carolina, Tennessee, Texas, and Vermont.

[22] Slovenko, "Psychiatry and a Second Look at Medical Privilege," *op. cit.,* p. 181. However, these groups have, in recent years, successfully obtained the privilege as professions in their own right in several states.

[23] *Ibid.,* p. 184.

[24] Slovenko, *Psychiatry and Law, op. cit.,* p. 254.

names of drug-dependent patients must be reported, and on and on *ad infinitum.*[25] Slovenko concludes that "there is virtually nothing covered by the privilege."[26]

CLERGYMEN

One might assume that clergymen have traditionally had the right of privileged communication, especially the Catholic priest in his confessional role. However, this is not the case; individual states have had to enact separate legislation to assure the confidentiality of clergyman-penitent communications. As of 1968, forty-seven states had done so.[27] It is interesting to note that where no such law existed, the courts have traditionally treated clergy as if they were in fact covered by privilege statutes, simply not requiring them to testify. Slovenko points out that the community expects absolute confidence between clergyman and counselee and that the courts dare not violate this expectation:

A priest-penitent communication may be relevant to an issue in a case, but the disclosure is nonetheless not demanded because of the deference given by the community to the relationship. Even in jurisdictions where there is no statutory priest-penitent privilege, an attorney would hardly dare subpoena a priest to testify regarding communications made by a penitent. It would not set right with judge or jury. It is not the enactment of a statutory privilege, but rather the feeling in the community about the relationship that makes a relationship sacrosanct.[28]

Where privilege statutes cover clergymen, they contain few exceptions; they confer the right to keep virtually everything confidential in both civil and criminal proceedings.[29] The primary exception is that the communication, to be privileged, must be made by a person who is a member of the church in which the clergyman presides.

One problem is to define just what is meant by a "clergyman." Obviously this would include pastors, rabbis, and priests. But what about Christian Science practitioners, Zen Buddhist leaders, occult religionists, and leaders of other, less well-known groups? Unfortunately, few states have made any significant attempt to set up criteria for meeting the definition of

[25] *Ibid.,* Chapter 23, p. 436. For a state-by-state breakdown of privileged communication for physicians as of 1966, with exceptions and the actual statute included, see Gerd Schroeter, "An Exploratory Analysis of Privileged Communication," master's thesis in sociology, Vanderbilt University, 1966, Table 1: "Statutory Survey of Physician-Patient Privileged Communication Laws," pp. 21–32.

[26] Slovenko, *Psychiatry and Law, op. cit.,* p. 63.

[27] Gerd Schroeter, "Protection of Confidentiality in the Courts: The Professions," *Social Problems,* Vol. 16 (Winter 1969), pp. 376–385.

[28] Slovenko, *Psychiatry and Law, op. cit.,* p. 67.

[29] Schroeter, "An Exploratory Analysis of Privileged Communication", *op. cit.*

a clergyman for purposes of dealing with the privileged-communication issue.

PSYCHIATRISTS

Almost everyone seems to assume that psychiatrists have the right of privileged communication, but this is not so. These professionals are covered only if they are practicing in one of the states that grant privileged communication to physicians in general or to psychiatrists as such. Psychiatrists have not been fully comfortable with the general "physician" privilege, and courts have occasionally refused to recognize the psychiatrist-patient relationship as having or needing special privileges. Thus, there has been increasing pressure for states to adopt statutes granting the privilege to psychiatrists and their patients as a separate group.

Numerous articles in the psychiatric and legal literature assert that psychiatrists need some protection from having to disclose patient confidences;[30] several position statements have been issued reflecting the desire to develop appropriate privileged-communication statutes.[31] State regulations for psychiatrists are subject to many of the same exceptions noted for physicians in general, and even the special statutes for psychiatrists have proved to contain so many loopholes as to be of limited value in many situations.[32]

PSYCHOLOGISTS

Psychologists have also been very active in pressing for the right of privileged communication, and they met with success in 1948 when Kentucky became the first state to grant it to them.[33] By 1971, thirty-five states had similar statutes.[34] It is interesting to note that in sixteen states the statute is patterned after that for attorneys, and in five, psychiatrists and psycholo-

[30] I.e., see the writings of Slovenko previously cited. See also Danny G. Davis, "EVIDENCE: Privileged Communication—a Psychiatrist Has a Constitutional Right to Assert an Absolute Privilege Against Disclosure of Psychotherapeutic Communications," *Texas Law Review,* Vol. 49 (May 1971), pp. 929–942; and Abraham Goldstein and Jay Katz, "Psychiatrist-Patient Privilege: The GAP Proposal and the Connecticut Statute," *op. cit.,* pp. 175–189.

[31] For example, see Group for the Advancement of Psychiatry, *Confidentiality and Privileged Communication in the Practice of Psychiatry, op. cit.;* and "Position Statement on Confidentiality and Privilege with Special Reference to Psychiatric Patients," *American Journal of Psychiatry,* Vol. 124, Part II, No. 7 (January 1968), pp. 1015–1016.

[32] See Slovenko, *Psychiatry and Law, op. cit.;* and "Psychotherapist-Patient Testimonial Privilege: A Picture of Misguided Hope," *op. cit.*

[33] Ralph Slovenko and Gene L. Usdin, "Privileged Communication and Right of Privacy in Diagnosis and Therapy," *Current Psychiatric Therapies,* Vol. 3. (New York: Grune and Stratton, 1963), note 26, p. 311.

[34] "Privileged Communications: A Case by Case Approach," pp. 448–449.

gists operate under similar regulations.[35] It has been pointed out that there is considerable inconsistency from state to state in psychologist privilege statutes due to lobbying by special-interest groups striving for professional status and, occasionally, acting out of professional jealousy.[36] As a result, in many states privileged-communication statutes for psychologist-patient communications are actually much stronger than those for physicians and psychiatrists, and this, understandably, has led to some envy on the part of other professions. The statutes contain comparatively few exceptions and, unlike similar laws for physicians and psychiatrists, the privilege applies in most states to both criminal and civil actions.[37]

SOCIAL WORKERS

Social work is one of the most recent of the helping professions to seek privileged-communication coverage. New York became the first state to grant this to licensed social workers, and by May 1976 ten states had accorded social-worker–client communications privilege in conjunction with a licensing or regulatory statute.[38]

There are some historical precedents dating back quite a few years.[39] In the early 1900's Mary Richmond stated, "In the whole range of professional contacts, there is no more confidential relation than that which exists between [the] social worker and the person or family receiving treatment."[40] In 1930 a situation arose in which the right of privileged communication was at stake, even though it was not so described at the time. A social worker refused to produce a court-requested case record, arguing the merits of maintaining confidentiality. The court allowed the record to remain confidential, but this initial ruling was later reversed.[41] As early as 1942, one author reviewed concepts of privileged communication and implied that this

[35] *Ibid.,* pp. 449–450.

[36] *Ibid.,* p. 450. See also Slovenko, "Psychiatry and a Second Look at Medical Privilege," p. 202, for an assertion in 1960 that psychologists do not need privileged communication coverage as much as do psychiatrists. The ability of psychologists as therapists is also compared most unfavorably with that of psychiatrists.

[37] Schroeter, "An Exploratory Analysis of Privileged Communication," *op. cit.,* Table 3: "Statutory Summary of Psychologist-Client Privileged Communication Laws," pp. 54–58.

[38] The ten states are Arkansas, California, Colorado, Idaho, Illinois, Kansas, Louisiana, Michigan, New York, and South Dakota. Additional states have licensing or regulatory acts but no privilege while in others, social workers are in the process of lobbying for privilege. Letters from Robert H. Cohen, Senior Staff Associate, NASW, Washington, D.C., May 25, 1976, and November 11, 1976, to the author.

[39] For a review of historical precedents to privileged communications for social workers, see Alves, *Confidentiality in Social Work, op. cit.,* pp. 74–91.

[40] Mary Richmond, *What Is Social Casework?* (New York: Russell Sage Foundation, 1922), p. 29.

[41] See *Perlman v. Perlman,* Index No. 5105, N.Y. Supreme Court, Bronx County, June 30, 1930, and *In the Matter of the City of New York* (Sup. Ct. Bronx County) 91 N.Y.L., February 1, 1934, p. 529, Col. 7 (reversing Perlman). See the Discussion of these cases in Logatto, "Privileged Communication and the Social Worker," *op. cit.,* p. 5.

was needed in social work practice.[42] As psychiatrists and psychologists began insisting that professional counseling-relationship communications met Wigmore's four criteria for being considered privileged, it became increasingly evident that the same arguments could apply to social work as well. In more recent years, several additional articles concerning the right of privilege for social-work communications appeared.[43] Such articles have been very rare in the social-work literature; the most in-depth discussions on the right of privileged communication for social workers have been found in legal rather than social work journals.[44]

In 1964, Geiser and Rheingold discussed privileged communication as it applied to psychologists, and expressed their feeling that it was inequitable for some professions to have the privilege when others also in the field of mental health do not: "Perhaps the greatest inequity of all is that no American jurisdiction grants a privilege to social workers."[45] Another author in 1973 specifically argued that in California the right of privileged communication already granted to psychologists and their patients should be extended to the clients of the psychiatric social worker as well.[46] The NASW has now adopted a Model Licensing Act for Social Workers (1973) designed to assist states in setting up appropriate statutes.[47] Most recently, in 1976, Mildred Reynolds reviewed privileged communication as a concept, discussed briefly who has it and who does not, and mentioned a few of the many exceptions.[48] She concludes by urging social workers to continue striving for privileged-communication coverage in their respective states. Where statutes do declare social-work communications privileged, the ever-present exceptions that plague psychiatry and psychology are there as well (see pp. 104–105).

OTHER PROFESSIONALS

There are other professions which have gained the right of privileged communication in at least one state each. These include: chartered account-

[42] A. Delafield Smith, "Reintegrating Our Concepts of Privileged Communication," *Social Service Review,* Vol. 16 (June 1942), pp. 191–211.

[43] For example, see Robert Plank, "Our Underprivileged Communications," *op. cit.,* and Mildred Reynolds, "Threats to Confidentiality," *op. cit.,* pp. 108–113. There is also an extensive discussion of privileged communication in Alves, *Confidentiality in Social Work, op. cit.* Bear in mind however, that his text was written before any state had granted the privilege to social workers.

[44] For example, see "NOTE: Social Worker-Client Relationships and Privileged Communications," *op. cit.;* and "COMMENTS: Underprivileged Communications: Extension of the Psychotherapist-patient Privilege to Patients of Psychiatric Social Workers," *California Law Review,* Vol. 61 (1973), pp. 1050–1071.

[45] Geiser and Rheingold, *op. cit.,* p. 835.

[46] "Underprivileged Communications: Extension of the Psychotherapist-Patient Privilege to Patients of Psychiatric Social Workers," *op. cit.*

[47] See Appendix B–2. Unfortunately, this Model Act concerns itself primarily with licensing regulations and contains only four short paragraphs on privileged communication.

[48] Mildred Reynolds, "Threats to Confidentiality," *op. cit.*

ants,[49] marriage counselors,[50] school guidance counselors,[51] and registered nurses.[52]

As of 1967, journalists were covered by the privilege in fourteen states.[53] These statutes pertain primarily to the source of the reporter's information, and most read that "persons engaged in or employed by newspapers, radio or television stations shall not be required to disclose sources of information procured and published or broadcast."[54] Laws for the press differ from most others in that the privilege is granted to the journalist rather than the informant. Reporters first acquired their right to secrecy of souces in 1896; however, this has come under increasing attack from attorneys and others, and no new statutes covering reporters have been passed since 1949.[55]

Vocational rehabilitation counselors gained privilege in one state simply by virtue of the fact that a public law existed requiring that all records of the rehabilitation agency be kept confidential. The state decided that to assure compliance, it would grant privileged communication to these counselors, even though as a group they did not meet the requirements for being a distinct profession.[56]

Husbands and wives in a legal marital relationship have traditionally had the right of privileged communication in that they cannot be made to testify against each other. This is considered necessary for preservation of the family.[57]

[49] As of 1968, sixteen states granted accountants the right of privileged communication: Arizona, Colorado, Florida, Georgia, Idaho, Illinois, Iowa, Kentucky, Louisiana, Maryland, Michigan, Nevada, New Mexico, Pennsylvania, and Tennessee. Gerd Schroeter, "Protection of Confidentiality in the Courts: The Professions," *op. cit.*

[50] Four states granted this privilege as of 1973. "Underprivileged Communication: Extension of the Privilege to Patients of Psychiatric Social Workers," *op. cit., note 11, p. 1052.*

[51] Nine states granted this privilege as of 1973. Fearqueron, *op. cit.*

[52] "NOTE: The Social Worker-Client Relationship and Privileged Communication," *op. cit., p. 366.*

[53] Selma Arnold, "Confidential Communication and the Social Worker," *Social Work,* Vol. 15, No. 1 (January 1970), pp. 61–67.

[54] Schroeter, "An Exploratory Analysis of Privileged Communication," *op. cit.* See Table 5: "Statutory Survey of Reporters-Informant Secrecy Laws," pp. 67–70.

[55] *Ibid.*

[56] Fearqueron, "A Study of Selected Aspects of Privileged Communication as Related to School Counselors, with Particular Reference to Florida," *op. cit.*

[57] Selma Arnold, "Confidential Communication and the Social Worker," *op. cit.* The fact that the husband-wife relationship is treated differently from others by the courts is shown in a reported case in which a couple sued for divorce. Both had been under the care of the same psychiatrist, who was called to testify. The husband argued that the information shared between him and the psychiatrist was privileged and ordered the professional not to testify, claiming his right to privileged communication. The wife argued that since both spouses were present during some of their sessions, the information was not confidential and the psychiatrist should testify. The Tennessee court ruled that "when a confidential relationship exists between a psychiatrist and a patient, the communications are privileged even though made in the presence of a spouse. The spouses should be able to approach a psychiatrist with the knowledge that what is communicated in an examination will be strictly confidential. This would mean that neither the spouses nor the psychiatrist should be allowed to subsequently disclose the contents of that communication" *Ellis v. Ellis,* 472 S.W.2d 741 (Tennessee App. Ct. 1971). For further discussion of this principle, see "Evidence—Privileged Communication in Divorce Ac-

Records and information regarding school pupils were considered privileged by two states in 1965.[58] Legislators have also been asked to grant the privilege to newscasters, school teachers, special clerks, stockholders, detectives, public officials, trust companies, and researchers.[59] Because researchers have encountered some rather frightening repercussions from their lack of protection, strong recommendations are beginning to appear demanding that some form of privilege be enacted for this group.[60]

Slovenko points out the absurdity of present privileged-communication statutes and the tendency to grant the coverage to everybody and anything. He devotes several pages to the facetious proposition that pet-master communications should be privileged:

> Privileged status dependent on the professional designation is not warranted. What difference does it make whether a person achieves a "corrective emotional experience" by talking with a psychiatrist, psychologist, social worker, preacher, or a good friend? Some people may have only a pet, purebred or mongrel, two-legged or four-legged, to turn to. Little Orphan Annie seems to talk only to Sandy, her dog. A pet lover who fashions a pet into a confidant may wonder whether communications to the pet are privileged and if not, why not, or why there is no owner-pet shield. After all, the law shields the lawyer-client, husband-wife, and priest-penitent relationships. Using Dean John Wigmore's oft-cited criteria for privilege, it may be said that the law inadequately protects owner-pet communications: it can be demonstrated that a communication between owner and pet is made in confidence, that violation of the confidence is detrimental to the purpose of the relationship, that the relationship is one that should be fostered, and that the injury to the relationship through public disclosure of the communication is greater than the benefit to justice to be derived therefrom.[61]

Thus, it appears that declaring every form of communication privileged—whether human or animal, filmed, tape-recorded, computerized, written, or what-have-you—is not the answer to the problem of disclosure of confidential information in the courtroom.

---

tions: Psychiatrist-Patient and Presence of Third Parties," *Tennessee Law Review,* Vol. 40 (Fall 1972), pp. 110–118. However, it should be noted that not all courts have ruled this way.

[58] Schroeter, "An Exploratory Analysis of Privileged Communication," *op. cit.*

[59] Slovenko, *Psychiatry and Law, op. cit.,* p. 61.

[60] See James D. Carroll and Charles R. Knerr, "The APSA Confidentiality in Social Science Research Project: A Final Report," *Political Science* (Fall 1976), pp. 416–418. These authors indicate that the privacy of certain types of research data is protected by various statutes, but that coverage for researcher-subject communications needs to be broadened (p. 417). See also James D. Carroll and Charles R. Knerr, "A Report of APSA Confidentiality in Social Science Research Data Project," *Political Science* (Summer 1975), pp. 258–261; and Paul Nejelski and L. M. Lerman, "A Research-Subject Testimonial Privilege: What to Do Before the Subpoena Arrives," *Wisconsin Law Review* (1971), p. 1085.

[61] Slovenko, "Psychotherapist-Patient Testimonial Privilege: A Picture of Misguided Hope," *op. cit.,* pp. 665–666. The discussion continues for several pages and even describes the testimonial problems presented by talking parrots.

THE CLIENT HIMSELF

It must be remembered that in most privileged-communication statutes, it is the client or patient, rather than the professional, who has the right of privilege. Thus, *the client must claim this right in order to prevent the professional from testifying.* Some thoughtful questions have been raised in response to this rather obvious fact: If the client has the right to claim the privilege, why is it that some professionals are covered and others are not? Several articles have appeared favoring a broader interpretation:

> We believe that a privilege should exist for the clients of psychologists functioning as diagnosticians or therapists, but in this connection we would like to recall an earlier statement that we made. The privilege logically should be granted to the client seeking services, regardless of what professional person he consults, and not to the professional offering services, regardless of who his client is. Thus, it would be our position that a privilege should exist for any person who consults a recognized professional (psychiatrist, psychologist, social worker, marriage counselor) for the purpose of the diagnosis of a mental, emotional, or adjustment difficulty, or for the treatment by psychotherapy, counseling, casework, etc., of said condition.[62]

As a result, the following model statute is proposed:

> A client, or his authorized representative, has a privilege to prevent a witness from disclosing, in any judicial, administrative, or legislative proceeding, communications pertaining to the diagnosis or treatment of the client's mental or emotional disorder, or difficulty in personal or social adjustment between the client and any of the following: a member of a mental health profession, any other professional or lay person who participates with such a member of a mental health profession in the accomplishment of individual or group diagnosis or treatment, or members of the client's family, or between any of these persons as concerns diagnosis or treatment.[63]

A feeling is also expressed here that if the client is really the one holding the privilege, then the professional involved should not have to be licensed in order for privileged communication to be in effect, since the legal coverage belongs to the patient and not the practitioner.[64] If this trend continues, soon it may not be necessary for individual professions to fight for the right of privileged communication, as one comprehensive statute could grant it to all consumers seeking their services.

[62] Geiser and Rheingold, "Psychology and the Legal Process: Testimonial Privileged Communications," *op. cit.,* p. 836.

[63] *Ibid.*

[64] *Ibid.* For a similar viewpoint, see "Privileged Communications: A Case by Case Approach," *op. cit.;* Craig Kennedy, "Psychotherapist's Privilege," *Washburn Law Journal* Vol. 12 (Spring 1973), pp. 297–316; and Sandra G. Nye, "Privilege," *op. cit.,* and the "Model Law on Confidentiality of Health and Social Service Information," Appendix B in *Confidentiality of Health and Social Service Records: Where Law, Ethics and Clinical Issues Meet, op. cit.,* pp. 260–282.

PROFESSIONALS NOT COVERED BY PRIVILEGED COMMUNICATION

A few moments' thought will bring to mind a number of professional groups who deal with highly confidential information and yet do not have privileged communication in any state. Consider, for example, personnel staff who handle vast volumes of data about employees. Much of this information is generated by or borrowed from records maintained by persons who are covered by the privilege (e.g., psychiatrists and psychologists), but once the material reaches the personnel officer it is fair game for the courts.[65] Only in settings under the jurisdiction of the Federal Privacy Act of 1974 is there some degree of protection. Public-school teachers often acquire highly confidential information in their day-to-day contacts and yet are without privileged-communication rights. However, the recent enactment (1974) of the Family Educational Rights and Privacy Act with its accompanying Rules and Regulations has helped to fill this gap.[66] Businessmen are without legal protection of confidential material, as are many members of the allied health professions (i.e., physical therapists, speech therapists, dieticians, and others). However, as has already been illustrated, it is possible to carry the concept to extreme. What, then, is the real meaning of the right of privileged communication and who should have it? We turn to this subject in the next chapter.

[65] See Mordechai Mironi, "Confidentiality of Personnel Records: A Legal and Ethical View," *Labor Law Journal,* Vol. 25 (May 1974), pp. 270-292, for a rather startling report on this problem. See also Chapter 9.

[66] Family Educational Rights and Privacy Act of 1974. This amends Public Law 93-568, effective November 19, 1974 ("The Buckley Amendment").

8. Privileged Communication: Common Exceptions to State Statutes

As INDICATED IN PREVIOUS CHAPTERS, privileged-communications statutes do not always provide absolute protection against disclosure of confidential material in legal actions. There are many exceptions and loopholes. Some are written into the statute itself. Others are subsequently determined by the courts, based on an examination of specific case situations. A few exceptions to the mandate to keep information confidential give the professional an option—he does not have to maintain secrecy but he is not obligated to release the data either. Others compel the practitioner to disclose the information—he has no choice. In such cases state or federal law, or a court order, almost always protects him from legal action for having violated confidentiality. On the other hand, should a professional divulge information in an unauthorized manner in violation of privilege statutes, he could be successfully prosecuted. Thus, it is necessary for practitioners to research the laws in their own states carefully in order to become familiar with their rights and limitations in maintaining the confidentiality of various communications.

It is impossible to list all the exceptions to privilege. Here we simply present the kinds of situations that most often limit the ability of a mental health professional to keep something confidential from the courts, with the purpose of providing some guidance as well as an awareness of the complexity of privileged-communication statutes. The list is rather lengthy; the examples indicate clearly that a right of privileged communication often offers little real protection.

1. THE CLIENT WAIVES PRIVILEGE

As has been noted, most privileged-communication statutes grant the privilege to the client, not the treating professional. Thus, it is the consumer who controls the privilege; he can exercise it or he can relinquish his right to

111

have certain information treated as privileged, freeing the professional to disclose that data, and only that data, in court. Some questions have arisen over whether or not a client's claim to privilege is automatic. For example, when a suit is brought, is the professional free to testify unless the client claims his right of privilege, or does the professional assume that he cannot testify unless the client expressly waives his right to the privilege? Some definitions of privileged communication seem to suggest that information is privileged until the client waives it; others read as if the privilege applies only when the patient invokes it.[1] The most common application seems to be that the privilege exists unless and until it is specifically waived by the client. Obviously, such a waiver should be obtained in writing.

The definition of the term "client" can present some problems. For example, in California the holder of the privilege, and thereby of the right to claim or waive it, is "the patient, a guardian or conservator of the patient when one exists, and the personal representative of the patient if the patient is dead."[2] Thus, a minor child or a legally incompetent adult might have a legal guardian who controls the right of privilege. The fact that the person himself no longer controls the information does not mean that it is not confidential. Rather, it is the guardian who determines whether or not certain information shall be disclosed. Some statutes broaden the definition of the term "client" to include the person making the communication, those hearing it (i.e., the professional himself), the personal representative of the client, and any third parties present when the communication is made.[3]

There are some other complications associated with waiver of privilege. It has been suggested that communicants might waive privilege without being fully "informed" (see Chapter 4). In other words, the client might not remember what he told the professional, and therefore is not certain just what he is authorizing for release to the court. In addition, he might not realize the significance of the disclosure and might waive privilege rather naively. A masochistic patient might waive privilege as part of his dysfunctional behavior—his need to punish or hurt himself could result in disclosure of damaging material.[4] Thus, it is argued that the professional who receives the confidential communication should also have the right to claim privilege and prevent its disclosure, even if the client has waived privilege. However, the courts have not accepted this opinion. In one well-known California case (*Lifschutz*) a psychiatrist, covered by privileged communi-

[1] See pages 98–99 and also "Psychiatrist-Patient Privilege: A Need for the Retention of the Future Crime Exception," *Iowa Law Review*, Vol. 52 (June 1967), pp. 1170–1186.

[2] Cal. Ev. Code §1013 (West 1966) quoted in Danny G. Davis, "EVIDENCE: Privileged Communication—A Psychiatrist Has a Constitutional Right to Assert an Absolute Privilege Against Disclosure of Psychotherapeutic Communications," *Texas Law Review*, Vol. 49 (May 1971), p. 932n.

[3] I.e., see "Privileged Communication: A Case by Case Approach," *Maine Law Review*, Vol. 23 (1971), pp. 443–462.

[4] American Psychiatric Association, *Confidentiality: A Report of the 1974 Conference on Confidentiality of Health Records* (Washington, D. C.: APA, 1975), pp. 39–41.

cation, was subpoenaed.[5] Legally, he was perfectly free to disclose certain information, as the patient had already waived his right to the privilege according to California law. However, the psychiatrist refused to testify because he felt that his patient's consent was not really fully informed and that it would not be in the best interests of the therapeutic relationship for the information to be revealed. Under a rather strict interpretation of the law on several points, the court ruled that he had to testify. Thus, when a client chooses to waive his privilege, the courts will generally enforce compliance by the professional.

2. CLIENT INTRODUCES PRIVILEGED MATERIAL INTO LITIGATION

A person waives his right to privileged communication when he himself mentions that he has been treated for a certain condition and thereby introduces it to the court. This happens most frequently in personal-injury suits when the individual acknowledges having received treatment and uses the information in his claim for damages.[6] In numerous suits centering around this issue, the courts have rather consistently ruled that when a plaintiff or defendant introduces his own mental condition as an issue in a lawsuit the need for complete disclosure of pertinent facts must take priority over the treating professional's right to keep confidential what he knows.[7] Also, it could be construed that the patient's introduction of the material is a form of permission to explore it further and bring out all the related facts necessary to study the case fully.

3. A COMMUNICATION DOES NOT MEET WIGMORE'S FOUR CRITERIA

A communication must meet all four criteria before it can be treated as privileged (see p. 99). Client communications to professional helping per-

[5] *Re: Lifschutz*, 2 California 3d 415 (1970). See also the discussion of this case in *Time Magazine*, April 27, 1970, p. 60, as well as by Ralph Slovenko in *Psychiatry and Law* (Boston: Little, Brown, 1973), pp. 65–66, and in "Psychotherapist-Patient Testimonial Privilege: A Picture of Misguided Hope," 23 *Catholic Univ Law Review*, (1974) pp. 656–658. It is interesting to note that the psychiatrist was eventually able to avoid testifying based on issues of relevancy rather than privilege.

[6] Slovenko, "Psychotherapist-Patient Testimonial Privilege: A Picture of Misguided Hope," *op. cit.*, p. 656.

[7] See *Hall v. Alameda*, 20 Cal. App. 3d 362 (1971) and *In Re: Cathey*, 55 Ca. 2d 679, 361 p. 2d 426 (1961) discussed in Slovenko, "Psychotherapist-Patient Testimonial Privilege: A Picture of Misguided Hope," *op. cit.*, pp. 656–659. See also Slovenko, *Psychiatry and Law*, pp. 65–66, and especially note 7 on pp. 72–73, where various case examples are discussed. See also *People v. Fenerstein* (1936) 293 New York Supplement 239 discussed in Alves, *Confidentiality in Social Work*, for an early case involving a recipient of public relief. At the time, New York State had a law on its books attempting to protect the "confidential communications of

sons are usually given with an expectation that they will remain confidential. One way of assuring that this first prerequisite is met would be for the helping professional to discuss his ethical and/or legal obligations regarding confidentiality with his client during their first session together.[8]

There are numerous articles arguing that communications with counselors, social workers, therapists, and other "professional helping persons" must be confidential in order for the relationship to be maintained.[9] These same articles also extol the value of professional counseling to society, thus meeting Wigmore's third criterion. Such statements are often accepted by the courts and can be somewhat difficult to attack.

Unfortunately, the fourth criterion is often questioned. If the court finds that it must have full information in order to study the facts in a case, it will rule that the benefit gained in regard to the correct disposal of litigation is greater than the injury that would occur to the relationship as a result of disclosure. Thus, the key issue becomes: Which is more important—the relationship between a professional and his client, or the need for society to have a fair and correct decision rendered in the legal action in question? The latter often emerges the victor, especially if criminal, rather than civil, elements are involved.[10] An article arguing for the right of privileged communication for social workers sums up the issue as follows:

> Against these facts and speculations as to the harm that results from forced disclosure and the frequency with which disclosure occurs, society's interest in the correct disposal of litigation must be balanced. That interest is obviously great, but does not seem to have a constant value, i.e., society as a whole has a greater interest in the correct disposal of a charge of murder than it has in a charge of peace disturbance arising from a marital quarrel. Thus the answer to Wigmore's fourth requirement can be viewed as depending upon the facts of the particular case rather than a predetermined evaluation. For example, the correct disposal of the murder charge probably outweighs any injury that would inure to the social worker–client relation. But the desirability of preserving a marriage of

---

relief recipients." However, the court ruled that the client waived his confidentiality rights when he himself disclosed his relationship with the relief program (pp. 76–77).

[8] I.e., see *State v. Driscoll* 193 N.W.2d 851 (Wisconsin 1972), where this became an issue when a social worker was asked to testify when his client was accused of indecent behavior with a child. When the client admitted to this behavior in a conference with his social worker, he was promised confidentiality. This satisfied Wigmore's first condition. Unfortunately, the practitioner was compelled to testify because the communication failed to meet the fourth criterion.

[9] For example, see "COMMENTS: Underprivileged Communications: Extension of the Psychotherapist-Patient Privilege to Patients of Psychiatric Social Workers," *California Law Review*, Vol. 61 (June 1973) "NOTE: Social Worker-Client Relationship and Privileged Communications," *Washington Univ. Law Quarterly*, (1965) pp. 362–395; and David W. Louisell and Kent Sinclair, Jr., "The Supreme Court of California 1969–70; Forward—Reflections on the Law of Privileged Communication—The Psychotherapist-Patient Privilege in Perspective," *California Law Review*, Vol. 59 (1971), pp. 30–55.

[10] See *Humphrey v. Norden*, 359 N.Y.S. 2d 733 (Sup. Court 1974) discussed supra note 12 on p. 100 for an example where this ruling forced a social worker, covered by privileged communication statute, to testify.

thirty years seems to override the benefit which would be gained by the correct disposal of the charge of peace disturbance.[11]

4. THE SOCIAL WORKER IS CALLED TO TESTIFY IN A CRIMINAL CASE

Many state statutes contain exceptions whereby the professional must testify if the litigation involves a criminal rather than a civil offense. Communications involving clergymen and psychologists tend to have greater privilege in criminal cases than do those involving physicians, psychiatrists, and others.[12] Thus, practitioners must research their own particular state statutes, but must still bear in mind that these regulations could be overruled by a court should it decide that the needs of society must take precedence in a particular case over confidentiality of information.

5. A CLIENT SUES HIS COUNSELOR

Most statutes permit a professional to disclose confidential information if a consumer brings suit against him (e.g. for malpractice). Even the American Bar Association, in its Canon of Ethics on preservation of client confidences, permits disclosure without client consent by an attorney when necessary "to defend himself or his employees or associates against an accusation of wrongful conduct."[13] The NASW "Model Licensing Act" also recognizes the need for violating confidentiality when "the person waives the privilege by bringing charges against the licensed certified social worker, the social worker, or the social work associate."[14] This can create more of an ethical than a legal dilemma for the professional involved, who may recognize that it would be harmful to the client to introduce certain material, and who on the other hand may feel he has little choice if he is to protect his professional reputation and his pocketbook.[15]

6. A CLIENT COMMITS OR THREATENS A CRIMINAL ACT

A professional may be permitted or required to abandon privilege when a client admits to a past or intended criminal act. This exception exists in

[11] "NOTE: Social Worker-Client Relationship and Privileged Communications," *op. cit.*, pp. 386–387.

[12] For a complete breakdown for various professions as of 1966, see Gerd Schroeter, "An Exploratory Analysis of Privileged Communication," master's thesis in sociology, Vanderbilt University, 1966, Tables 1 through 5.

[13] *Code of Professional Responsibility*. Canon Four: "A Lawyer Should Preserve the Confidences and Secrets of a Client" (Chicago: American Bar Association, 1975), pp. 21c–23c.

[14] NASW, "Model Licensing Act for Social Workers," reprinted from *Legal Regulation of Social Work Practice* (Washington, D. C.: NASW, (1973), p. 8.

[15] See pp. 170–171 and 195–196 for further discussion of confidentiality issues involved when a consumer brings charges against a social worker or a superior.

most state statutes and model statutes of professional groups, including social workers. Yet it has generated more controversy than all the others combined. How serious must a crime be before there is an obligation or a duty to report it? Is the professional merely *permitted*, but not *required*, to violate confidentiality in order to protect the client, the intended victim, and society, or must he report the intended crime? Can he be held responsible for failure to do so? What if he reports it and the crime fails to take place— could the professional be held liable for violation of confidentiality? And just how far is the practitioner required to go in his efforts to report the intended crime and prevent it from occurring? Finally, how competent are professional helping persons in predicting the dangerousness of their patients? The legal and psychiatric literature is replete with articles heatedly debating these and related issues.[16]

The controversy came into full bloom when the California Court reached its decision in the case of *Tarasoff v. Regents of the University of California* (1974). A university student told his psychiatrist he intended to kill his girlfriend as soon as she returned from out of town. The therapist advised the campus police of the student's threat and asked them to take appropriate action. However, he did not warn the intended victim or her parents. The student was subsequently picked up by the campus security but soon released because he "appeared rational." Shortly thereafter he murdered his girlfriend. When her parents sued the psychiatrist, the Supreme Court ruled:

> When a doctor or a psychotherapist, in the exercise of his professional skills and knowledge, determines, or shall determine that a warning is essential to avert danger arising from a medical or psychological condition of his patient, he incurs a legal obligation to give that warning.[17]

The court also concluded that

> the public policy favoring protection of the confidential character of patient-psychotherapist communication must yield in instances in which disclosure is essential to avert danger to others. The protective privilege ends where public peril begins.[18]

Thus, the court held the psychiatrist liable for failure to warn the intended victim and set a precedent that has stirred considerable controversy.

How serious must a crime be in order for the professional to take protective measures? Obviously, crimes involving someone's life are sufficiently serious. But what about destruction of personal property, theft, and the hundreds of misdemeanors that are so minor that they are rather easily overlooked? Unfortunately, there seems to be no clear-cut definition of

[16] See pp. 257–266 of the Bibliography for an extensive list of readings.

[17] *Tarasoff v. Regents of the University of California*, 13 Cal. 3d 177 (1974). See the discussion of this case in *"Tarasoff v. Regents of University of California*: The Psychotherapist's Peril," *University of Pittsburgh Law Review*, Vol. 37 (Fall 1975), p. 159.

[18] *Ibid.*, p. 161.

what constitutes a serious crime, and it appears that this will have to be determined by the courts in individual case rulings.

Several authors argue that the mental-health professional must be allowed an exception to privileged communication when a client reveals an intended crime of a serious nature. However, only a few go so far as to express the view that disclosure *must* be made.[19] Many psychiatrists, psychologists, and attorneys recognize their duty to warn, but would not like to see this become mandatory. Slovenko's view is rather typical of those encountered:

> The doctor's role in society is to save life, not to destroy it. The physician, according to his oath, may reveal a confidence when it becomes necessary in order to protect the welfare of the patient or the community. The psychiatrist must however be permitted to make this judgment. In such situations, the revelation is made only to the person who should have it in order to avert the catastrophe.[20]

Another argument postulates that professions which have absolute privilege and are not required to report intended crimes might attract potentially dangerous individuals who would then feel freer to disclose such actions. Thus, the professional must let the patient know the limits of confidentiality at the beginning of the therapeutic relationship. The overriding concern then becomes "the protection of these unwary patients from self-threatening disclosures."[21] This author goes on to suggest that no action should be taken by the therapist until danger is imminent, and then the form of intervention least harmful to the patient's interest should be selected.

Several model statutes contain clauses clearly indicating the duty of the professional to take action to protect society when he deems it necessary. However, they do not make this action mandatory, and largely leave it up to the treating professional to determine, in his own best judgment, when a client's actions or communications warrant protective measures and what

[19] For one such opinion, see Michael Glassman, "Recent Cases—Privileged Communication—Psychiatry: Psychotherapist Has a Duty to Warn an Endangered Victim Whose Peril was Disclosed by Communications between the Psychotherapist and Patient," *University of Cincinnati Law Review*, Vol. 44 (1975), p. 369. Referring to *Tarasoff v. Regents of University of California*, 118 Cal Rptr 129, 529 p2d 553 (1974), he states: "A psychotherapist treating a mentally ill patient bears a duty to give threatened persons such warnings as are essential to prevent forseeable violent attack arising from the patient's condition or treatment." Melvin Lewis, in an article discussing confidentiality issues in a community mental health center, also maintains that confidentiality must be broken when "there is bona fide evidence that failure to disclose the relevant information would result in death, serious injury or illness to the patient, the therapist or a third person." Melvin Lewis, "Confidentiality in the Community Mental Health Center," *American J. of Orthopsychiatry*, Vol. 38, No. 5 (October 1967), p. 954.

[20] Ralph Slovenko, "Psychiatry and a Second Look at Medical Privilege," *Wayne Law Review* (Spring 1960), p. 198. See also Robert M. Fisher, "The Psychotherapeutic Professions and the Law of Privileged Communication," *Wayne Law Review*, Vol. 10, No. 4 (1963-1964), pp. 609-654.

[21] John Fleming and Bruce Maximov, "Patient or His Victim: The Therapist's Dilemma," *California Law Review*, Vol. 62 (May 1974), p. 1060.

those measures should be. For example, the Committee on Ethics of the American Psychiatric Association in its statement concerning the release of confidential material dictates:

> When, in the opinion of the psychiatrist, it becomes necessary, in order to protect the welfare of the patient or the community, to reveal confidential information disclosed by the patient (for example, when he believes that the future behavior of the patient may constitute a risk of future injury to the patient or others), it is desirable, where possible, to obtain the authorization of the appropriate person, such as the next of kin, legal guardian, legal counsel, or by order of the court. In emergencies, it may be necessary, and is ethically correct, for the psychiatrist to take action without such authorization in order to protect the patient and others by preventing the patient from carrying out a criminal act. An example of such action is emergency detention of the patient in a hospital under proper statutory authorization such as an "emergency" or "temporary" certificate.[22]

The National Association of Social Workers "Model Licensing Act" also includes a clause permitting licensed social workers to violate confidentiality when an intended crime is confessed. Again, it allows, but does not require, a disclosure:

> A licensed certified social worker, licensed social worker, or licensed social work associate shall not be required to treat as confidential a communication that reveals the contemplation of a crime or harmful act.[23]

Bear in mind that this is a proposed statute; individual states may or may not adopt it as quoted here.

Thus, there are arguments, statutes, and position statements which indicate that there is a definite duty, if not a requirement, to warn intended victims. On the other hand, there are those who feel that confidentiality should *not* be violated even in these situations, and there should be no ethical or legal obligation to disclose this information. Opponents of the "duty to warn" point out that if psychotherapists *must* warn of dangers, a break in the therapeutic relationship will occur, and this will sabotage the best chance of preventing crime—through continued therapy. "The real 'public peril' may arguably be the loss of psychotherapy as an effective tool for treating the mentally ill. A duty to warn third persons of threats made by patients destroys the trust relationship between psychotherapist and patient."[24]

Another problem with the duty to warn is that of malpractice insurance and the type of coverage provided. The psychotherapist's insurance may cover him if he fails to warn an intended victim and is held liable, but

---

[22] "Position Statement on Guidelines for Psychiatrists: Problems in Confidentiality," *American Journal of Psychiatry,* Vol. 126 (April 1970), p. 1545. The duty to warn is also discussed in Patrick Sean Cassidy, "Liability of Psychiatrists for Malpractice," *University of Pittsburgh Law Review,* Vol. 36 (Fall 1974), p. 117.

[23] NASW, "A Model Licensing Act for Social Workers," *op. cit.* pp. 7–8.

[24] *"Tarasoff v. Regents of University of California*: The Psychotherapist's Peril," *op. cit.,* pp. 162, 164.

there is a possibility that it would not cover the doctor's intentional revelation of a privileged communication if such revelation was found to be without justification. If such is the case, the doctor, aware of the limitations of his insurance policy, may choose not to warn, risking liability and subsequent total indemnification (within the limits of his policy) rather than to risk being without defense in the revelation of a privileged communication and being forced to bear the entire judgment.[25]

Then there is the whole question of the ability to predict dangerousness in patients. As one author puts it,

> Given the inability of psychotherapists to predict acts of violence and psychiatrists' lack of special training in the prediction of dangerous behavior, no reason exists for psychotherapists to be singled out for a special duty apart from that imposed upon laymen.[26]

Another article comments that since it is difficult to predict dangerousness, therapists must use their own judgment as to whether or not any action should be taken, and there should be no duty to warn.[27] In an article in the *University of Pennsylvania Law Review*, Bernard Diamond raises serious questions regarding the ability of psychiatrists to predict dangerousness, and uses this to argue that there should be no duty to warn:

> There are a number of statistical studies which amply demonstrate that the predictions by psychiatrists are unreliable. . . . The findings so consistently demonstrate that psychiatrists over-predict dangerousness by huge amounts that the reports must be taken seriously.
>
> There seems to be no convincing study to show that we can predict really dangerous behavior with any amount of reliability.[28]

The Alcohol, Drug Abuse and Mental Health Administrations of the Department of Health, Education, and Welfare stated in a press release:

> Although the psychiatric profession is frequently called upon to predict the potential dangerousness of persons brought before the courts, no scientifically reliable method for predicting dangerous behavior exists.[29]

Bernard Diamond concludes that

> neither psychiatrists nor other behavioral scientists are able to predict the occurrence of violent behavior with sufficient reliability to justify the restriction of freedom of persons on the basis of the label of potential dangerousness.[30]

[25] *Tarasoff v. Regents of the University of California*, "TORTS: The Dangerous Psychiatric Patient—The Doctor's Duty to Warn," *Land and Water Law Review*, Vol. 10 (1975), pp. 605–606.

[26] Joseph L. Latham Jr., "TORTS: Duty to Act for the Protection of Another—Liability of Psychotherapists for Failure to Warn of Homicide Threatened by Patient," *Vanderbilt Law Review*, Vol. 28 (April 1975), pp. 631, 639.

[27] "*Tarasoff v. Regents of University of California*: The Psychotherapist's Peril," *op. cit.*

[28] Bernard L. Diamond, "Psychiatric Prediction of Dangerousness," *University of Pennsylvania Law Review*, Vol. 123 (December 1974), pp. 444–445, 451.

[29] U.S. Department of Health, Education and Welfare, *HEW News* (News release, August 8, 1974).

[30] Diamond, "Psychiatric Prediction of Dangerousness," *op. cit.*, p. 452.

Perhaps the pros and cons of a duty to warn and the problems of inadequate definitions are best summed up in the concluding remarks of an article by Michael Glassman:

Under *Tarasoff*, a patient's threat to kill a third person requires disclosure, but how far courts are willing to expand this duty remains unresolved. Threatened crimes which are less serious in nature, such as shoplifting, should not require disclosure; but as the gravity of the crime increases, the argument to make disclosure compulsory becomes correspondingly more persuasive. Where to draw the line is one major problem presented by *Tarasoff*, and is an issue that either the legislature or the courts must address so that the psychotherapist has precise guidelines to know when to act. Another problem raised by *Tarasoff* concerns the difficulty in establishing an appropriate standard of negligence. How far a psychotherapist must go to determine who the intended victim may be or where the potential victim is located is not clear. With these uncertainties the psychotherapeutic profession [is] burdened heavily both in terms of rendering effective treatment and the imposition of personal liability upon the individual psychotherapist.

The *Tarasoff* court, nevertheless, justifiably imposed a duty to warn one in danger. Those who fear *Tarasoff* now "puts psychiatrists in a position where they have to respond even to idle threats" may be reading the decision far too broadly. *Tarasoff* does not require a warning in response to every threat, but only those which in the psychotherapist's professional and skilled judgment present a real danger to an identifiable person. This offers a viable compromise which may protect human lives while preventing any wholesale erosion of the psychotherapist-patient relationship.[31]

Some additional factors must also be taken into consideration. When a patient discloses his intention to commit a crime, the therapist must evaluate the meaning of the revelation. Is it testing or manipulative behavior? Is it a bid for someone to help the patient control impulses he cannot handle himself? Is he seeking punishment to assuage his guilt feelings? Ethically speaking, the therapist must advise the patient of the extent and limits of confidentiality and should address therapeutically any reactions this precipitates on the part of the patient. Such a stance is supported in the literature; for example, a statement by the National Federation of Societies for Clinical Social Work maintains that confidential information should be revealed

to the appropriate professional people only when there is an immediate danger to an individual or society in the judgment of the clinical social worker. The fact that this information will be revealed is shared with the client.[32]

A client may confess to a crime already committed for which he has not

---

[31] Michael S. Glassman, "Recent Cases—Privileged Communication—Psychiatry: Psychotherapist Has a Duty to Warn an Endangered Victim whose Peril was Disclosed by Communications Between the Psychotherapist and Patient," *op. cit.*, p. 375. Obviously Glassman favors some type of duty to warn.

[32] "News of the Societies: National Federation of Societies for Clinical Social Work: Ethical Standards of Clinical Social Workers," *Clinical Social Work Journal*, Vol. 2, No. 4 (Winter 1974), pp. 312–315.

been prosecuted. Since this is not an intended crime (it is too late to protect the victim), the professional may not be obligated to take any particular action unless a third party is being wrongfully accused of the crime or is otherwise suffering as a result of the patient's undisclosed act.[33] However, the helping professional should consider whether he needs to reveal the information in order to avoid criticism should the client's criminal act be discovered later on along with the fact that the practitioner knew about it and did not reveal it.

In summary, a professional whose client confesses an intended or past crime can find himself in a very delicate position, both legally and ethically. There are enough conflicting beliefs on how this should be handled so that clear guidelines are lacking. Social workers who receive a communication about a serious criminal act by a client would be wise to consult an attorney for a detailed research of appropriate state statutes and a review of recent court rulings that might help determine the desired course of action.

7. A PATIENT THREATENS SUICIDE

Suicidal threats could force a therapist to violate confidentiality if this is necessary to save the individual's life. Again, while the treating professional is encouraged to come to the aid of his patient, there is not necessarily a legal requirement that he do so.

Several authors cite a rather interesting case concerning the qualifications of the therapist for intervention. A student was receiving therapy from a "counselor" who was actually a professor of education. Treatment was terminated at the educator's suggestion. When the student later committed suicide, the parents sued, claiming negligence on the part of the "counselor" for failure to prevent this event or warn the parents of the danger. The court ruled that the educator was not liable because he was not professionally trained to assess suicidal potential and therefore could not be held responsible.[34] This issue certainly could have ramifications for unlicensed persons calling themselves "social workers" who, in reality, have no professional social-work training and yet are doing counselling. It would be most interesting could we know how the court would have ruled had the counselor been a trained therapist instead of an educator. In view of some of the previously discussed concerns regarding ability to predict dangerousness, it could be argued that even psychiatrists might not be able to predict suicidal potential accurately.

[33] This is suggested in "NOTE: Social Worker-Client Relationship and Privileged Communications," *op. cit.*, p. 393.

[34] *Bogust v. Iverson*, 10 Wisconsin 2d 129 N.W.2d 228 (1960). See also the reference to this case in Mildred Reynolds, "Threats to Confidentiality," *Social Work*, Vol. 21, No. 2 (March 1976), pp. 108–113; and Fearqueron, "A Study of Selected Aspects of Privileged Communication as Related to School Counselors, with Particular Reference to Florida," *op. cit.*

8. A CLIENT THREATENS TO HARM HIS THERAPIST

Obviously this is intention to harm another. The professional must evaluate the seriousness of the threat and take appropriate action to protect himself.

9. PHYSICIANS MUST REPORT CERTAIN MEDICAL CONDITIONS AND TREATMENTS

This situation rarely affects a social worker directly. However, mental-health professionals employed in interdisciplinary settings should be aware of the legal obligations of their physician-psychiatrist colleagues. The kinds of conditions that must be reported have already been listed (see pp. 102–103). While some state or federal laws require the reporting of certain medical conditions or treatments, others may simply permit disclosure without making it mandatory. Thus, physicians have been able to violate confidentiality in order to report venereal disease to spouses[35] and tuberculosis to landlords[36] without being held liable. However, in one case reported by Slovenko, a physician warned a woman that her fiancée (the patient) had a psychopathic personality. The professional was held liable on the basis that the protection of society did not require such a disclosure.[37] On the other hand, there may be obscure laws on the books requiring physicians to report certain conditions which, in light of modern medical knowledge, should not need reporting. For example, as recently as 1967 eight states still had laws requiring physicians to report all cases of epilepsy to the state department of motor vehicles regardless of how long the patient had been seizure-free. As of 1967, two states even forbade persons with seizure disorders to marry.[38] Thus, under certain circumstances physicians in these jurisdictions could conceivably find themselves forced to disclose privileged information, though not necessarily to a court of law.

10. A MINOR IS INVOLVED IN CRIMINAL ACTIVITY

When minors commit crimes, are used by adults as accessories in illegal activities, or are the victims of criminal actions, most states require that the information be reported. NASW's "Model Licensing Act" recognizes that state laws may force a social worker to violate privilege in these situations:

[35] See A.B. v. C.D. 7F (Scott) 72 (1905).

[36] *Simonsen v. Swenson*, 104 Nebraska 224, 177 N.W.831 (1920).

[37] *Berry v. Moench* 8 Utah 2d 191, 331 p.2d 814 (1958), discussed in Slovenko, *Psychiatry and Law, op. cit.*, p. 437.

[38] Ruth S. Barneis and Suanna J. Wilson, "A Study of Social Attitudes Towards Epilepsy," master's thesis, Syracuse University School of Social Work, 1968, p. 24.

[If] the person is a minor under the laws of this state and the information acquired by the licensed certified social worker, licensed social worker, or licensed social work associate indicates that the minor was the victim or subject of a crime, the licensed certified social worker, licensed social worker, or the social work associate may be required to testify fully in any examination, trial, or other proceeding in which the commission of such a crime is the subject of inquiry.[39]

Again the question, "How serious must the crime be?" arises. In reality, many professional helping persons who learn of minor infractions of the law by children and adolescents choose not to report the violations because the damage to the relationship and the helping process would be too great. Thus, petty thievery, marijuana use, and other offenses often go unreported.

11. CHILD ABUSE OR NEGLECT IS SUSPECTED

Many states require that any professional who encounters child abuse or neglect must report it to a designated child-protection organization. These authorities then evaluate the situation and recommend appropriate action to prevent further injury to the child, or else they give clearance that there was no abuse. Toll-free numbers to these organizations are now provided, and laymen as well as professionals are urged to report suspicious cases under the promise of complete anonymity. Professionals, however, must often identify themselves, and in legal actions—i.e., custody hearings or prosecution of the abusing adult—they may be required to testify. Thus, most states grant immunity from breach of confidence suits to the practitioner for having to disclose confidential information in these cases.

12. A CLIENT IS USING CERTAIN TYPES OF DRUGS

Some state and federal laws require that users of certain types of drugs be reported. In fact, some jurisdictions require submission of full identifying data on patients under a physician's care who are "drug-dependent." A psychiatrist brought suit against the state of Connecticut on behalf of all physicians practicing there, seeking a reversal of this requirement on the basis that it

infringed upon physicians' rights to privacy and confidentiality with patients and violated physicians' rights of due process of law. In addition, . . . the law fails to provide a definition of the term *drug-dependent*, conflicts with the state's privileged-communications law, and constitutes "an unreasonable exercise of police power."

However, the court ruled against the psychiatrist:

[39] NASW "Model Licensing Act for Social Worker," *op. cit.*, p. 8.

[T]here is no constitutional basis for privacy, privilege, or confidentiality between physician and patient and the matter rests entirely in the power of the legislature to enact laws related to these matters. While some matters of privacy have recently received constitutional protection in Supreme Court decisions, this court ruled that the physician-patient relationship is not so protected.[40]

Some drug use is clearly a violation of state or federal law (e.g., possession of marijuana, heroin, etc.) and therefore an obligation exists to report it because it constitutes a criminal activity. Social workers as well as physicians encounter these offenses rather regularly in their daily practice. Again, in reality, it would probably be safe to assume that many such offenses go unreported.

13. A CLIENT'S CONDITION MAKES HIS EMPLOYMENT HAZARDOUS TO OTHERS

A treating professional may be aware of a client's desire to engage in an occupation that is contraindicated by the presence of a medical or psychiatric disorder such that the individual would be a clear danger to himself or others at work. Thus, it may be necessary to violate confidentiality for the protection of all concerned. In *Clarke* v. *Geraci* a physician had knowledge that an alcoholic patient was unable to carry out his duties as an airplane pilot safely and was endangering the lives of others. In spite of the fact that the patient objected to the disclosure of his medical condition, the physician reported it to his employer, who subsequently fired him. The courts ruled in favor of the physician's violation of confidentiality.[41] However, several cases have occurred in which a physician released information to a patient's employer without patient consent and the courts held the physician liable for violation of privacy. Apparently, the hazard to society was not considered great enough to warrant disclosure.[42]

14. THE COURT ORDERS A PROFESSIONAL EXAMINATION

The American Medical Association, in its "Principles of Medical Ethics," states that if a patient is being examined for security purposes, to determine his suitability for various jobs or to evaluate his legal competence,

---

[40] Slovenko, *Psychiatry and Law, op. cit.*, p. 437. He is discussing *Felber v. Foote*, 321 F. Supp. 85 (D. C. Connecticut 1970). See also pp. 451–452.

[41] *Clarke v. Geraci*, 208 N.Y.S.2d 564 (Sup. Ct. 1960).

[42] See *Horne v. Patton*, 287 So.2d 824 (Alabama 1973) and the discussion by Arthur H. Bernstein, "Unauthorized Disclosure of Confidential Information," *Hospitals*, Vol. 48 (November 1, 1974), p. 26, and by Mildred Reynolds, "Threats to Confidentiality," *op. cit.*, p. 111. See also *Carr v. Watkins*, 227 Me. 578 177 A.2d 841 (1962), cited by Slovenko in *Psychiatry and Law, op. cit.*, p. 437.

the psychiatrist must explain to the patient that the results will be reported to the person requesting the examination.[43] Because a therapist may be called as an expert witness by the court, in such situations he must advise the client that he cannot keep confidential the information learned from his examination or contact with him. However, only information that is relevant to the purpose of the examination must be disclosed.[44] Several state statutes contain specific exceptions in this regard.[45]

When mental competency is an issue, professionals involved in court-ordered evaluations are not bound by privileged communication. Once the determination has been made, the privilege once again applies, though if the patient is found incompetent it may be the guardian who holds it.

15. INVOLUNTARY HOSPITALIZATION IS NEEDED FOR SOMEONE'S PROTECTION

When a psychiatrist determines that involuntary hospitalization is required for the protection of the patient or others, he may release necessary information. Many statutes free the professional from privilege requirements in these situations. Thus, confidentiality can be violated in some states when a psychiatrist determines that a patient must be involuntarily hospitalized for his own protection or the safety of others.[46]

16. THE CLIENT DIES

The literature of the 1960s presented the view that an individual's claim to privileged communication ended with his death:

> The rule in many jurisdictions is that death terminates the privilege. Thus, a legatee to a will in testamentary actions, or a beneficiary of a life insurance policy, cannot claim the privilege of the deceased patient, and the doctor cannot insist on remaining silent. The privilege belongs to the patient, and not to the physician.[47]

However, the more recent trend appears to be toward retention of the privilege following the client's death. Even in the early 1960s heirs could

---

[43] "The Principles of Medical Ethics with Annotations Especially Applicable to Psychiatry," *American Journal of Psychiatry*, Vol. 130 (September 1973), pp. 1058–1064.

[44] See Slovenko, *Psychiatry and Law, op. cit.*, p. 446.

[45] For example, see Schroeter, "An Exploratory Analysis of Privileged Communication," *op. cit.*

[46] Irwin N. Perr, "Current Trends in Confidentiality and Privileged Communications," *Journal of Legal Medicine*, Vol. 1, No. 5 (November–December 1973), pp. 44–47. Also see Schroeter, "An Exploratory Analysis of Privileged Communication," *op. cit.*

[47] Slovenko, "Psychiatry and a Second Look at the Medical Privilege," *op. cit.*, p. 182. See also *Rhodes v. Metropolitan Life Ins. Co.*, 172 F.2d 183 (5th Cir. 1949); and the discussion

claim or waive the privilege in behalf of the dead patient in some states.[48] George W. Holmes, in a letter to the Editor of *Social Service Review* in 1964, discusses a situation faced by his mental health clinic when a client died and the surviving family members wanted to get at certain information in the clinic's files. After careful consideration, the clinic refused to release the information, taking the stand that "death does not terminate an agency's obligation regarding confidentiality."[49] Earl Rose, in discussing confidentiality of pathology and autopsy reports (1972) expresses the feeling that phsysicians must abide by privileged communication regarding a patient after his death and that only heirs, divisees, and executors can waive the privilege. Furthermore, he points out that the surviving spouse or the next of kin has legal custody of the corpse; this person, then, can authorize an autopsy and control the release of information learned from it.[50] The federal provisions for the confidentiality of alcohol- and drug-abuse records have also adopted this stance:

> [W]hen consent is required for any disclosure . . . such consent in the case of records of a deceased patient may be given by an executor, administrator, or other personal representative. If there is no appointment of a personal representative, such consent may be given by the patient's spouse, or, if none, by any responsible member of the patient's family.[51]

While this does not refer specifically to privileged communication, it certainly implies that if a record of a deceased patient were to be subpoenaed and the employee involved had the right of privileged communication, the authorized representative or family member mentioned would undoubtedly be consulted as to his wishes regarding disclosure.

The NASW "Model Licensing Act" states that information can be released

> with the written consent of the person or persons or, in the case of death or disability, of his own personal representative, other person authorized to sue, or the beneficiary of an insurance policy on his life, health, or physical condition.[52]

---

in Slovenko and Usdin, "Privileged Communication and Right of Privacy in Diagnosis and Therapy," *op. cit.*, p. 282.

[48] Slovenko and Usdin, "Privileged Communication and Right of Privacy in Diagnosis and Therapy," *Current Psychiatric Therapies*, Vol. 3 (New York: Greene and Stratton, 1963), note 14, p. 309.

[49] George W. Holmes, Letter to the Editor under "Correspondence," in *Social Service Review*, Vol 38 (June 1964), p. 221.

[50] Earl F. Rose, "Pathology Reports and Autopsy Protocols: Confidentiality, Privilege and Accessibility," *American Journal of Clinical Pathology*, Vol. 57, No. 2 (February 1972), pp. 144–155.

[51] "Department of Health, Education and Welfare, Public Health Service: Confidentiality of Alcohol and Drug Abuse Patient Records—General Provisions," found in the *Federal Register*, Vol. 40, No. 127 (July 1, 1975), Part IV, p. 27808, Sec. 2.16 (b) (1).

[52] NASW "Model Licensing Act for Social Workers," *op. cit.*, p. 7.

This, too, would appear to place the control over disclosures in the hands of the authorized survivors, but it also adds the beneficiary of an insurance policy. Hopefully such individuals could only authorize release of information directly related to their claim and would not have consent control over an entire therapeutic record.

In sum, it appears that death need not terminate the privilege:

> The general rule still seems to be that at the death of a person holding the privilege it passes to his representatives and may be waived or asserted by them. In this case, the privilege is not available to persons antagonistic to the interest of the deceased. But, it should be remembered there is no cause by a deceased person's estate either for libel or for invasion of privacy of a decedent, nor can a claim be made by members of the decedent's family for their own anguish based upon statements concerning the decedent.[53]

However, there do appear to be a few situations where privilege regarding a deceased patient might not apply. The following is taken from a model statute:

> There is no privilege for any communications otherwise privileged under this act when evidence of a deceased patient's mental condition is introduced as an issue by any party claiming by testate or intestate succession or inter vivos transaction through or from the patient, provided that the judge finds that the social harm done by requiring the disclosure of confidences in the particular situation is overbalanced by the desirability of disclosure.[54]

Thus, if someone with authority to waive or claim privilege for the deceased introduces the patient's mental condition into litigation, the case is similar in principle to a client's introducing confidential information in a court case and thereby waiving privilege (see p. 113).

17. A TREATING PROFESSIONAL NEEDS TO COLLECT FEES FOR SERVICES RENDERED

A professional may need to secure the services of an outside collection agency to obtain payment for past-due bills. To do so requires disclosure of certain patient-identifying information. However, the courts have generally determined that the legalities of privileged communication and confidentiality should not prevent the professional from disclosing information necessary to obtain payment for his services.[55]

[53] Letter from Ralph Slovenko to the author dated January 12, 1977, in response to a question as to whether death of a client terminates the privilege.

[54] Craig Kennedy, "Psychotherapist's Privilege," *Washburn Law Journal*, Vol. 12 (Spring 1973) p. 315.

[55] For example, see *Yoder v. Smith*, 112 N.W.2d 862 (Iowa 1962). For further discussion on bill collecting, see also *Confidentiality and Privileged Communication in the Practice of*

18. INFORMATION IS LEARNED OUTSIDE THE PROFESSIONAL TREATMENT RELATIONSHIP

Practitioners sometimes acquire information regarding their clients prior to, outside of, or after termination of the formal treatment relationship. Obviously, professional ethics dictate that such information be kept confidential. However, the therapist could disclose the data in court without being held liable for violation of privileged-communication statutes. On the other hand, even if these statutes require the reporting of certain information, the professional would not in this case be obligated to do so. For example, it has been pointed out that should a psychotherapist learn at a cocktail party prior to the initiation of therapy of a patient's intention to commit a serious crime he is not required to keep the information confidential, nor is he under any more legal obligation than the average citizen to take action to prevent the intended crime.[56]

19. INFORMATION IS SHARED IN THE PRESENCE OF A THIRD PERSON

Problems can arise in this area, especially in family and group therapy. As this matter is discussed in more detail later (pp. 133–137) it will not be explored here.

20. THE FEDERAL GOVERNMENT NEEDS CERTAIN INFORMATION

The list of exceptions to absolute privilege under this item is virtually endless. The Internal Revenue Service can get at medical records if they are needed to settle a tax dispute, regardless of state laws to the contrary. At least one case has been reported in which the state law was overturned.[57] The FBI can gain access to just about anything it wants. Slovenko reports in his 1973 text that

> any federal agency can exercise the legal authority given the government to examine records of patients in Veterans Administration hospitals; it is done not only for purposes of treatment or for determination of disability payments, but also even when the patient makes application for any type of federal employment.[58]

Psychiatry, GAP Report No. 45, (New York: Group for the Advancement of Psychiatry, June 1960), p. 105; and Slovenko and Usdin, "Privileged Communication and Right of Privacy in Diagnosis and Therapy," *op. cit.*, pp. 302–303.

[56] *"Tarasoff v. Regents of University of California*: The Psychotherapist's Peril," *op. cit.*

[57] See *U.S. v. Kansas City Lutheran Home Association*, 297 F. Supp. 239 (D. D. Mo. 1969); and the discussion by Mildred Reynolds, "Threats to Confidentiality," *op. cit.*, p. 111.

[58] Slovenko, *Psychiatry and Law, op. cit.*, p. 443.

With the advent of professional standards review organizations, the government is now amassing volumes of computerized data on many Americans who seek health care, and medical information that would ordinarily be privileged must be released to them in compliance with the review process. Even though the program has elaborate confidentiality safeguards of its own, there are concerns that they are not adequate. Some suits have even been brought attempting to gain access to peer-review and PSRO records. Thus, complete privilege may be lost.[59] Unfortunately, these examples are only the surface of a massive iceberg of privilege-loopholes that exist due to the federal government's seemingly unlimited access to confidential data.

21. THE RIGHT OF PRIVILEGED COMMUNICATION IS NOT TRANSFERABLE FROM ONE STATE TO ANOTHER

Suppose that a therapist with privileged communication in state A moves to state B, which does not grant the privilege to his professional group and its clients. He is no longer covered as he conducts business in state B. However, suppose a matter comes up in the courts pertaining to confidential information obtained while he was in state A. At least one court has ruled that the privilege would apply.[60]

22. PRIVILEGE DOES NOT USUALLY APPLY TO THE FACT THAT A COMMUNICATION WAS MADE

It has been pointed out that

the medical privilege applies only to the communication itself, and not to the fact that a communication was made. Thus, under the orthodox medical privilege, the fact of the physician-patient relationship, that the patient was under treatment, the number of visits, and the duration of treatment, are not privileged areas.[61]

This position has led some to argue that mental-health professionals need privilege statutes different from those of attorneys and physicians in

[59] For example, see the discussion in Helen Creighton, "Legal Implications of PSRO's," *Supervisory Nurse*, Vol. 6, No. 5 (May 1975), p. 19; and in John M. Rumsey, "Confidentiality: The Patient's Trust Must be Protected," *Prism*, Vol. 2, No. 6 (June 1974), pp. 22–26. See also Chapter 4 for more details on maintaining confidentiality of PSRO materials.

[60] *Queen v. OrtMeyer*, N.Y. (Sup. Ct., 1962). Also see Geiser and Rheingold, "Psychology and the Legal Process: Testimonial Privileged Communications," *American Psychologist*, Vol. 10, No. 11 (November 1964), p. 833.

[61] Slovenko and Usdin, "Privileged Communication and Right of Privacy in Diagnosis and Therapy," *op. cit.*, p. 303.

order to protect the identity of clients.[62] It has also been argued that "because there may sometimes be a social stigma attached to visiting a social worker, it might be desirable to shield the identity of clients."[63] One might wonder how many persons hesitate to seek treatment for fear that the mere fact of their doing so will be disclosed. Under existing privilege statutes, it appears that in most instances the fear is well justified.[64]

Furthermore, the existence of this exception can be used to manipulate patients into withdrawing suits or engaging in other actions that may not be in their best interests:

> The primary purpose of the attorney issuing the subpoena, in effect, is not to investigate but rather to intimidate the opposing party into foregoing or settling the case. Privilege offers no protection against such blackmail. Since the privilege covers only the content of a communication and not the fact of a relationship, the identity of a treating psychiatrist can be elicited under a discovery demand. Pressure then can be brought to bear which frightens the patient, notwithstanding assurances from his attorney, into thinking that all his statements made in psychotherapy will be revealed in open court. It is impossible to estimate the number of cases which patients have dropped or feared to initiate because of the apprehension of disclosure.[65]

23. EMERGENCY ACTION IS NEEDED TO SAVE A CLIENT'S LIFE

This is similar to the exception granted when a patient is suicidal. Various state and federal regulations permit confidentiality violations when necessary to save a person's life. This occurs quite frequently in medical settings where an individual, for example, may enter the system confused, comatose, or otherwise unable to give consent for release of information or for medical treatment.[66]

24. LEGAL ACTION IS NEEDED FOR PROTECTION OF A MINOR

Minors are often considered unable to protect themselves and in need of adult decision-makers to make certain that actions taken are in their best in-

[62] For example, see Slovenko, "Psychiatry and a Second Look at Medical Privilege," op. cit., pp. 188–189.

[63] "NOTE: Social Worker-Client Relationship and Privileged Communications," op. cit., p. 392.

[64] I.e., see Slovenko, "Psychotherapist-Patient Testimonial Privilege: A Picture of Misguided Hope," op. cit., pp. 653–654.

[65] Ibid., pp. 653–654. See also Confidentiality and Third Parties, Task Force Report 9, American Psychiatric Association, Washington, D. C., June 1975, for some frightening examples of the effects of disclosure of treatment to third parties, particularly insurance carriers and employers.

[66] See Patrick Sean Cassidy, "Liability of Psychiatrists for Malpractice," University of Pittsburgh (Law Review, Vol. 36 (Fall 1974), pp. 108–137. Also see the Federal regulations for confidentiality of Alcohol and Drug Abuse records and the Federal Privacy Act which also permit unauthorized disclosures in medical emergencies.

terests. Thus, in child-custody cases, for example, privilege may have to take a back seat to the need to look out for the child's welfare.[67]

25. A CLIENT ENGAGES IN TREASONOUS ACTIVITIES

Federal law makes it a criminal offense not to report knowledge of such activities. The FBI has gone one step further and has actively solicited reports of subversive activity from physicians. "Wanted" notices have appeared rather frequently in publications of the American Medical Association, asking physicians to help the FBI find persons engaging in treasonous activity who may be seeking treatment for a known medical problem. Thus, there is active solicitation for violation of privileged communications. As might be expected, this has generated some criticism from inside and outside the medical profession.[68]

26. A PRE-SENTENCE INVESTIGATION REPORT IS PREPARED

These reports are usually prepared by probation departments and whatever specialty groups they may call upon for assistance in evaluating an individual. The sentencing judge must have full access to the material to assist him in his decision. However, several groups, including the American Bar Association, have taken a stand that the report must be made available to the defendant and his attorney, and some states and courts have been enforcing this requirement.[69]

27. THE TREATING PROFESSIONAL IS EMPLOYED IN AN AGENCY/INSTITUTION

When a mental health professional is employed by a larger institution, he may be required to disclose privileged information to others within the setting. Most social workers will identify readily with this situation. A certain amount of intra-agency or intra-institutional sharing must take place for effective delivery of services to occur. However, not all professionals and persons handling confidential data in these settings are covered by a privilege statute. Therefore, in 1963, Slovenko and Usdin warned psychiatrists that

> the attorney-client privilege covers the attorney's agent, but in most states the physician's agent, the nurse, is not generally included within the medical privi-

[67] Slovenko, "Psychotherapist-Patient Testimonial Privilege: A Picture of Misguided Hope," *op. cit.*, p. 656.

[68] Slovenko, *Psychiatry and Law, op. cit.*, p. 445 and note 16, p. 454.

[69] *Ibid.*, pp. 447–448 and note 20, p. 455.

lege, unless expressly provided by statute. Likewise, psychologists, social workers, counselors and stenographers may not come within the scope of the medical privilege, even when working under psychiatric supervision. Communications to these persons may be compelled in court. This is important to the psychiatrist, who often relies on such persons.[70]

Thus, these individuals may be subpoenaed in an effort to get at privileged information.

Another problem occurs when mental-health professionals are employed in private industry to counsel employees on personal problems. The employer may insist on some feedback from the practitioner and may make it part of his job requirement. Prisons may look to the professional therapist as a good inside source of information about past and future criminal activities and the general mood of the prisoners.[71] The Group for the Advancement of Psychiatry has expressed its feeling that a psychiatrist cannot ethically work in such an environment and should seek employment elsewhere if he is not permitted to maintain confidentiality of patient communications.[72]

Supervisors with privileged-communication coverage who are of different disciplines may require that certain confidential information be obtained by employees who do not have the coverage. It has been argued that these internal communications should be privileged:

> [C]ommunications from patients to psychiatric social workers administering therapy under the direction of a supervisor covered by the privilege should also be privileged under this rule. Many psychiatric social workers interview patients and family members in order to help determine which patients are to be admitted to mental health facilities and which are ready to be discharged. In doing so, they usually answer to the physician in charge of admitting and discharging patients. Other psychiatric social workers work directly with patients in outpatient clinics, in consultation with a director who is a psychiatrist. In both cases, communications received by the social worker should be privileged under the agency principle. Of course, psychiatric social workers who practice independently would not receive privilege under this rule, and some social workers might qualify for privilege in connection with some of their duties but not others.[73]

28. A SOCIAL WORKER IS EMPLOYED IN A MILITARY SETTING

As of 1963,

a privilege is not recognized in military law for communications made to medi-

[70] Slovenko and Usdin, "Privileged Communication and Right of Privacy in Diagnosis and Therapy," *op. cit.*, p. 288.

[71] Slovenko, *Psychiatry and Law, op. cit.*, p. 448.

[72] *Confidentiality and Privileged Communication in the Practice of Psychiatry*, GAP Report No. 45, *op. cit.*, p. 106.

[73] "COMMENTS: Underprivileged Communications: Extension of the Psychotherapist-Patient Privilege to Patients of Psychiatric Social Workers," *op. cit.*, pp. 1060-1061.

cal officers and civilian physicians, although military law does recognize the privilege relationships of attorney-client, husband-wife, and priest-penitent.[74]

There is as of now still no privilege for psychotherapeutic communications.[75] Social workers are urged to observe ethics of confidentiality, but "information obtained by the social-work officer is not privileged information in the legal sense. . . . [H]e is in an official position [and] information he obtains about a patient is available for use by courts-martial and civilian courts if properly called for."[76]

Thus, mental-health professionals functioning in a military setting must be aware of the armed services' unique confidentiality and privilege regulations.

29. CLAIMS ARE FILED FOR LIFE AND ACCIDENT INSURANCE BENEFITS

Some insurance companies have the applicant sign blank consent forms as a prerequisite for receiving insurance coverage. Such forms may contain a clause whereby the insured waives his and his beneficiary's right to claim privilege. Thus, when someone files claim to the benefits provided by the policy, medical and mental-health professionals may be forced to testify, since the privilege has already been waived.[77]

Privileged Communication and Group Therapy

A communication is usually not considered privileged if it is made in the presence of a third person.[78] There are a few exceptions, such as when the third individual is acting as a professional's agent (i.e., a secretary, or a member of another discipline) or when the third party is the client's legal spouse. However, fellow group members and "co-counselees" have not come under the definition of "an agent for the professional" in most state statutes. Thus, group members could theoretically be called as witnesses and made to disclose confidences during group therapy sessions. Amazingly enough, however,

[74] Slovenko and Usdin, "Privileged Communication and Right of Privacy in Diagnosis and Therapy," *op. cit.*, p. 289.

[75] Slovenko, *Psychiatry and Law, op. cit.*, p. 63, referring to the *Manual for Courts-Martial*.

[76] *Army Social Work*, TM 8-241, Department of the Army Technical Manual, Headquarters, Department of the Army, January 1958, p. 19.

[77] Slovenko and Usdin, "Privileged Communication and Right of Privacy in Diagnosis and Therapy," *op. cit.*, p. 282.

[78] I.e., see Leila M. Foster, "Group Psychotherapy: A Pool of Legal Witnesses?," *International Journal of Group Psychotherapy*, Vol. 25, No. 1 (January 1975), pp. 50–53.

while in the dyadic, one-to-one situation, there have been many subpoenas of therapists, it is rather remarkable that notwithstanding the large number of people in group therapy, there apparently has been no subpoena of any member of a group anywhere in the country.[79]

In another article, Slovenko also points out that there have been very few reported problems with abuse of confidentiality in group therapy situations.[80]

In a survey of ninety-two group therapists, one author reported that none of those responding reported any significant breaches of confidentiality during the previous year.[81] It has also been said that therapists are "far more concerned about confidentiality than members of the group."[82] Perhaps this illustrates the naivete of consumers regarding privacy rights and how easily these rights might be violated. Perhaps it is also a reflection of the clients' absolute trust in the therapist. In an interview with several individuals who had been in group therapy for a number of years, Slovenko reports that they repeatedly indicated that when confronted with a thorny confidentiality problem they would look to the therapist for guidance.[83] These same counselees commented that they considered their relationships with one another as being even more intense than that between a man and wife. They felt they should have the same legal protection as spouses so they could not be forced to testify against one another. How can this protection be provided? Several approaches have been suggested for dealing with the problem, and some suggestions have found their way into various model statutes.

Several authors have suggested that group members sign a contract between themselves and the therapist pledging to maintain confidentiality. The agreement might be a very simple one dictating that "statements made and advice rendered can not be used in any legal proceedings."[84] Supposed-

[79] Ralph Slovenko, "Interview of Group on Confidentiality," unpublished transcript obtained from the author, dated January 5, 1977.

[80] Ralph Slovenko, "Group Therapy: Privileged Communication and Confidentiality," paper presented at the Annual Meeting of the American Group Psychotherapy Association, February 3, 1977, San Francisco.

[81] Nan Mykel, "The Application of Ethical Standards to Group Psychotherapy in a Community," *International Journal of Group Psychotherapy,* Vol. 21 (1971), p. 248, discussed in Slovenko, "Group Therapy: Privileged Communication and Confidentiality," *op. cit.* However, clients can experience actual or alleged confidentiality violations and react strongly. The day before completion of this chapter, an individual related that when she was a participant in group therapy, another group member talked about her outside the sessions and used things she had said against her. She blamed the therapist for "maintaining inadequate control over the group members and allowing certain things to go on that shouldn't have" and subsequently terminated treatment.

[82] Slovenko, "Group Therapy: Privileged Communication and Confidentiality," *op. cit.,* p. 1.

[83] Slovenko, "Interview of Group on Confidentiality," *op. cit.*

[84] Selma Arnold, "Confidential Communications and the Social Worker," *Social Work Journal,* Vol. 15, No. 1 (January 1970), pp. 61–67.

ly, if all group members are adults and sign such a statement, everyone would be legally bound by confidentiality. Some of the proposed contracts are much more sophisticated, however:

> We, the undersigned, in consideration of and return for receiving group psychotherapy and its possible benefits, and in consideration of and return for similar promises by other members of the psychotherapy group, consciously and willingly promise never to reveal the identity of any group member (listed below) to anyone who is not in group therapy, other than staff of the psychiatric agency from which we receive services. We realize that to relate specific problems of a group member to a nongroup member, even though the name of the group member may not be directly revealed, may at times lead to the eventual disclosure of the group member's identity. Therefore, we promise to avoid speaking of any group member's problems in any manner which would even remotely risk revealing the identity of that group member. We fully realize and strongly agree that in the event of a lawsuit for breach of contract, we give the offended party the right to recover for damage to his/her reputation the minimum amount of $_____. Also, such party may recover for any other damages which can be proved.[85]

Another approach is to have all group members declared agents of the therapist and thus bring them under existing privileged-communication statutes.[86] One model statute reflecting this view proposes that clients can treat as privileged the communications

> between any other professional or lay person [who participates with such a member of the mental health profession] in the accomplishment of individual or group diagnosis or treatment, or members of the client's family, or between any of these persons as concerns diagnosis or treatment.[87]

Another defines confidential information to include communications between

> persons who participate in the accomplishment of the objective of diagnosis, fact-finding, or service provision under the supervision of, or in cooperation with, the service provider.[88]

Another prefers to treat all group members as primary clients and declare

[85] J. Morrison, M. Frederic, and H. J. Rosenthall, "Controlling Confidentiality in Group Psychotherapy," *Forensic Psychology*, Vol. 7 (1975), pp. 4–5.

[86] I.e., see Leila Foster, "Group Psychotherapy: A Pool of Legal Witnesses?," *op. cit.*; Robert Jay Braman, "NOTES: Group Therapy and Privileged Communication," *Indiana Law Journal*, Vol. 43 (Fall 1967), pp, 93–105; and Leila M. Foster, "Confidentiality of Group and Family Psychotherapy Records," Chap. 6 in *Confidentiality of Health and Social Service Records: Where Law, Ethics & Clinical Issues Meet* (Chicago: University of Illinois at Chicago Circle, December 1976), p. 131.

[87] Robert L. Geiser and Paul D. Rheingold, "Psychology and the Legal Process: Testimonial Privileged Communications," *American Psychologist*, Vol. 19, No. 11 (November 1964), p. 836.

[88] Sandra G. Nye, "Model Law on Confidentiality of Health and Social Service Information," *op. cit.*, p. 261.

outright that all communications made in the presence of fellow group members are confidential and privileged:

> (iii) . . . Where the psychotherapeutic relationship is such as to require the participation of more than one of such persons, "patient" shall be interpreted as meaning more than one of such persons; (iv) "Psychotherapeutic relationship" means a relationship which exists between two (or more) persons where one (or more) is a patient seeking help from a psychotherapist in the solution of his (their) problem(s).[89]

Still another proposal is that those with a right to claim privilege should include

> third parties present when the communication was made with the knowledge of the person making the communication and whose presence was reasonably believed to be necessary either to the person hearing the communication or to the person making the communication;
>   third parties present when the communication was made without the knowledge of the person making the communication.[90]

An additional proposal includes the following as persons who may receive disclosures that will remain legally "privileged":

> those to whom disclosure is reasonably necessary for the transmission of the information or the accomplishment of diagnosis or treatment, including group therapy; and members of the client's family; supervisors or other persons participating in consultation, examination or interview, diagnosis, or treatment, or other service provided under the direction of the provider; third party payers. . . .[91]

However, Foster points up a possible problem that could arise if all group members have the right to exercise or waive privilege: suppose one group member wants a certain piece of information kept confidential and another waives privilege—what would the therapist do?[92]

Since there have been no legal actions to date subpoenaing group members for disclosure of confidential communications, it remains to be seen how much of a problem this will be and whether some mechanisms other than those mentioned here for avoiding disclosures would be necessary and effective.

One attorney has suggested that the fact that many group workers do not keep records of the process would make it difficult for courts to get at the content of group sessions. Furthermore, it might be argued that group members are not usually qualified to give professional assessments of others

[89] Kennedy, "Psychotherapist's Privilege," op. cit., p. 315.

[90] "Privileged Communications: A Case by Case Approach," op. cit., p. 458.

[91] Nye, "Model Law on Confidentiality of Health and Social Service Information," op. cit., pp. 263-264.

[92] Foster, "Confidentiality of Group and Family Psychotherapy Records," op. cit., p. 133.

in therapy and that their statements are subject to error because several people often speak at once in group discussions. Finally, a group member could conveniently suffer "loss of memory" without the attendant stigma and repercussions that the therapist–group-leader would encounter.[93]

Nonprivileged Situations Where Confidentiality Still May Be Preserved

Confidential information received by a professional not covered by a general privileged-communication statute is usually readily available to the courts through the subpoena process. However, courts sometimes rule that non-privileged information does not have to be disclosed, in effect treating it as if it were privileged. The situations are highly specific and do not necessarily carry over from one case to another; they are often adjudged after an in-depth analysis of the existing statutes in the state. However, a few of the more common instances in which such communications have been treated as privileged or otherwise exempt from disclosure in court are presented here.

1. A COMMUNICATION MEETS WIGMORE'S FOUR CRITERIA

When the communication is found to meet the four Wigmore criteria, privilege may be granted in a particular situation. This would mean that society's need to know must be less important than the need to preserve confidentiality. As this point has already been explained, it will not be repeated here.[94]

2. THE SUBPOENAED INFORMATION IS NOT RELEVANT TO LITIGATION

When confidential information is not relevant to a litigation, it does not have to be disclosed. This is one of the mental-health professional's strong-

[93] Suggested by Robert H. Cohen in a letter to the author dated 5-18-77. However, group members who are professional, trained helping persons or therapists themselves might find it more difficult to plead inability to make diagnostic assessments. In addition, some group members do keep personal notebooks that may describe content as well as reactions to group therapy sessions. This may be done at the therapist's suggestion, but can also occur without his knowledge.

[94] See p. 99 and pp. 113–115. See also *Simrim v. Simrim*, 43 Cal. Rptr, 376 (Dist. Ct. App. 1965) discussed in "NOTE: Social Worker-Client Relationship and Privileged Communications," *op. cit.*, pp. 374–375. In this case a Rabbi had promised confidentiality to a couple receiving marital counseling. When the wife sought modification of a prior custody action in-

est defenses against having to disclose confidential communications in court, even if they are not protected by a privilege statute. If he can show that the court really does not need his data to rule on the case or that the requested information is more than is necessary, he may be able to avoid testifying. Slovenko feels rather strongly about this point:

> In every case where the testimony or records of a physician or psychotherapist have been required by a court, it was because the evidence was deemed relevant or material to an issue in the case. As a consequence, in the last analysis, the confidentiality of a physician-patient or psychotherapist-patient communication is protected from disclosure in a courtroom only by a showing that communication would have no relevance or materiality to the issues in the case.[95]

It would appear then, that the relevancy issue holds more hope for preventing disclosures in court than do privileged-communication statutes.

3. DATA SOUGHT BY THE COURT CAN BE OBTAINED FROM SOME OTHER SOURCE

When data sought by the court can be obtained through some other source, a professional who has been subpoenaed may not have to disclose his confidential data. If the practitioner freely relinquishes his confidential though non-privileged data with little or no objection, the courts may not even check to see if the information can be obtained elsewhere. If the professional resists disclosure, however, the court may investigate to see if it can get the data from some other source. This may then let the professional "off the hook."[96]

4. SPECIALIZED COMMUNICATIONS MAY HAVE BEEN DECLARED PRIVILEGED

State and federal regulations may have granted privileged status to certain specialized types of communications. These exceptions vary widely

volving their four children, the court asked the rabbi to testify. He refused, based on the fact that the relationship was entered into with an expectation of confidentiality. The trial court and later the appeal court upheld his right not to disclose the information because of the importance of preserving marriages and the importance of the counseling process. Thus, society's needs for preserving confidentiality outweighed the need to get all the facts in this particular situation.

[95] Slovenko, "Psychotherapist-Patient Testimonial Privilege: A Picture of Misguided Hope," *op. cit.*, p. 659.

[96] See *Re: Kryschuk & Zulynik*, 14 D.L.R. 2d 676 (Sask., Canada Magis. Ct. 1958). A social worker was subpoenaed in a paternity suit. A number of issues were involved, including some debate over whether the communication should be considered privileged. However, the social worker protested against having to testify, and the court finally felt that it had enough other evidence to render its decision and therefore did not require that the social worker testify. See the discussion of this case in "NOTE: Social Worker-Client Relationship and Privileged Communications," *op. cit.*, pp. 373–374.

from state to state and are subject to change. Among the kinds of communications that various states have declared privileged are adoption proceedings and treatment for certain conditions (i.e., venereal disease, abortions, contraception).[97]

Many state legislatures, either in conjunction with federal grant-in-aid programs or on their own initiative, have enacted statutes granting a privilege to participants in particular welfare programs. Information may be privileged if it was given to adoption or health and safety agencies, mental institutions, maternity hospitals or departments of unemployment compensation; or if it appears in drug addiction, alcoholism, venereal disease, eye disease, probation and parole, or child welfare records; or in the records of social welfare, vocational rehabilitation, juvenile court, probation and parole or domestic relations proceedings.[98]

Practitioners should review their own state's statutes and current federal legislation if they are faced with a subpoena and seek an "out" under this type of clause.

5. SOCIETY TRADITIONALLY EXPECTS THE COMMUNICATION TO BE PRIVILEGED

When society traditionally expects certain communications to be kept confidential, most courts will treat them as privileged. The priest-penitent relationship is generally viewed as sacred, and even when privileged communication does not exist few courts will ever ask a priest to testify. Another exempt role is that of secretary:

An attorney rarely, if ever, subpoenas a secretary, even though the boss-secretary relationship is not protected by a statutory privilege, for the relationship is considered sacrosanct. (The word *secretary* is from Latin *secretum*, secret.) The physician-patient or psychotherapist-patient relationship is not considered untouchable by the community and therefore does not stand on the same footing as the priest-penitent or secretary-boss relationship.[99]

If even psychotherapists are not accorded untouchable status, one needn't wonder where social workers would be rated on such a scale!

6. A WITNESS IS MENTALLY INCOMPETENT

Incompetent testimony will not be heard by the courts and thus does not have to be disclosed. If a witness is mentally incompetent, his disclosures

[97] See Adele D. Hofmann, "Confidentiality of the Health Care Records of Children and Youth," *Psychiatric Opinion*, Vol. 12, No. 1 (January 1975), pp. 20–28.

[98] "NOTE: Social Worker-Client Relationship and Privileged Communciations," *op. cit.*, pp. 367–368.

[99] Slovenko, *Psychiatry and Law, op. cit.*, pp. 67–68.

are considered valueless and he will not be compelled to testify. However, one author would like to broaden the term "incompetency" to include the ability to testify meaningfully and competently.[100] When a psychiatrist is called to testify, time pressures and the method of questioning used by the attorneys may make it difficult for him to give meaningful, "professionally competent" testimony. His own resistance to having to disclose the information in the first place could make the professional helping person a very poor and ineffective witness. Thus, Slovenko wonders why psychiatrists could not argue at times that they are unable to testify competently and thus avoid making the disclosure.

7. THE CLIENT MAKES HIS DISCLOSURE INVOLUNTARILY

When disclosures are made involuntarily by a client and/or under threat, courts will rule the information inadmissible. If a professional or attorney can prove that his client made a communication under extreme duress or under threat the court will rule it inadmissible. For example, in one case a probation officer applied pressure to get his client to "tell me the truth" and elicited a confession to several crimes which the individual had previously denied committing. When called to testify, the probation officer explained what had happened. His testimony was required, but "the Supreme Court of California reversed the trial court's decision because the probation officer's statement to the defendant constituted a threat or an implied promise of leniency and therefore his admissions were involuntary and inadmissible."[101]

8. AN INDIVIDUAL IS ACTING AS AN AGENT OF THE PROFESSIONAL COVERED BY PRIVILEGED COMMUNICATION

Communications to persons acting as agents of a professional who is covered by privilege may also be privileged. As previously indicated, in order for such communications to be considered privileged, the privileged-communication statutes should specify that the professional's agents are also covered. Several authors point out the need for such coverage for all

[100] See Slovenko and Usdin, "Privileged Communication and the Right of Privacy in Diagnosis and Therapy," op. cit., pp. 294–297. The authors present several arguments supporting their feeling that various circumstances can affect the psychiatrist's testimony.

[101] People v. Quinn 61 Cal. 2d 551, 39 Cal. Rptr. 393, 393 p.2d 705 (1964). The case is discussed in "NOTE: Social Worker-Client Relationship and Privileged Communications," op. cit., p. 375. See also the cases of Leyra v. Denno, 347 U.S. 556 (1954), and of Oaks v. Colorado 371 p. 2d 443 (Colorado 1962) cited in Slovenko, Psychiatry and Law, op. cit., p. 446, for two other examples when psychiatrists used rather manipulative methods for obtaining information from patients, causing the courts to declare the communication inadmissible.

professionals, including social workers.[102] Also, several model statutes propose that agents of professionals be covered under privilege statutes.

For example, "Privileged Communications: A Case by Case Approach" lists the following as being able to claim the privilege:

1. the person making the communication;
2. the person hearing the communication, unless he is instructed otherwise by the person who made the communication or his personal representative or guardian or unless there is neither a person who made the communication nor his personal representative in existence;
3. a guardian or conservator of the person who made the communication;
4. the personal representative of the person who made the communication if that person is dead;
5. third parties present when the communication was made with the knowledge of the person making the communication and whose presence was reasonably believed to be necessary either to the person hearing the communication or to the person making the communication.[103]

Thus, practitioners without the privilege would do well to check their state statutes concerning privilege for other disciplines with which they work closely, in order to determine whether this association also declares their clients' communications privileged. Note, however, that such a privilege would apply only to communications taking place in connection with the association with the other professional.

9. THE INFORMATION IS HEARSAY

If a professional learns something about his client from a third person and is subsequently asked to disclose the content in court, it is usually considered hearsay evidence and declared inadmissible.[104] Furthermore, if a practitioner reports third-party information in court and it proves to be wrong, he may be sued for libel or slander if someone should decide to seek damages. Therefore, he should try to avoid giving this evidence by stating at the outset that it is hearsay.

[102] See "COMMENTS: Underprivileged Communications: Extension of the Psychotherapist-Patient Privilege to Patients of Psychiatric Social Workers," *op. cit.*, pp. 1060–1061; Slovenko and Usdin, "Privileged Communication and Right of Privacy in Diagnosis and Therapy," *op. cit.*, pp. 287–288; and Earl F. Rose, "Pathology Reports and Autopsy Protocols: Confidentiality, Privilege and Accessibility," *op. cit.*

[103] *Op. cit.*, p. 458. See also Sandra G. Nye, "Model Law on Confidentiality of Health and Social Service Information," where it is stated that "confidential information" means "information relating to diagnosis, facts necessary to the provision of service, or treatment transmitted between any of the persons specified [above] and persons who participate in the accomplishment of the objectives of diagnosis, fact-finding, or service provision under the supervision of, or in cooperation with, the service provider" (p. 261).

[104] Robert E. Boyd and Richard D. Heinsen, "Problems in Privileged Communciation," *Personnel and Guidance J.*, Vol. 50, No. 4 (December 1975), pp. 20–28.

10. AN ATTORNEY FILES DOCUMENTS IN A MALPRACTICE LAWSUIT

Documents filed by attorneys in certain malpractice suits have been declared privileged. One author reports a ruling that documents filed by attorneys in malpractice suits against physicians are privileged communication.[105] One wonders if the same would apply if the defendant were a social worker instead.

11. A CLIENT HAS SIGNED A BLANKET "CONSENT FOR RELEASE OF INFORMATION" FORM

When a client has "waived privilege" by signing a blanket consent-for release-of-information form, the court may rule that no waiver of privilege has occurred. Blanket consent forms are coming under increasing criticism; mental-health professionals can become very frustrated when they are called to testify and are forced to disclose confidential, perhaps damaging, material because a client has signed "one of those cursed forms." However, Maurice Grossman, in an article giving guidance on how to respond to subpoenas, reports a case where the court ruled that the blanket consent was not a waiver in a specific case because it was intended for other purposes. According to Grossman, "this begins to apply the doctrine of 'informed consent' to such written waivers."[106] The ramifications of this could be quite significant. If every consumer who felt information had been disclosed without his "informed consent" were to bring suit for violation of confidentiality, the courts would be jammed. Likewise, if professionals could claim privilege because "the client really didn't waive privilege at all," very little would have to be disclosed.

[105] Joseph E. Simonaitis, "Documents Filed in Lawsuits Are Privileged Communication," *Journal American Medical Association*, Vol. 228, No. 10 (June 3, 1974), p. 1332.

[106] Maurice Grossman, "The Psychiatrist and the Subpoena," Bulletin of the *American Academy of Psychiatry and the Law*, Vol. 1, No. 4 (December 1973), p. 248, discussing *Roberts v. Superior Court of Butte County*, 9 C.3d 330 (Calif. Sup. Ct., April 11, 1973). See also Chapter 4 for a detailed discussion on the concept of "informed consent" and the use of blanket consent forms.

9. Lawsuits, Subpoenas, and the Right of Privileged Communication for Social Workers

Lawsuits Involving Confidentiality Actions

THERE ARE NUMEROUS SUITS in which confidentiality becomes an issue after legal action has been initiated for some other reason. For example, the victim of an auto accident sues for damages and asks the defendant's psychiatrist to testify regarding a past history of psychiatric treatment. When the psychiatrist refuses, claiming that the material is confidential and/or privileged, confidentiality becomes an issue as the court determines whether or not the information must be disclosed. In this instance confidentiality is really a side issue—the primary cause for action is something else.

There have been several studies reviewing the nature of malpractice suits directed against physicians. One reported that during the period from 1794 to 1900, only 224 reported cases of suits against physicians occurred, but from 1900 to 1955, 1,712 cases were reported. None of the suits revolved around violation of confidentiality or privilege.[1] Another study looked at malpractice suits directed against psychiatrists from 1946 to 1961. It reported that four to five hundred malpractice claims reached the appellate courts, but that the actual number of original claims would be much higher as "only one out of 100 claims reaches the appellate court."[2] Thirteen cases were directed against psychiatrists specifically, and all involved problems in treatment, commitment, suicide, or "miscellaneous." However, none of the "miscellaneous" included actions for violation of confidentiality or

[1] "Review of Medical Professional Liability Claims and Suits," *Journal of American Medical Association*, Vol. 167, No. 2 (May 10, 1958), pp. 227–229.

[2] William A. Bellamy, "Malpractice Risks Confronting the Psychiatrist: A Nationwide Fifteen-year Study of Appellate Court Cases, 1946–1961," *American Journal of Psychiatry*, Vol. 118 (March 1962), p. 769.

privilege.[3] In fact, there have been at least two actions brought because a professional failed to violate confidentiality, resulting in harm to someone.[4]

Thus, suits brought for the reason that "someone violated my confidentiality and I want to sue him for it" are rare and have occurred only in recent years. Some examples (most of these have been mentioned earlier in other connections): A patient overheard two physicians talking about her out in the hallway, became so upset that her surgery had to be cancelled, and subsequently sued;[5] an individual wrote an article for the *Reader's Digest* naming an accomplice in a crime without disguising identifying data and was sued successfully for his indiscretion;[6] a patient authorized a physician to make a film of her in childbirth to be shown to medical societies, and sued when the doctor violated her privacy by showing it in public;[7] another patient sued when a psychiatrist published a detailed account of his family's treatment.[8] Employees have sued when physicians have disclosed adverse information to their employers without their consent.[9] In another case a therapist treating a man and wife gave the husband a report on his spouse's mental condition; when the husband's attorney confronted the wife with it a year later, she sued because the disclosure caused her harm and mental distress.[10] A plastic surgeon published a picture of a patient's nose in a medical journal without the patient's consent and was sued for invasion of privacy.[11] Another patient sued and collected damages when his physician made an unauthorized disclosure to an insurance company.[12]

Most of these cases involved physicians. I have been unable to learn the details of any cases in which a social worker was specifically sued by a client for breach of confidentiality.[13] An inquiry to the malpractice-insurance carrier for the National Association of Social Workers revealed that several cases involving confidentiality issues are currently in litigation; however,

[3] *Ibid.*, pp. 769–780.

[4] See *Tarasoff v. Regents of University of California*, 13 Cal. 3d 177 (1974), and *Bugust v. Iverson*, 10 Wisconsin 2d 129 N.W. 2d 228 (1960).

[5] Frances Ginsberg and Barbara Clarke, "Patients Need Privacy—and May Sue If They Don't Get It," *Modern Hospital*, Vol. 118, No. 6 (June 1972), p. 110.

[6] "Invasion of Privacy—Former Criminal's Name Entitled to Protection," *Briscoe v. Reader's Digest Association Inc.*, Supreme Court of California, April 2, 1971. Reported in the *Social Welfare Court Digest*, Vol. 16, No. 6 (June 1971), p. 1.

[7] *Feeney v. Young* reported in "CASE NOTES: *Roe v. Doe*: A Remedy for Disclosure of Psychiatric Confidences," *Rutgers Law Review*, Vol. 29 (Fall 1975), p. 195.

[8] *Roe v. Doe, ibid.*, p. 190.

[9] *Horne v. Patton*, 287 So.2d 824 (Alabama 1973).

[10] *Furness v. Fitchett* (*New Zealand Law Rev.* 396, 1958). Reported by Patrick Sean Cassidy in "Liability of Psychiatrist for Malpractice," *University of Pittsburgh Law Review*, Vol. 36 (Fall 1974), pp. 115–116. However, a review of appropriate legal references failed to turn up the report on this case.

[11] *Griffin v. Medical Society of New York*, 11 NYS 2d 109 (1939).

[12] *Hammonds v. Aetna Casualty and Surety Co.*, 243 F. Supp. 793 (D. C. Ohio, 1965).

[13] This applies for the period through 1976. See note 14.

specifics were unobtainable.[14] Thus, it is not known whether confidentiality is a primary or secondary issue in these suits.

In summary, it appears that social work has thus far escaped any significant volume of suits for breaches of confidentiality. The fact that violations by social work practitioners occur *is* well documented in the literature,[15] and it is only a matter of time before someone brings legal action for damages. The Federal Privacy Act of 1974 carries definite penalties for confidentiality violations and a mandate for consumer education regarding this fact. If extended to the private sector, the clause would add fuel to the potential fire of confidentiality suits against social work practitioners or agencies.

WHAT TO DO IF SUBPOENAED

There have been two significant articles which offer specific guidance to the professional who is subpoenaed;[16] the concerned mental-health practitioner would do well to study them carefully before a subpoena arrives.

Far too many social-work settings view the subpoena as "an act of God." Everyone stands in awe as all other important matters take a backseat to the urgent need to respond to the subpoena. As most social workers, and many other mental-health professionals as well, are poorly informed on legal procedures, they often overreact, and hastily and dutifully gather together everything the subpoena requests. In the process, much unnecessary and highly confidential information is often disclosed. Consider Maurice Grossman's comments on the nature of the subpoena:

> If the recipient knew how easy it was to have a subpoena issued; if he knew how readily the subpoena could demand information when there actually was no legal right to command the disclosure of information; if he knew how often an individual releases information that legally he had no right to release because of intimidation—he would view the threat of the subpoena with less fear and

[14] Letter to the American Professional Insurance Agency produced the following reply:

There have been law suits brought against social workers concerning confidentiality of records and right of privileged communication. I cannot provide you with the exact nature of the legal action as this is confidential as is the outcome and the current status of the case.

I can however, tell you that there have been several cases of this type and that none of them at this point are settled.

Letter from Richard C. Imbert, Senior Partner, to the author, dated 7-1-76. The letter indicated that NASW had some of the data in summary form and was preparing a report; however, followup inquiries to the NASW failed to produce any specifics.

[15] For example, see Joseph Alves, *Confidentiality in Social Work,* (Washington, D.C., Catholic University of America Press, 1959), pp. 198–200, where subjects of his survey rather freely admitted to a variety of violations.

[16] See Maurice Grossman, "The Psychiatrist and the Subpoena," *Bulletin of the American Academy of Psychiatry and the Law,* Vol. 1, No. 4 (December 1973), pp. 245–253; and Barton E. Bernstein, "The Social Worker as a Courtroom Witness," *Social Casework,* Vol. 56, No. 9 (November 1975), pp. 521–525.

greater skepticism. A lawyer may merely attest that he believes a certain individual has certain information that is relevant to the issue at court to get a subpoena issued. These forms are transmitted to the office of the clerk of the court routinely and the clerk of the court has a staff that routinely makes out the subpoena to be served by organized processors. No one reviews the request for the subpoena. No one examines the basis for the request. No one discusses with anyone else whether there is a legal right for disclosure. No one raises the question whether information is protected by law against disclosure before the subpoena is issued. The subpoena is requested and routinely issued on the principle of law that there is a right for discovery of any and all facts relative to the issue at court.[17]

Subpoenas must be responded to in some manner; otherwise the legal penalties are very real. However, it *is* possible to respond with the argument that all or part of the requested material should *not* be disclosed, based on concepts presented in this book and on existing state and federal statutes. The list of unexpected situations in which communications might be treated as privileged (see Chapter 8, pp. 137–142) suggests some available tactics that might prove more powerful and effective in preventing disclosures than privileged-communication statutes. Professionals ignorant of such matters often blindly comply with subpoenas, and their attorneys, who may not have had occasion to research the intricacies of privileged communication and confidentiality from a legal perspective, might not even suggest that the subpoena be questioned. Thus, the practitioner may need to initiate the suggestion and stimulate the attorney's desire to pursue it further. An in-depth awareness of the issues presented in this entire text, and especially the chapters on privileged communication, should go a long way towards helping the social worker respond appropriately and effectively to subpoenas.

It is important to distinguish between subpoenas and court orders. A subpoena says, "Come and/or furnish certain materials." If the professional wants to take issue with the subpoena, his attorney will present appropriate arguments to the court, which will then rule whether or not the information must be disclosed and in what manner. If the court orders it revealed, the battle is over, unless the professional chooses to take the issue to a higher court or spend some time personally studying the living conditions of prison inmates.

Should Social-Worker–Client Communications Be Privileged?

The naive practitioner will immediately respond with a resounding "Yes, of course!" If only the answer were really that simple! As we have seen, there

[17] Grossman, "The Psychiatrist and the Subpoena," *op. cit.* p. 245.

are strong arguments in support of privileged communication for mental-health professionals, which would certainly include social workers. However, this author has some concerns about the social work profession's readiness for privileged communication, the effectiveness of such coverage, and thus, the need for it. A few key questions will help define the issues:

Do social-worker–client communications satisfy the four Wigmore criteria for privileged-communication coverage?

Professor Wigmore did not have the psychotherapeutic professions in mind when he postulated his four prerequisites. Thus, much effort has been devoted to "making them fit" the communications of mental-health professionals. The answer as to whether social-work communications meet the four criteria is not quite as obvious as it might appear, and an examination of each of the four items is required:[18]

1. *"The communications must originate in a confidence that they will not be disclosed."* There must be some expectation of, commitment to, or communication of the fact that what transpires between social worker and client will be kept confidential. Several authors maintain that the very existence of social-work relationships and communications fulfills this requirement. For example:

> Communications between a psychiatric social worker and his patients are imparted in the expectation of deepest confidence. The authorities agree that therapy requires complete candor of the patient, who must reveal compulsions, fantasies, fears, obsessions, and guilt feelings of such a private nature that he probably has never revealed them before, even to his closest friends.[19]

However, this general statement has been questioned. Do clients really expect confidentiality when they seek out social-work services? Apparently this is an assumption that has not been adequately researched:

> [I]t is arguable whether the *expectancy of confidentiality* in the social-worker–client relationship is inherent or emanates from the social worker's explicit or implicit assurances of secrecy. If evidence were uncovered which revealed that the majority of clients do not go to a social worker expecting confidentiality but only desiring it, then some doubt would exist as to whether the social work profession fulfills Wigmore's first requirement. However, the answer may be that because the social worker probably assures his client of confidentiality at the outset of an interview, most communications are made after a "confidence that they will not be disclosed" has been established, thus satisfying the requirement.

[18] Wigmore, *Evidence in Trials at Common Law*, Vol. 8 (revised by J. T. McNaughton) (Boston: Little, Brown, 1961), p. 52.

[19] "COMMENTS: Underprivileged Communications: Extension of the Psychotherapist-Patient Privilege to Patients of Psychiatric Social Workers," *California Law Review*, Vol. 61 (June 1973), p. 1057.

But it may be that at least some clients come to the social worker knowing that they have no privilege, because they have consulted a lawyer in contemplation of litigation or are already experienced in such matters. Communications made under such circumstances could never originate "in a *confidence* that they will not be disclosed."[20]

Slovenko points out that for many clients the things they discuss with their social workers make up the substance of their everyday conversations with just about everybody else; such clients seem to have no concern for confidentiality:

Except when afflicted with syphilis and other loathsome diseases, the patient seeks out opportunities to discuss his ailment with family, friends, neighbors and, in fact, with anyone who will listen.[21]

It is necessary to examine Wigmore's second point before a full conclusion can really be rendered regarding satisfaction of the first prerequisite.

2. *"This element of confidentiality must be essential to the full and satisfactory maintenance of the relation between the parties."* Earlier chapters in this text as well as many other social work writings clearly indicate that confidentiality is an important concept for social work practice. Advocates of privileged communication for psychiatrists and psychologists have expressed their belief that therapy also cannot take place without a promise of secrecy. Following is one typical example:

Psychotherapy by its very nature is worthless unless the patient feels assured from the outset that whatever he may say will be forever kept confidential. Without a promise of secrecy from the therapist, buttressed by a legal privilege, a patient would not be prone to reveal personal data which he fears might evoke social disapproval.[22]

If this concept is carried one step further, we would have to say that many persons would refuse to seek professional counseling if they felt confidentiality could not be assured. It has been pointed out that "unlike the patient suffering an organic illness, a person in psychotherapy, by and large, visits his psychiatrist with the same secrecy that a man goes to a bawdy house."[23]

It could be said that there is a certain stigma attached to visiting a social worker as well. Slovenko expresses his concerns regarding psychiatry:

[20] "NOTE: Social Worker-Client Relationship and Privileged Communications," *Washington University Law Quarterly* (1965), pp. 384–385. In addition, see Robert Plank, who also feels too much has been taken for granted regarding client expectations, in "Our Underprivileged Communications," *Social Casework*, Vol. 46, No. 7 (July 1965), p. 431.

[21] Ralph Slovenko, *Psychiatry and Law* (Boston: Little, Brown, 1973), pp. 68–69.

[22] Ralph Slovenko, "Psychiatry and a Second Look at the Medical Privilege," *Wayne Law Review*, Vol. 6, No. 2 (Spring 1960), pp. 186–187, quoting an address delivered by Judge Luther Alverson of the Atlanta Superior Court to the North Georgia Chapter of the National Association of Social Workers in Atlanta, October 21, 1958.

[23] Slovenko, *ibid.*, p. 188, note 46.

Without confidentiality, a person would hesitate to see a psychiatrist, much less to make revelations to him. Confidentiality in court as well as out is essential not only for successful treatment but also to induce a person to visit a psychiatrist. It is vital to maintain confidentiality as to the fact of treatment as well as to communications made in treatment. By and large, people in the community, even those who are well-informed on other matters, consider a person's treatment by a psychiatrist as evidence of his "queerness" or even insanity. A person may hesitate to visit a psychiatrist out of fear that he will be set apart from his fellow men.[24]

Another author expresses his views concerning psychiatric social workers and the need for confidentiality:

[P]reservation of confidentiality is essential to the success of the relationship. Without the security of a strong foundation of trust, the client will be unwilling, sometimes unable, to cooperate with his therapist in bringing to the surface painful repressed material, or in participating uninhibitedly in therapeutic measures designed to hasten his recovery.[25]

Unfortunately, a few questions have again been raised. "[S]ocial workers have always assumed that confidentiality is necessary to the casework relationship—but do they actually know this to be true?"[26] Would lack of confidentiality really deter consumers from seeking social-work services? It has been reported that "no statistical evidence was uncovered which suggested or weakened [this] assumption, but common sense apparently supports [it]."[27] In a 1962 study, the *Yale Law Journal* looked at privileged communication as it pertained to various professions, and examined consumer feelings about consulting a professional functioning under privilege statutes versus one who was not. The results showed that 51 out of 108 persons would be less likely to reveal confidential information to a social worker if he did not have privilege; 45 would be less likely to reveal such material if it were a psychiatrist; 47 if a psychologist were involved; and 55 if the professional were an attorney.[28] Thus, there appears to be some deterrent, though not an overwhelming one.

While most social workers can relate situations they feel would be damaging to clients if confidentiality had to be violated, is it really known just how the *consumer* feels about the importance of confidentiality and privileged communication? Given the public's probable lack of awareness of the ramifications of privileged-communication statutes, it could be reasonably

---

[24] *Ibid.*, pp. 187–188.

[25] "COMMENTS: Underprivileged Communications: Extension of the Psychotherapist-Patient Privilege to Patients of Psychiatric Social Workers," *op. cit.*, p. 1057.

[26] Plank, "Our Underprivileged Communications," *op. cit.*, p. 431.

[27] "The Social Worker-Client Relationship and Privileged Communications," *op. cit.*, p. 365.

[28] "NOTES AND COMMENTS: Functional Overlap between the Lawyer and Other Professionals: Its Implications for the Privileged Communication Doctrine," *Yale Law Journal*, Vol. 71 (May 1962), p. 1268.

argued that a given professional's lack of privilege would not in and of itself necessarily constitute a significant deterrent to patients seeking counseling services.

3. *"This relation must be one which in the opinion of the community ought to be sedulously fostered."* To meet this criterion, one would have to establish that the social work profession serves an effective and useful function in society—that the services of social workers are needed. There is so much literature supporting this view that it would be redundant to mention it here. What is significant is that attorneys and members of other professions also recognize the need for social workers.[29] However, along with this recognition and acceptance the basic issue remains, one that should be of concern to a profession that has had some difficulty in proving that what it does is really effective:

> If the social work profession is capable of helping such persons learn to make their lives more useful to themselves and society, then there is little doubt that the social-worker–client relationship "ought to be sedulously fostered." *If it is not able to help them, then no privilege should be granted.*[30] [Emphasis added.]

It does appear that Wigmore's third criterion is met, as long as there is continued acceptance of the premise that social workers really do help people.

4. *"The injury that would inure to the relation by the disclosure of the communications must be greater than the benefit thereby gained from the correct disposal of litigation."* This issue has already been discussed in some detail; we will not repeat that discussion here. It is the most difficult criterion to satisfy; however, at least one author feels that social work satisfies this final condition, as well as the other three.[31] A more realistic view would be that the satisfaction of the fourth prerequisite depends on the issues involved in each specific case.

It is obvious that there are many situations in which all four criteria will be met by social-worker–client communications. On this assumption, we can then move on to a few more questions.

Why should other groups have privileged communication while social workers do not?

If other professions meeting Wigmore's criteria are granted privileged communication, it certainly seems unjust to exclude social workers. If privi-

[29] For example, see "COMMENTS: Underprivileged Communications: Extension of the Psychotherapist-Patient Privilege to Patients of Psychiatric Social Workers," *op. cit.*; and "NOTE: Social Worker-Client Relationship and Privileged Communications," *op. cit.*

[30] "NOTE: Social Worker-Client Relationship and Privileged Communications," *op. cit.*, p. 386.

[31] "I.e., see "COMMENTS: Underprivileged Communications: Extension of the Psychotherapist-Patient Privilege to Patients of Psychiatric Social Workers," *op. cit.*

lege statutes are a viable means of preventing unauthorized disclosure of confidential data, then all professional helping persons should be so covered. If such statutes are not effective in accomplishing their purpose, it really matters little whether social workers are included or not.

Are social workers knowledgeable enough to handle the complications of privileged-communication responsibly?

The answer to this question must be a firm "no."

In 1959, Joseph Alves conducted interviews with forty-eight caseworkers in four different cities regarding confidentiality-awareness and practices. Among other things, he concludes that

> there was widespread ignorance of the requirements and privileges of civil law with respect to confidentiality of case records. Caseworkers were often ignorant of facts such as whether and when they were legally obligated to volunteer information about crimes to law enforcement authorities, many feeling that they were so obligated to a greater extent than is in fact true. They were generally mistaken about provisions of civil law making confidences entrusted to ministers and physicians "privileged communications," assuming such statutes to exist where they did not.[32]

In a questionnaire administered to the respondents, Alves found that

> sixty percent of these caseworkers correctly replied that they and their records were subject to subpoena. However, the fact that nearly thirty per cent of them did not know whether they or the agency case records could be so subpoenaed, and that another ten per cent were wrongly convinced that they could not is not a very happy discovery when one draws some of the implications that might follow. The harshest observation that could be made as a consequence of these responses would be that, potentially, the communications of up to forty per cent of the clients served by the caseworkers involved in this study were in jeopardy because of the ignorance of the caseworkers themselves. Those who erroneously believed that case records were protected under the statute law of privileged communications very likely included in the record material, which, if released, might be most injurious to the client or someone else and which would never have been so recorded if the caseworkers might not have encouraged clients to reveal some types of information about themselves or others if they knew in advance that they could be forced to divulge this information.[33]

In 1962, the *Yale Law Journal* reported that twenty social workers were asked if they had privileged communication or not. Three believed they did, fifteen knew they did not, and two did not know. Thus, one-fourth were incorrect in their understanding of privileged communication. (In 1962, no

[32] Alves, *Confidentiality in Social Work, op. cit.*, pp. 248–249.

[33] *Ibid.*, pp. 217–218. See also pp. 240–242 showing the responses to specific questions dealing with privileged communication. The results indicate not only ignorance, but a total lack of uniformity as to how various situations should be handled. Page 210 also has more of the same.

state had extended the privilege to social workers.)[34] The article further comments that, as of 1962, the National Association of Social Workers had not officially embraced privileged communication for social workers. The author goes on to speculate that perhaps this was due to the fear that if the privilege were adopted a social worker not knowing about it might be held liable for violations. This concern seems justified even today. In November of 1977 this author gave a presentation on confidentiality to a national audience of MSWs and NASW members from throughout the country.[35] Fifty-four attendees completed a special questionnaire testing knowledge about privileged communication and other confidentiality issues. The majority had over ten years of post-MSW social work experience. Many were agency executives and supervisors. Twenty-eight percent thought they did not have the right of privileged communication and were in fact practicing in one of the states that grants it to social worker-client communications. Nine percent believed they had the right of privileged communication when in fact they did not. Another nine percent did not know whether they had the right of privileged communication or not. A total of 26% of respondents correctly defined the term "right of privileged communication" when a generous approach was taken in evaluating the responses. When these same answers were reviewed by an attorney-MSW, he declared that only 11% had defined the term correctly, based on a strict legal definition. Perhaps the explanation for this rather widespread lack of knowledge is the fact that 78% of these respondents (most having over ten years post-MSW experience) reported that they had *never* received any training on confidentiality. Furthermore, sixty-seven percent reported that their agency did not have specific, written guidelines on confidentiality.

During 1974–1975, of 106 persons surveyed by the author (all were working in the state of Florida), including direct-service practitioners, graduate and undergraduate students in social work, supervisors, administrators, field instructors, social work educators, and at least one board member and consultant, only thirteen (12%) could give a precise written definition of the term "privileged communication." Seventy-seven (72%) gave an obviously incorrect answer; eleven (10%) wrote "I don't know," and six (6%) left the question blank. If the last three categories are combined, we find that 88% of the social workers in this unusually diverse, though not necessarily random, sample did not know what privileged communication is. Of those who guessed, most responded incorrectly because they simply defined "confidentiality" without distinguishing it from privileged communication.

[34] "NOTES AND COMMENTS: Functional Overlap between the Lawyer and Other Professionals: Its Implications for the Privileged Communication Doctrine," *op. cit.* p. 1268.

[35] Suanna J. Wilson, "Confidentiality: Human Rights vs. Effective Service Delivery; Legal Aspects of Privileged Communication and Confidentiality," Invitational Presentation at the 1977 NASW Fifth Biennial Professional Symposium "Social Work Skills: Humanizing the Human Services," San Diego, November 19–22, 1977.

Thus, the evidence indicates that social workers continue to be quite uninformed about confidentiality and privileged communication, and the profession therefore appears to be fighting for something that it does not even fully understand itself.

Is it discriminatory to consumers for some to be served by a profession with privileged communication while others are denied this right?

One author has suggested, in arguing for privileged communication for psychiatric-social-worker–client communications in California, that for this group to be without protection leads to discrimination against poor patients who cannot afford psychiatrists and psychologists for private mental-health care.[36] Instead, they are seen by psychiatric social workers who often practice in governmental settings (non-federal as well as federal) or who, if in private practice, charge less than do other psychotherapists. It seems improbable that many of these poorer patients even realize that the relationships of economically advantaged persons to their therapists may have a legal status that their own do not have. This area needs further research before any sweeping conclusions can be drawn.

Concluding Remarks

Several conclusions can be drawn concerning privileged communication and helping professionals:

1. Privileged communication statutes *sometimes* prevent the disclosure of confidential information in the courtroom. More often than not, the court rules that it must have full disclosure, and forces the professional to testify regardless of privilege statutes. While most disciplines are fighting *for* privileged communication, one of the most prolific and outspoken critics, Ralph Slovenko, finds the whole concept virtually meaningless for psychotherapeutic relationships and communication because it so rarely holds up in court. After giving a long list of exceptions to the privilege for physicians, Slovenko states that "there is virtually nothing covered by the privilege."[37] In another article he concludes that

> the concept of privilege, while it may offer a sense of security, should be abandoned as a means of determining whether disclosure of communications made in psychotherapy should be required.[38]

[36] "COMMENTS: Underprivileged Communications: Extension of the Psychotherapist-Patient Privilege to Patients of Psychiatric Social Workers," *op. cit.*, pp. 1053–1055.

[37] Slovenko, *Psychiatry and Law, op. cit.*, p. 63

[38] Ralph Slovenko, "Psychotherapist-Patient Testimonial Privilege: A Picture of Misguided Hope," *Catholic University Law Review*, Vol. 23 (1974), p. 672.

This author's research and exhaustive review of the literature substantiate this viewpoint.

2. In the long run, factors other than privileged-communication statutes are more likely to prevent disclosures of confidential material in court. The practitioner should study these other factors, calling upon them when appropriate, rather than rely on privileged-communication statutes or confidentiality ethics alone to come to the rescue.

3. There are a number of indications that the social work profession and its thousands of practitioners are poorly informed and not yet ready to determine if privileged communication is "the answer" or to assume the complex responsibility that goes along with acquiring the coverage.[39]

4. If privileged communication is in fact the best way we have of preventing unauthorized disclosures in legal actions, then the coverage should be equally available to all consumers of services from professional helping persons. The best way to achieve this would be to do away with separate privileged-communication statutes for the professions and adopt a uniform, comprehensive statute that would grant the coverage to all consumers.

[39] I.e., see Appendix B and reread NASW's "Model Licensing Act for Social Workers," especially the four paragraphs concerning privileged communication. A number of key issues are not addressed, and yet these guidelines are being used by many states as social workers strive for privileged communication in their respective jurisdictions.

10. Confidentiality Problems Faced by Supervisors and Administrators

> *John is sure lousing up his cases. I thought he was a caseworker when we hired him, but he can't counsel any more than the man in the moon. He's so passive-aggressive when I try to help him that it's hopeless. I'm gonna let him go if he doesn't straighten out soon.*
>   —Remarks overheard by a non-supervisory social worker.

CONFIDENTIALITY ISSUES are primarily thought of as affecting the direct-service practitioner. Some, though minimal, attention has been given to the need for privacy of personnel records and related documents (see Chapter 11). However, an area that is virtually overlooked in the professional literature is that of confidentiality problems encountered by supervisors and administrators as they carry out their duties. Some of these have been alluded to in Chapter 2 and are considered further in Chapters 11 and 12. Certain of them must be considered carefully, since management personnel deal with them on a daily basis. The giving and receiving of references, requests for information about employees, conflicts between obligations to an individual employee and duty to the larger organization, "leaks" within a setting whereby confidential information is being disclosed via unknown channels, and employee-employer grievances and lawsuits are fraught with opportunities for careless or deliberate confidentiality violations.

Giving and Receiving References

I have a personal philosophy that when I am asked for evaluations or references, everything I feel and have experienced with that employee and/or student should be put into black and white. This way the person knows what's being said and can defend himself. I'm opposed to all this informal oral exchange

that takes place where the person being talked about doesn't know what's be-
ing said about him by whom and has no way to defend himself. What do you
think of this philosophy?

References are usually obtained by written statements, phone calls, or personal contacts with individuals whose names are provided by an applicant for a position. But what about the rather common practice of seeking information from persons whom the applicant did *not* list as references? Does this violate anyone's confidentiality?

Let us assume that an individual has applied for a job in a rather large social-work setting. It is not unusual for current employees and/or students in the agency to know the applicant. They may even come forth and volunteer this fact. It certainly is tempting for the administrator to follow up with, "How did he do when he worked for XYZ agency?" or even, "Do you know why he left there?" In one setting, recent graduates of a nearby school of social work were often asked their opinion of former classmates who were seeking jobs in the agency. They eventually became uneasy with the position administration was placing them in and expressed their concern about the practice. In another instance, a senior staff member had actually supervised an applicant when they were in a different setting together. The applicant did not know that his former supervisor now worked for the agency where he was seeking employment and had not given her as a reference. Is it a violation of confidentiality to seek unofficial references from such an individual?

If the person who is being asked to supply the unofficial reference was employed in a federal program at the time his knowledge of the applicant was acquired, a violation of confidentiality as defined by the Privacy Act of 1974 could occur if the information is shared without the applicant's knowledge and consent. Look again at the definition of a "record"—which must be kept confidential:

> . . . any item, collection, or grouping of information about an individual that is maintained by an agency, including, but not limited to his education, financial transactions, medical history, and criminal *or employment history* . . . .[1]

An applicant does not always announce to his supervisor that he is seeking another position. Thus, it is important to determine whether it is permissible to approach his current employer for a reference. Should an administrator do so without the applicant's permission or through an unofficial source, and should the employer thus learn that his staff member is job-hunting, the applicant will certainly feel that his confidentiality has been violated. If no federal employees are involved, there will be no legal infraction, but a violation of ethics will have occurred.

[1] Federal Privacy Act of 1974, §552a(a). [Emphasis added.]

The reverse situation can also occur. Social work administrators often keep in close contact with one another. If one has a vacancy and is hiring, he may contact his management-level friend seeking qualified applicants. This usually works to the applicant's advantage. However, evaluative feelings are often exchanged as well as names. "Well, I saw John Doe yesterday and he seems quite capable." Suppose the second administrator knows Mr. Doe and has a less-than-positive picture of him. Should this view be volunteered to his fellow manager? The ideal ethical practice and the realities of professional survival often clash viciously in these instances, and reality-factors almost always emerge victorious. Ideally, no unsolicited sharing of references should occur. However, the reality is that managers do use personal contacts and inside information to help them make the best possible decisions for their organizations. This is basic to human nature and no amount of legalizing or moralizing will change it. Thus, both applicants and administrators need to accept the existence of informal exchanges, but must also be willing to deal with any repercussions that might arise.

Finally, since informal giving of references can influence the employer either negatively or positively as regards the applicant, bias may occur before the individual is interviewed. How many applicants are eliminated by this mechanism without even being officially considered? How many others are hired without a full, formal review of their credentials? Unofficial information, whether solicited or unsolicited, often proves highly accurate, but it can also be unreliable. Should an applicant discover that he failed to get a position because of malicious, untrue statements about his performance or character from one of these informal reference-givers, he could initiate legal action for libel or slander. Even if he did not win, the experience could prove quite unpleasant for everyone involved.

Even if references are given through formal channels and using proper procedures, problems can arise. Some large institutional employers have reported suits or grievances over reference disputes. In most instances, suits are threatened but do not materialize. Most experienced administrators have encountered employees who totally deny unsatisfactory job performance and perhaps even their dismissal. When that individual then seeks another position, he may challenge the references given by his former employer, calling them "malicious," "untrue," or "discriminatory" when in fact they present an accurate and unbiased picture of his performance and reason for leaving. This denial of reality can be so complete that all kinds of absurd accusations can be made, and prospective employers in the local area may come to believe that the applicant's former employer really is "a rotten guy who is blackballing him." Some employers have become so sensitive to this problem that they are severely restricting the manner in which references are given. Settings having a personnel department may require that all inquiries be directed to their office for response, forbidding the individual supervisor to give out any information. In some settings, the standard response to reference requests has become so sanitized that only the former employee's dates of employment, job title, salary, and reason for leaving are given—with no details provided. Should this become standard practice in too many settings, it won't be very long before the reference-giving process becomes totally meaningless.

On the other hand, there are employees and applicants who are genuinely maligned by inaccurate, biased, or incomplete references. Thus, whenever an individual expresses a concern that this has happened, it cannot be ignored—it must be investigated. Thus, it appears that employers are choosing to avoid the expense and headaches associated with these investigations by giving out harmless references that no one would want to challenge.

In the usual application process, applicants submit resumes and are interviewed. References are checked if the candidate looks promising or if questionable areas come up needing further exploration. As the social-work job market tightens, applicants become more aggressive in pursuing job applications—if they are not hired, they may want to know why. What if the administrator has secured an unfavorable reference? Should the individual be told this is the reason for his rejection? Should the content and giver of the reference be shared?

The situation can become quite complicated. If the setting where the individual was previously employed is a federally administered program, he has the legal right to his own personnel file and to any written reference material contained therein (with a few exceptions). Therefore, one could assume that such a person already knows what kind of references are being given about him. If he raises this question with a prospective employer, he should be referred back to his former governmental supervisor. Other applicants may not realize they have the right of access to their old personnel records and prepared references. In those settings which unfortunately do not allow employees access to personnel records, if communication between employee and supervisor was not effective, the individual may have no idea of what kind of reference he is receiving.[2] If questions arise, the applicant should be referred back to his former employer.

Most references are given in strictest confidence. Even the Federal Privacy Act of 1974 permits the contents of references to remain secret from the employee before and after he is hired if such references were given with the promise of confidentiality or were elicited prior to a date specified by the act.[3] However, the NASW maintains that all references must be shared with the employee. The 1975 version of the *NASW Standards for Social*

---

[2] This practice would violate *NASW Standards for Social Work Personnel Practices*, which states that "a copy of the letter of reference shall be made available to the subject of the reference on his request. The letter of reference should be prepared by the agency and received by the employee prior to leaving the agency" (Washington, D.C.: National Association of Social Workers, 1975), p. 28.

[3] See the Federal Privacy Act of 1974, Section 552a(k) (5).

Work Personnel Practices requires that employees be advised what kind of reference will be given on them after leaving an agency and that references received from outside sources must be shared as well:

> material provided to or offered to the agency on a "confidential only" basis shall not be accepted or solicited by the agency or any members of the staff, except when required in law or federal regulation.

More specifically,

> references provided with a request that they not be shared should be returned and not considered.[4]

This represents a complete reversal of NASW's earlier position that "in the course of evaluating a candidate for a position, written references shall be obtained. These shall be held in confidence by the recipient."[5] What if an agency which has gathered references under a promise of absolute confidentiality later adopts a policy permitting employees access to their records? Will not the reference-giver's confidentiality be violated? It would appear more desirable to follow the principle of allowing applicants to waive their right to see their references, or else employ some other method for protecting those references solicited in confidence prior to the adoption of an open-record policy.

Is it ever permissible to have "secret" references? Although as mentioned above, the Federal Privacy Act does permit some confidentiality of references in federal programs, it is neither necessary nor desirable for all references to be maintained in secrecy. Many are highly positive, and the reference-giver may have already shown a copy to the employee. When employees have access to their personnel files, agencies must find some way of letting the reference-giver know in advance about this policy and that references may be shared with the applicant. Many social-work employers and schools of social work are resolving this problem by preparing written statements to accompany the reference request. The following was received from a school of social work requesting a reference on a student applying for admission to a graduate program:

> As you prepare a letter of reference you should be aware that all information received must be made available to the student to inspect and review if he/she so requests, under the provisions of the amendments to the Federal Family Education Rights and Privacy Act of 1974. The law, however, also makes it possible for the student to waive the right of access to letters of recommendation written after 1-1-75. In the event the student chooses to waive his right of access, he/she will complete and sign the form on "Student Waiver of Right to Inspect and

---

[4] *NASW Standards for Social Work Personnel Practices* (1975), *op. cit.*, p. 28.

[5] *NASW Standards for Social Work Personnel Practices* with "Revisions in *NASW Standards for Social Work Personnel Practices*," policy statements amended or adopted by the NASW Delegate Assembly, April 1969, p. 2 New York: National Association of Social Workers, 1958).

Review Educational Records'' and present you with copies to be attached to your letters of reference. Unless a completed Waiver Form is attached to *each* letter and copy you prepare we are required by law to make the letter available to the applicant for his/her inspection and review.[6]

If a setting already has references on file which were gathered under old regulations or to which the employee has waived his right of access, they should be destroyed if at all possible. Keeping them in a separate file would preserve confidentiality, but goes against the principle that there be no secret records. If such material must be kept, one solution might be to include a statement in the record to which the employee has access to the effect that "three references are not in this file under the exception permitted by law" or that they exist but are unavailable "because the student waived his right of access."

Applicants may apply persistent, sometimes unpleasant, pressure to find out why they were not hired. It can be tempting to tell an applicant that he was passed over because of a poor reference in order to "get him off one's back." A more effective response would be the simple statement that reference content cannot be shared with applicants; a suggestion might be given that the individual contact the reference-giver directly if he has additional questions. On the other hand, with increasing concern about discrimination in hiring practices, there is today greater pressure to tell applicants why they were not hired so that they can determine if some form of illegal discrimination was a factor. Most applicants know when references given will be negative, though they may not agree with them. Individuals who have been fired from their previous job will sometimes start out an employment interview by stating this fact and presenting their side of the story. Many applicants will find some way to let the interviewer know that their references "won't be so good," so they can have an opportunity to present their views. The effective personnel interviewer will explore the situation thoroughly with the applicant. This discussion can take place quite meaningfully without any disclosure of information that the prospective employer might have obtained through references.

There is another aspect to this problem. The need to protect the content of references is rather obvious. However, when an administrator contacts someone for a reference, should statements that the *applicant* has made be shared with the reference-giver? Suppose an individual explains that he left his last job "due to the change in hours"—a valid-appearing problem that

---

[6] Wayne State University School of Social Work, Detroit: Statement regarding confidentiality on a mimeographed cover letter on reference request for persons applying for admission. For a complete study of the right of student access to school records and controls, see the Family Educational Rights and Privacy Act of 1974 and the Department of Health, Education and Welfare, "Privacy Rights of Parents and Students: Final Rule on Education Records," *Federal Register* (June 17, 1976), which took effect on June 17, 1976.

could affect almost anyone. If, however, the reference indicates orally that the person in fact was terminated for insubordination, should the administrator share the applicant's stated reason for leaving the job? Technically speaking, to do so would violate his right to confidentiality. In reality, such sharing may be necessary to fully explore the situation in question; however, there should be awareness of the fact that confidentiality issues are involved.

One outcome of the requirement that references must be shared with the individual about whom they are written is an increasing reliance on oral references. The era of written references may be drawing to a close. The telephone is probably the most common vehicle for this information exchange. The basic confidentiality aspects already described would obviously apply. However, there is a need for special caution on the part of the agency or supervisory person who receives a phone call soliciting reference material. Is he certain that the person at the other end of the line is who he says he is? Does that person have a legitimate right to the confidential information he is requesting? Agencies receiving such calls should not hesitate to verify the caller's identity, perhaps by asking for a written request, to be followed up later by a return phone call. The caller's phone number, agency, and position could be requested. A check with the appropriate personnel officer would then verify the individual's position.

Likewise, when a prospective employer is checking references by phone, he must be certain that the individual he talks with really is the person who evaluated the former employee's performance or acted as his supervisor. The voice on the other end of the phone may have acquired an instantaneous and very temporary promotion just for the purpose of giving a false reference.

Sometimes an agency must weigh the need to protect its own best interests, those of the consumers it serves or those of the larger social-work community against the need to maintain confidentiality in exchanging references. A strict preservation of confidentiality may enable an incompetent practitioner to move from agency to agency in a community, as he is repeatedly hired by employers unaware of the underlying problems. On the other hand, personnel policies may make it very difficult for a social work administrator to dismiss an employee whose incompetence or behavior is actually damaging to clients or interfering with the effective functioning of an entire program, department, unit, or agency. For example, social workers are uniquely trained to identify psychotic behavior and other psychodynamics that can interfere with employee functioning and create problematic situations. Unfortunately, a number of social work supervisors and administrators have encountered personnel department staff who do not understand the social worker's unique preparation for assessing and dealing with these kinds of problems and instead label the problem as a "personality clash" between supervisor and employee. When this happens, the supervisor's recommendation for dismissal or transfer is usually denied or extensively delayed. If the individual's behavior is creating a serious enough problem, the administrator may feel that the adverse effects upon his agency and its clients are such that he cannot afford a lengthy process of trying to get personnel to accept dismissal. Thus, when this employee becomes unhappy and seeks another job, the temptation to withhold severely negative information is very strong. The administrator may rationalize that perhaps the problem was unique to his setting or may even consciously realize that he is turning the individual loose to do harm elsewhere.

This questionable personnel practice may also be employed when an individual with considerable seniority has "been a problem for years" but nothing has happened that would justify dismissal. Perhaps the person has a personality that makes him hard to get along with and just barely manages to maintain a minimally satisfactory performance. Perhaps the supervisor has assigned him responsibilities "where he can do the least damage" but really wishes he were a stronger employee because he is needed for other responsibilities. Yet this person takes up a budgeted personnel position and prevents administration from hiring someone who would be a greater asset to the program. Thus, when this individual seeks another job, the employer is all too glad to do whatever is necessary to make it possible for him to move on, knowing that otherwise he will be "stuck with him for life." Perhaps the individual really would perform more effectively in a setting where the demands and job responsibilities are different. And so the administrator is able to produce a fairly positive reference on a marginal or problematic employee and often has few guilt feelings, even though he is fully aware of what he is doing and why. On the other hand, this same administrator will curse loudly when the same trick is pulled on him, and he hires someone only to discover the hard way that the references he obtained failed to give a complete picture.

Whether we like it or not, such personnel practices are fairly common, and social work supervisors and administrators who have had to interview, hire, and dismiss problem employees can present strong arguments both for and against the adjustment of confidentiality ethics to fit specialized situations when there appear to be no other reasonable approaches that will resolve a sticky and serious problem.

Requests for Information Regarding Employees

These inquiries usually come via telephone and are often received by a secretary who must decide what to do with them. Potential creditors may call to verify an individual's employment and salary. Clients, personal friends, and assorted others may ask for a staff member's home telephone or address. If the employee is behind in his bills, creditors may call seeking information to help them secure payment.

The *NASW Standards for Social Work Personnel Practices* states rather clearly and summarily the policy to be followed by social-work settings regarding employee information:

> No information on an employee or from a personnel record shall be furnished to persons outside the agency except when specifically authorized by the employee.[7]

Clerical staff must be trained to follow a policy of not giving out employee phone numbers or addresses. If it appears to be an emergency or the caller is especially insistent, the call should be referred to an appropriate supervisor if the employee is not available. The caller's name, his relationship to the employee, and his phone number should always be obtained. The employee is notified that someone has called seeking certain information, and he then has the option of following through as he desires. Professional staff who are involved in a counseling relationship with clients usually do not give out their home phone numbers for their own protection. Emotionally disturbed individuals and overly dependent clientele, for example, could create problems at all hours of the day and night if some precautions are not taken to protect the worker's privacy. A few practitioners do give out their private number to selected consumers, but the professional must be the one maintaining control over this.

Newly hired employees seeking local credit or others making major purchases often generate calls attempting to verify income and employment. In some settings this is handled by the personnel office. If not, someone in the agency should be designated to exercise this responsibility. Unfortunately, such information is often released rather freely if the caller appears legitimate. As most credit application forms contain a clause authorizing the release of the information in question, consent may have already been given. When there is doubt, the employee should be contacted and his consent obtained for the disclosure.

If creditors are aggressively pursuing an employee for payment of delinquent bills, state laws may determine the tactics they can legally use and what obligations, if any, the employer has in responding to such contacts. Certainly the employee needs to know that such calls are being received; counseling may be indicated. Personnel policies may prescribe certain actions for employees whose personal financial difficulties affect their job performance. These factors will all determine how much and what kind of information can be disclosed in response to creditors' inquiries.

[7] *NASW Standards for Social Work Personnel Practices* (1975), p. 28.

Confidentiality of an Employee Versus the
Needs of the Larger Organization

There are situations that can literally force the supervisor to choose between protecting the confidentiality of a supervisee or violating it for the good of the larger organization.

Management staff must often make decisions that affect a number of personnel. There is usually a well-thought-out reason for an action, but circumstances do not always permit sharing the rationale with grass-roots–level employees. This can create considerable anxiety and generate requests for information that cannot be released without violating someone's confidentiality. For example, consider the following question, often raised in various versions by social-work supervisors:

I have been supervising an employee who is very popular among staff. His performance has declined seriously in recent months. I have tried everything I know to help him, even counseling him, and I've tried to be fair and lenient. The director finally told me I couldn't fool with it any longer and the employee had to go. So, I went through all the proper personnel procedures and recently terminated him. He didn't voluntarily resign and I had to fire him with documentation of unsatisfactory performance.

This has precipitated quite a reaction among our other staff. I'm being viewed as the "hatchet man," and my other supervisees are very uneasy, obviously wondering if I'll do the same thing to them. If only I could explain why I had to do it—could defend myself and my actions—I'm sure they would understand that I only did what had to be done. But I cannot, because I can't violate my former supervisee's right of confidentiality. What can I do to ease my own discomfort and that of the staff over this incident?

This incident poses several challenging questions: How damaging will the employee unrest and resulting morale problems be to the overall functioning of the agency? Should the dismissed employee's confidentiality be sacrificed to resolve the problem? Is the supervisor strong enough to withstand the criticism his actions have precipitated? Should the former employee's privacy rights be relinquished to alleviate the staff's anxiety? Whose needs and rights are most important in this situation?

The hard-line administrator would argue that no defense is necessary—the supervisor did what he had to do and that's that—the other employees have no right to question or require explanations for supervisory actions. This may be valid, but it does not necessarily relieve the supervisor's anxiety. Social workers and members of counseling professions who also happen to be supervisors/administrators are trained to be unusually sensitive to people's feelings and needs, and the anxiety of others is keenly felt. Along with this empathy comes the inevitable ". . . and I've got to do something about it." Seasoned supervisors usually work this out privately, or ventilate with their superiors and peers, without having to resort to confidentiality violations. However, the inexperienced or insecure manager will undergo a real internal struggle, perhaps accompanied by the overwhelming desire to explain what happened as a means of defending himself.

One effective way to consider the consequences of violating the former employee's confidentiality would be for the supervisor to list on paper all the persons who might be affected should this action be taken, and all who would be affected if it were not, and then list the probable repercussions, both negative and positive, for everyone concerned, including himself. Which course of action offers the most positives and the fewest negatives? What about long-term as opposed to short-term repercussions?

It has been said that supervision is a very lonely job. Many want to be in charge, but few aspirants fully realize the responsibilities and private agonies that go along with the title. Some feelings can be ventilated to superiors and/or peers, but other questions and anxieties of subordinates may have to go unanswered. These can be handled in various ways, but not at the expense of a supervisee's confidentiality.

There is another rather common situation in which confidentiality becomes a key supervisory issue. Let us imagine a social-work supervisor sitting peacefully in his office minding his own business as he gets some work done that has been pending for days. He is interrupted by three workers under someone else's supervision. During the next hour, they reveal in gory detail a number of rather serious incidents indicating that their immediate superior is "having problems." The disclosure is quickly followed by the proverbial plea, "But don't tell anyone we told you these things!" The supervisor's previous blissful state comes to an abrupt end. What now? The problem obviously needs attention. Does he deliberately violate the request for confidentiality so he can deal with it?

The obvious solution to this dilemma is to avoid it in the first place. If a complainant begins with, "I'm going to tell you something in confidence. . . ." he can be stopped right there while the supervisor explains the rules of the game. "OK, but you must realize that if it's anything you want me to take action on, you'll have to be willing to let me share the information as I feel it necessary in order to resolve the problem. Otherwise, there's no point in your telling me about it." A naive employee may genuinely believe that he can extract a pledge of absolute confidentiality from a supervisor and still expect that his complaint will be magically resolved.

Suppose the individual drops the problem in the supervisor's lap without warning and then asks for total confidentiality. Again, the supervisor's position must be explained—if something is to be done, the complainant must be willing to take some risks. The supervisor may realistically promise not to reveal the complainant's identity while expressing his desire to share the nature of the problem and explore it further. If the situation is serious enough, confidentiality may have to be violated, though this should never be done without first discussing this necessity with the complainant.

When an employee brings a pertinent problem to management's attention and then ties a superior's hands by asking him not to tell anyone about the matter, several questions must be examined. Why did the individual mention the problem at all if he is going to make it impossible for any action to be taken? Does he realize the bind he is creating for the supervisor? What does he think would happen if the supervisor were to act on his complaint? How badly does he really want the problem resolved? The supervisor would need to engage in a frank discussion with the complainant around these questions as one means of moving toward a course of action.

Confidentiality "Leaks"

All offices come equipped with built-in "grapevines." However, administrators should be able to keep certain confidential material out of the gossip channels when necessary. This is not always a simple matter, however. For example, consider the following problem, based on an actual incident in a very large social-service agency:

> *I am an administrator of a large setting employing well over 200 social workers and supportive staff. I have under my immediate supervision an Assistant Administrator and three Supervisor III's. Our agency is open to public scrutiny and has received some controversial publicity. Various events have been happening on the local, state, and national scene which have repercussions for us. I share as much as possible with all my staff so they can keep informed of things that might affect our clients, the service delivery system, or their jobs. However, occasionally I learn of "possibilities" that I don't want to share with anyone except my top-level supervisors. I'd rather wait and share fully when I have more information. I have had meetings with my Assistant and the three Supervisor III's behind closed doors as we discussed some of the "possibilities." As unbelievable as it may sound, within* hours *after our "confidential" meeting, the entire agency is alive with rumors regarding exactly what we talked about— even the clerical staff! Is it possible that one of my top people is violating confidentiality by taking back information from these rare but confidential meetings? What can I do?*

There is much emphasis on preserving basic privacy for consumers of services, but what about for administrators? Let us assume that none of the four top people in this setting is violating confidentiality. How else could confidential information be leaking out? The following checklist may prove helpful:

1. Is it possible to hear through the walls of the room where the meetings are held? Closed doors create a false sense of security—many offices are not soundproof and adjoin other rooms or clerical work-areas.

2. Are minutes taken or typed following the meeting? All who take down, type, file, or distribute the notes become potential sources of leaks.

3. Has material been typed or duplicated in preparation for the "top secret" meeting? Have there been in-coming phone calls concerning the topic of discussion, in planning for the meeting? The perceptive executive secretary can often piece together small but significant details in order to figure out what is taking place.

4. Recognizing that every office has its grapevine and that large settings probably have inner and not-so-inner channels of communication, look again at administrative clerical staff. Is someone there part of the unofficial inner grapevine, passing out juicy tidbits of confidential information?

5. It is not unusual for administrators to let off steam through informal banter with their secretaries. Are casual remarks being made in such a way that conclusions can be drawn and passed on to others by a curious secretary seeking status among peers?

6. Recognizing that virtually all secretaries who work closely with administration will eventually overhear things they shouldn't, have they been trained regarding their obligation to keep such material confidential?

7. Does one of the top administrators have an office with chairs just outside the doorway where people can sit while waiting to see him? Could such persons overhear a phone conversation taking place in the office and pass the content on to fellow employees, perhaps not even realizing that it was not for public broadcast?

8. In a large social-service agency, it is highly possible that at least one employee is friendly with "somebody high up in the system" or has outside contacts. Such an individual may be getting inside information even before the agency administrator does, and passing it on to his peers just as quickly. He may or may not be consciously aware of the difficulties this behavior creates for administration; he probably does not consciously consider it a confidentiality violation.

Grievances

Most employment settings and schools of social work provide mechanisms through which individuals may initiate a grievance if dissatisfied with personnel actions.[8] The process usually begins rather informally. Someone is dissatisfied with an action that has been taken regarding his role as em-

---

[8] NASW also has a grievance process that its members can use to bring action against agencies and professionals they feel are in violation of basic standards of social work practice as prescribed by their professional organization. See the *Manual for Adjudication of Grievances* (1973), available from NASW, 1425 H. Street NW, Washington, D.C.

ployee or student. If the complaint cannot be worked out through informal discussions with the superiors involved, the individual may request a meeting with persons higher up in the chain of command. If this fails to provide the desired results, steps may be taken to initiate a formal grievance. It is obvious that much confidential material, often laden with strong emotions, is shared before a grievance is begun. Promises may have been made to keep certain information confidential. What is the impact when the formal grievance is brought?

Strong pressure can often be applied to encourage pertinent individuals to testify; however, it may not be possible to subpoena them and force them to appear or reveal the full extent of their knowledge. Thus, unlike the situation in a courtroom, it may be possible for interested parties to keep certain information confidential if they wish. However, this may not be desirable. Obviously the individual being "accused" must be free to defend himself. The complaining supervisee or student will also want to bring out all the facts he can to support his claim. Thus, very little remains confidential. Only the most naive claimant would initiate a grievance under the illusion that only the information he wants brought out will be revealed. Likewise, management may find some of its dirty linen being aired publicly.

The individual bringing the grievance is often so unhappy with whatever precipitated his action that he freely verbalizes his dissatisfactions to anyone who will listen. This, of course, is his right, though such behavior does not always work to his benefit. Persons serving as witnesses and other interested parties would usually be wise to discuss the matter as little as possible with persons who are not directly involved. There is no law or professional ethic dictating such a guideline, but common sense reveals its appropriateness. However, selected agencies and/or schools may have policies stipulating confidentiality for these individuals.

A final area must be addressed. Those who serve on the grievance committee (staff who hear the case and render a decision) gather volumes of highly confidential material in the process. What are their obligations? Unless the process is taking place in a federal program coming under the jurisdiction of the Federal Privacy Act, there may be no legal guidelines whatsoever. If unions are involved, rules and regulations for grievances, including confidentiality regulations, should be quite clearly and strongly spelled out. Other settings may provide a brief statement on the topic, reminding grievance-committee members of the importance of confidentiality. However, many such policies lack "teeth"—what would actually happen to someone caught violating confidentiality? Is any action prescribed?

The following excerpt from NASW's *Manual for Adjudication of Grievances* sets forth its confidentiality requirements:

> The NASW *Procedures for Adjudication of Grievances* require the complainant and respondent "to keep the proceedings of the committee confidential except if it becomes necessary to share information in order to provide relevant

evidence." The same discipline is required of the Committee on Inquiry. It is the adjudication *proceedings* that constitute "classified" information. It is not possible to require that confidentiality be applied to the situation giving rise to the complaint; this situation is too often known to a number of people when it occurs or at least before a complaint is filed. It is not always possible either to maintain secrecy about the fact that a complaint has been filed. What is written in depositions by the complainant or respondent and what is said and by whom at the hearing and in the deliberation of the committee *must* be kept confidential for the protection of all concerned until the chapter officers take action to approve the final report and the thirty-day appeal period open to both complainant and respondent has expired.

When the findings of the inquiry exonerate the respondent, the agency or individual who has been charged by the complainant has the privilege of circulating the report as widely as necessary so that all those involved may become aware of the results. Certainly, everyone who participated in the hearing or provided written testimony should be informed. Again, this action to share the report must be withheld until the final appeal period has expired. When the findings support the complainant, recommendations to publicize the report are subject to the restrictions noted later.[9]

Another example is the following, taken from the grievance procedures developed by a school of social work:

> The subject matter of grievance hearings will be private. So that all parties may preserve the fairness of the proceedings, they should avoid public statements and publicity about the case until the proceedings have been completed. The hearing(s) will be held on campus, allowing only those directly involved to be present, and all participants will keep the proceedings entirely confidential.
>
> Minutes will be taken during all the meetings by a person appointed by the chairperson. These minutes will be available to principal parties following the hearing if appeals are under consideration. The chairperson will be responsible for maintaining these minutes and other evidence until the committee completes its proceedings. Following their conclusion, all minutes and evidence will be kept by the Dean in a folder separate from the student's official records. All minutes and evidence from the grievance proceedings will be destroyed by the Dean after all appeals have been exhausted, or if there are no appeals, at the end of the academic year.[10]

Thus, the need to keep grievance material confidential can be dealt with in various ways. Members of grievance committees obviously cannot talk about the proceedings with anyone outside the committee. This would require that all contacts with witnesses, informants, the grievance-bearer, and the defendant take place only as part of the formal proceedings—there should be no informal outside contacts where matters pertaining to the grievance are discussed. Grievances can lead to legal actions if the claimant

[9] *Ibid.*, Part Two: "Manual for Chapters in Handling Adjudication of Grievances," p. 6.

[10] Because this school is in the process of revising its guidelines, it shall not be identified.

or the defendant is dissatisfied with the outcome. Should this occur, the way in which the grievance was conducted may come under close scrutiny as defense and prosecution attorneys search for irregularities that might help them win their case. If confidentiality violations have occurred, the chances are excellent that they will be uncovered during the legal investigation. Such behavior could cause the courts to question the validity of the entire grievance procedure or, at the minimum, could enable information to be brought out from unofficial sources that could be used for or against a key person in the suit. Obviously, "informal" information and evaluative statements can be applied unfairly and unjustly as well as to the benefit of either party. Thus, confidentiality in grievance proceedings is a very serious matter.

Lawsuits

These are comparatively rare, but supervisees dissatisfied with management decisions do sometimes seek justice through the courts. Once this occurs, all the information and incidents occurring between supervisor, supervisee, and others who have been involved come under close scrutiny. In the social-work setting, there may have been intensive counseling (appropriately or inappropriately) regarding an employee's personal problems along with other sharing of confidential material. How is the confidentiality of what has transpired between supervisor and supervisee affected when a suit is brought?

A great deal of "secret" information becomes known to all attorneys and the court. Lawyers on both sides will aggressively pursue all the facts and unless a supervisor can convince them that certain information is not relevant or should not be disclosed, it must be revealed. The supervisor must be free to defend himself, and therefore should disclose whatever information is necessary for his defense. Witnesses may be subpoenaed and required to reveal what is known to them. The employee should realize that when he initiates a lawsuit or grievance there are no more confidences except those between him and his attorney—he is opening the door to a full investigation of *all* the facts, including some he may wish could remain secret.

Privileged-communication statutes do not at present cover suits between supervisors and supervisees. That is, a social-work supervisor covered by privileged communication would have to testify if subpoenaed, as would any other employee in the agency who may have interacted with the plaintiff. Most privileged-communication laws cover communications between the professional and his clientele, and interchanges between employees would not appear to meet this definition. An additional note of interest is that current malpractice insurance for social workers does not cover disputes between employers and employees or field instructors and students.[11] Should a client sue a social worker and also name that worker's supervisor in the suit, insurance protection would be available because the action involves a consumer of services. However, "professional liability insurance does not cover suits arising out of a supervisor-supervisee relationship in which the supervisee may bring suit for damages arising out of an evaluation, termination of work, or other work related incidents."[12] Thus, payment for legal representation and any damages assessed by the court would have to be through the supervisor's agency or from his own funds.

[11] However, at least one school of social work has recently obtained special malpractice insurance for its field instructors, covering disputes that might arise out of the agency-employed social worker's duties as a field instructor for the school. Others provide indemnification for field instructors through a written contract with the agency.

[12] Letter from Richard C. Imbert, Senior Partner, American Professional Agency, Amityville, N.Y., February 18, 1976 (the carrier for NASW malpractice insurance).

11. Confidentiality of Personnel Records

Surprisingly, according to present legal doctrines, the personnel records of employees are not confidential at all. To the best of my knowledge, the issue has been entirely neglected in professional literature. [1]

Mordechai Mironi

Information Contained in Personnel Files

IT IS IMPORTANT TO UNDERSTAND exactly what a personnel record is before the need for preserving its confidentiality can be fully appreciated. What kinds of things are in most employee files? According to the National Association of Social Workers,

> a personnel record must be maintained by the agency for each employee. It shall contain the application, contracts or agreements, description of work assignments, performance ratings, and pertinent correspondence. It shall be open and available to the employee and contain no material or information that cannot be shared with the employee. [2]

An attorney, discussing legal and ethical views of personnel records, offers the following description:

> Personnel records refer to all recorded information about employees kept by an employer, usually in the form of and under the name "personnel files." Files may include medical reports, criminal records, counseling protocols, and personal inventories. One writer has given just a taste of the thoroughness with which some organizations keep such files: "For each manager and employee, records detail initial application forms, results of physical examination, interviewer's notations, test scores, periodic appraisals, transfers and promotions,

[1] Mordechai Mironi, "Confidentiality of Personnel Records: A Legal and Ethical View," *Labor Law Journal*, Vol. 25 (May 1974), p. 270.

[2] *NASW Standards for Social Work Personnel Practices*, NASW Policy Statements 2 (Washington, D. C.: National Association of Social Workers, 1975), Section 20.0, p. 28.

disciplinary actions, releases and hirings, wages, salaries, taxes paid, contributions and other similar items."[3]

By combining the ideas and experiences of various administrators and authors, a frightening list of the data found in many personnel records can be compiled:

1. The employee's written application for the position and related correspondence.
2. Written references obtained in connection with the application.
3. Notes regarding impressions gained from an employment interview. If prepared by a professionally trained social worker, these may be inappropriately diagnostic, not simply factual.
4. Results of psychological and personality tests.[4]
5. Results of polygraph (lie detector) tests. Their use in private industry has long been a source of controversy.
6. Results of miscellaneous tests measuring aptitude and intelligence.
7. Reports from outside credit agencies employed to do background checks on prospective employees. Data gathered by such agencies is often highly personal, very judgmental, and obtained from questionable sources.[5]
8. Copies of medical/psychiatric reports. If an applicant admits to having a history of medical or psychiatric treatment that could affect his performance on the job or that is otherwise of interest to a prospective employer, he may be asked to sign a waiver granting permission for disclosure of the data. Unfortunately, these are often "blanket consent forms" and required as a condition to employment.[6]
9. Fingerprints and clearances for past criminal records. Government employers routinely fingerprint employees and check for infractions of the law by applicants; if an individual is hired and the search subsequently reveals a criminal offense that the employee did not indicate, he may be subject to dismissal for giving false information on the application form.
10. Data processing forms and other documents that officially add the individual to the payroll, assign him to a position, area, or depart-

[3] Mironi, "Confidentiality of Personnel Records: A Legal and Ethical View", *op. cit.*, pp. 270–271, quoting Dale Yoder, *Personnel Management in Industrial Relations*, 6th Ed. Prentice-Hall, Englewood Cliffs, N.J.: 1970), p. 711.

[4] A study conducted in the middle 1960's surveying 300 corporations of various types found that 46% used personality tests. Mironi, *op. cit.*, p. 272.

[5] For example, see *ibid.*, p. 273.

[6] See Chapter 5, pp. 57–64. Once this highly confidential (and often privileged) information gets into a personnel file, it is no longer protected from disclosure to others, except by the employer/agency's own personnel policies and any federal or state laws mandating confidentiality of personnel record material. However, such laws are virtually absent unless the setting comes under the Federal Privacy Act's jurisdiction.

ment, and give him various identifying numbers. A job description may also be included.

11. Income tax withholding forms, items regarding insurance coverage (both optional and mandatory), retirement funds, and related job benefits.
12. Various documents (often computerized) reflecting changes in status, position, or pay.
13. Performance evaluations—both scheduled and unscheduled.
14. Copies of letters of commendation or notations of special accomplishments and awards.
15. Various forms, memos, notations, and evaluations regarding performance difficulties and disciplinary actions.
16. Written responses by the employee to performance evaluations or disciplinary actions.
17. Reports of grievances or special hearings related to disagreement with a performance evaluation or disciplinary action.
18. Data regarding sick leave, annual leave, leave without pay, and other absences or excess hours worked. Such reports are often computerized. However, they may be highly personal and confidential. For example, if an individual has suffered a "nervous breakdown" and had an extended absence from work, there may be copies of medical/psychiatric reports recommending a leave of absence or indicating the nature of the treatment received and evaluating the employee's readiness to return to work.
19. Medical/psychiatric data supplied to an employer by an insurance carrier following an employee's claim for services covered by his policy. Many employers provide health insurance to employees as part of the benefit package. If the employer pays the premiums, he may maintain that he has a right to know how staff are using their coverage. A rather free exchange of information may occur between insurance carrier and employer, all without the employee's knowledge, and in some situations, in direct opposition to his request that no such disclosures occur. The American Psychiatric Association has reported twenty-nine case examples. Nine concerned damages resulting from release of confidential information by insurance companies to employers when claims were filed. Other cases are mentioned wherein individuals desperately needing psychiatric care will not seek it or will not claim reimbursement through their insurance carriers for fear of unauthorized disclosures to their employer.[7]
20. The employee's letter of resignation.
21. A final performance evaluation done at the time of the employee's

[7] *Confidentiality and Third Parties*, Task Force Report 9 (Washington, D. C.: American Psychiatric Association, June 1975), Appendix H: "Samples of Reports from Psychiatrists of Injuries to Patients Resulting from Breaches of Confidentiality."

separation or shortly thereafter. It often recommends whether or not the individual should be rehired.

22. A written summary of comments made by an employee during an exit interview.

23. References written by the employer after the individual has left.

24. Other miscellaneous specific data kept by various employers for specialized purposes.

Thus personnel records often contain more highly confidential data than do many client case records, and yet they have far less protection legally and ethically from confidentiality violations.

Notice that items (1) to (9) are generated even before an individual is hired. Thus, the unsuccessful job applicant may leave behind a trail of highly confidential, half-completed personnel records as he moves from setting to setting seeking employment.

Social workers are noted for their thoroughness in information-gathering and history-taking activities. Unfortunately, this same tendency often enters into personnel practices as well. How relevant is the information being gathered on applicants and placed in personnel files? One major corporation has taken steps to eliminate the collection of unnecessary personnel data:

> Only what we think is necessary to make the employment decision—name, address, previous employer, education, and a few other basic facts [are] gathered. We don't even ask for date of birth at this time, although if the person is hired we will need to get his or her age. We don't ask about the employment of the applicant's spouse, about relatives employed by IBM, or for previous addresses. We don't ask about any prior treatment for nervous disorder or mental illness. We don't ask about arrest records or pending criminal charges or criminal indictments. We do ask about convictions—but only convictions during the previous five years.[8]

When asked why IBM adopted this policy, the response was:

> We were getting a lot of data we really didn't need. It was cluttering up the files. Worse than that, it was tagging along after people. Particularly in the case of unfavorable information about an employee, there's a tendency for the material to follow the person around forever and to influence management decisions that it shouldn't. It's better not to have the data in the files in the first place.[9]

How many social-work employers have taken such a stand? Have steps been taken to sort out relevant from irrelevant personnel data? How can the confidentiality of such masses of personnel data be preserved?[10]

---

[8] "IBM's Guidelines to Employee Privacy: An Interview with Frank T. Cary," *Harvard Business Review*, (September–October 1976), p. 85.

[9] *Ibid.*

[10] It is significant to note that the NASW in its *Standards for Social Work Personnel Practices* fails to address this issue. This thirty-nine-page pamphlet contains only three short paragraphs on "Personnel Records" (see pp. 172 and 177 of this book), and no guidelines are pro-

Safeguarding Personnel Files

The precautions for physically safeguarding personnel files should be similar to those observed for case record materials (see Chapter 4). The Federal Privacy Act of 1974 certainly makes it clear that personnel records must be treated the same as other files. All federal regulations concerning the release of information to others and to the employee himself must be applied. Thus, employees in federal programs have some protection under law. Such protection is virtually absent for personnel data maintained in non-federal settings, and the Federal Privacy Protection Study Commission has been holding hearings on the possible need for extending the Privacy Act regulations to personnel records in the private sector as well.

One company which testified regarding employee privacy was IBM. While recognizing that more stringent regulations may very well have to come from the federal government, it was argued that "such legislation should be designed to result in improved employee privacy while considering the implementation costs and potential inflationary impact." In opposing extension of the Privacy Act in its present form to private industry, the IBM representative went on to state:

> The value of maintaining records of internal uses made of employee data and a listing of those allowed access to every system would appear within IBM to be burdensome, costly and unnecessary. This is especially true when data is used only for employment purposes, when its release outside the enterprise is highly restricted, and when general rules of access are known to employees. Our employees have not requested this type of record.[11]

It appears, however, that some type of legislation will be forthcoming, as so many private settings have failed to build in adequate safeguards for confidentiality of personnel information. A review of business-management literature as well as that of the social work profession has revealed very few articles covering this topic. Those found, however, were alarming in their descriptions of the lack of attention to privacy of personnel information and the occurrence of daily abuses.[12]

In the absence of clearly defined guidelines for private settings, social workers must turn to their primary professional organization—NASW— for guidance. With the exception of three sentences regarding employee ac-

---

vided for data gathering or retention. *NASW Standards for Social Work Personnel Practices* (1975), *op. cit.*, p. 28.

[11] "IBM—The Managing of Employee Personal Information and Employee Privacy," oral statement of Walton E. Burdict, Vice President, Personnel Plans and Programs, IBM Corporation, presented before the Privacy Protection Study Commission—Employment and Personnel Record-Keeping Practices Hearing on 12-10-76. Pages 11 and 12 of a transcribed copy.

[12] For example, See Mironi, "Confidentiality of Personnel Records: A Legal and Ethical View," *op. cit.*; and the APA's *Confidentiality and Third Parties, op. cit.*

cess to certain materials, the following paragraphs, plus the one on page 172 above, present the primary policy of NASW regarding personnel records:

> Material provided to or offered to the agency on a "confidential only" basis shall not be accepted or solicited by the agency or any members of the staff, except when required in law or federal regulation.
>
> The written evaluation and the employee's statement, if any, shall become an integral part of the employee's personnel record. The personnel record shall be kept strictly confidential and be available to authorized persons only. No information on an employee or from a personnel record shall be furnished to persons outside the agency except when specifically authorized by the employee.[13]

What steps must be taken to keep the record "strictly confidential," especially since neither privileged-communication statutes nor other state or federal laws, with a few exceptions, protect employee records? Is it really possible to keep such records confidential? What physical safeguards are recommended? Who are "authorized persons"? The mandate to make no disclosures without employee consent appears unrealistic and unenforceable—employee records are subject to subpoena, and insurance carriers, the Internal Revenue Service, unions, and others may gain access to certain data without employee knowledge and consent. Once again, the social work profession is guilty of espousing an ideal with little consideration of how it might be achieved or what problems might be encountered along the way. What should be the penalty for individuals who violate confidentiality in handling personnel data on social-work employees? Again, no prescription is offered. The Federal Privacy Act, the Professional Standards Review Organization (PSRO) confidentiality guidelines, and others all postulate stiff penalties for confidentiality violators. If only the social work profession would take a firm stand as have some private industries:

> We try to make it very, very clear to managers what's expected of them [regarding confidentiality of personnel data]. The rules for handling personal information are incorporated in our management training programs. We describe the principles we want followed, and we walk them through the specific do's and don'ts of practicing the rules. We try to produce uniform understanding on this. Within 30 days of becoming a manager, every first-line manager begins to receive basic training.[14]

If an IBM employee violates one of the guidelines,

> depending on the violation, the manager may be subject to dismissal.

Furthermore,

> failures in ethics and integrity [at IBM] are less excusable than errors in performance. People can perform their jobs on a range from satisfactory to

---

[13] *NASW Standards for Social Work Personnel Practices* (1975), *op. cit.*, p. 28.

[14] "IBM's Guidelines to Employee Privacy: An Interview with Frank T. Cary," *op. cit.*, p. 84.

outstanding, but there's only one standard of ethics and integrity that we recognize.

The introduction to the NASW *Statement of Personnel Standards* states that

procedures have been established under which the association considers complaints filed by social workers against employers alleging violations of written personnel practices. When complaints are filed against an employer who does not have written personnel policies, these standards are used in the process of adjudicating the complaint.[15]

Could a social-work employee bring a grievance and effectively prove violation of confidentiality of data in his personnel file? The existing policies are so vague and unspecific that arguments pro and con would have to be based largely on interpretation, and it appears unlikely that a meaningful, enforceable outcome could be achieved.

Social-work agencies and settings maintaining personnel records of any kind must develop specific written policies addressing each of the following areas, in order for personnel data to be protected as fully as possible under present legal and ethical doctrines:

1. Identify the type of personnel records currently being kept.

2. Distinguish between: (a) information that is *absolutely essential* to the process of considering someone for employment and for maintaining him on staff, and (b) data that are interesting and which may be freely given or obtained, but which is *not relevant* to the employment process.

3. Determine how many copies of all personnel record material must be made. It is not unusual for several copies of personnel records to be floating around in large agencies. Are all these copies really necessary? Make public the number of copies in existence and the names of those authorized to hold them.

4. Set up a specific procedure governing what information can be placed in a personnel file and how it gets there. For example, some settings specify that employees must see everything that goes into their files.

5. Make any employee who uses information in a personnel record for any purpose other than that for which it was gathered subject to dismissal, and enforce this policy. The only permissible exception would be when the employee whose data it is has given written, fully informed consent for alternate use of the data.

6. Specify under what conditions and to whom personnel information may be disclosed *within the agency* (and/or its parent organization). Limit access to those individuals with a "need to know" and enforce restrictions to prevent curiosity seekers from gaining access.

[15] *NASW Standards for Social Work Personnel Practices* (1975), *op. cit.*, p. 12.

7. Specify under what conditions and to whom personnel information may be disclosed to sources *outside the agency*. Restrict third parties from releasing this information to anyone else. Differentiate between: (a) disclosures that can occur only with written, informed consent of the employee, and (b) disclosures that could occur without employee knowledge or consent due to existing laws and lack of legal safeguards.

Publicize to prospective and current employees item's identified in (a) and (b) and specify that employees will be notified whenever a disclosure is being requested or considered under (b).

8. Permit employees access to material in their personnel files and give them the right to correct or amend their record as necessary to insure its accuracy and completeness. Policy should provide for the employee to actually receive copies of most personnel materials if desired.

9. If certain materials cannot be shared with employees and are kept in a separate place, advise staff of the nature of such information and the reason why it is not routinely available to them. Consider adopting a policy permitting a representative of the employee's choosing to have some access to this material.

10. Develop and implement a procedure for physically safeguarding all personnel records and related data.

11. Spell out confidentiality policies concerning the writing, giving, and receiving of references, and make the guidelines known to all involved.

12. Set limits on record retention. List the kinds of data most commonly found in the agency's personnel records, and, for each kind, specify how long it is to be kept before it is destroyed. Effect destruction of outdated record materials in a manner that will preserve confidentiality.

13. Give careful thought to the process of typing performance evaluations and other highly confidential personnel material. Do not allow subordinates to type the evaluations of superiors; do not use steno pools or outside typing services for this task. Only clerical personnel who have been specially trained in confidentiality regulations should handle evaluatory material.

14. Establish mandatory training programs in all confidentiality procedures; establish personnel policies with disciplinary actions clearly spelled out for those who violate confidentiality regulations.

15. Research local, state, and federal laws to determine if any special confidentiality coverage is applicable, or if such laws contain clauses or loopholes that might make it difficult to maintain confidentiality of personnel record materials.[16]

[16] For example, in the state of Florida, there is a law declaring all state agency documents public and therefore open to public inspection. While consumer records are specifically excluded so their confidentiality can be preserved, personnel records are not, thus leaving them open to access by anyone. Efforts to fill the loophole have failed in the legislature for several years. Concern has been mounting, and it appears the law will soon be amended.

16. Publicize to potential and current employees the guidelines arrived at in items 1–15 along with the mechanisms available to those who feel there have been violations and wish to make their dissatisfactions known.

Thoughtful administrators may think of several items to add to this list.

Release of Personnel Data to Others

Disclosure of personnel data can occur both within and outside the agency maintaining the record.

WITHIN THE AGENCY

Personnel records tend to arouse curiosity. Actually, employees in a social-work setting would be much more interested in getting a glimpse of a co-worker's personnel file than that of someone's client. So much data in personnel files is "juicy" that it makes fascinating reading. If the records are not kept under lock and key, unauthorized persons within the agency may gain access to them, for example, a staff member or student working late. Supervisory-level staff who normally have access to personnel records may seek an individual's file for the wrong reason—to satisfy curiosity or to use the information against the employee—and thus, supervisory and management level staff must not have blanket access to all personnel files. When disputes arise between employees or between a supervisor and a subordinate, there may be an intense desire to know someone's past performance record. Clerical staff doing the filing may take a little longer than necessary as they read "interesting" performance evaluations, disciplinary reports, or perhaps documentations of past medical or psychiatric treatment. Thus, differential guidelines regarding record access must be developed.

The IBM Corporation has developed an approach that would seem desirable for other settings as well. It maintains two types of personnel records. One is strictly job-related and contains performance evaluations and similar material. Only those staff concerned with employee performance are allowed to see this material. A second file contains such data as wage and salary details, medical benefits, payroll deductions, etc. The immediate supervisor does not usually need to see this information, yet certain personnel-department staff must work with it intensively. Through this division, IBM "protects the individual from having facts about his or her life accessible to people who should only be concerned with specific areas."[17] The social work profession must also address this issue and

[17] "IBM's Guidelines to Employee Privacy: An Interview with Frank T. Cary," *op. cit.*, p. 87.

develop unified guidelines for protecting employee confidentiality within social-work settings.

DISCLOSURES OUTSIDE THE AGENCY

It is argued that consumers of services must give informed consent before information from their records can be released to others. If social-work clients have this right, then certainly the social-work employee is entitled to the same protection. Thus, the concepts discussed in Chapter 5 apply here as well; we need not repeat them here.

The NASW does support the position that no information should be released from personnel records without employee consent.[18] Mironi points out that "when insurance companies, credit bureaus, private investigators, mailing firms, debt collectors, and others" seek information from personnel files

> their position, occupation or type of business do not make them privileged. Nothing in the law requires an employer to make the information available to them. On the other hand, almost nothing can prevent him from revealing it either. The employer has complete discretion in this case and he takes no real legal risk by releasing information from his files.[19]

He goes on to suggest, however, that the employer should fear possible legal recourse from the applicant if such information is disclosed. The individual may argue that his privacy was violated, that defamation occurred, or that there was a breach of a confidential relationship. Unfortunately, Mironi concludes, none of the three possible arguments available to the consumer "appear to be an effective protection or remedy for the employee."[20] It might be logical to argue that information in personnel records should be treated as privileged communication and thereby afforded legal protection. However, privileged-communication statutes usually involve a professional group with definite professional ethics, and there is no profession of "personnel-record–handlers." In addition, a number of specifics would have to be nailed down—some data can be disclosed without harm and some is highly sensitive; certain information is crucial to the personnel process while other data is not, and so on. The entire area of confidentiality of personnel records has not been studied in sufficient depth to permit the development or implementation of relevant privileged-communication statutes at this time.

Release of confidential personnel information to union officials can present a special problem. Mironi quotes several court decisions that have granted them free access, and points out that

[18] *NASW Standards for Social Work Personnel Practices* (1975), *op. cit.*, p. 28.
[19] Mironi, *op. cit.*, p. 278.
[20] *Ibid.*, p. 288.

an employer must furnish to a union, after the union has been certified as his employee's exclusive bargaining representative, information which is relevant for collective bargaining, processing grievances, or contract administration. It may include highly sensitive information as found in medical records, wage histories, test results, investigation reports, and so forth. An employer's contention that the data is personal, private, or confidential is unavailing.

Furthermore,

it does not matter whether the employee agrees that the union representative should see his file or whether the information therein is sensitive. As long as it [is] relevant to labor union functions, the employer must surrender it.[21]

An employee who is *not* a union member but who works in a setting where there is a union may have his personnel record pulled by the union if it is considered relevant in any way to something the union is studying. All this may occur without his knowledge.[22] Thus, labor relations laws, anti-discrimination laws, and similar regulations may permit or require invasion of privacy of individual employees.

Receipt of Confidential Personnel Data from Other Sources

Solicited and unsolicited information of a highly confidential nature may find its way into personnel records.

All unsolicited reports and data should be carefully screened. If an insurance company, for example, volunteers information regarding a claim filed by an employee, it should not be automatically received and filed. Has the employee given permission for this information to be shared with the employer? Is it relevant, or is it going to be used against the employee without his knowledge? There are exceptions, however. If an individual's performance has been declining and the situation reaches a point where the employer requires him to undergo medical or psychiatric examination to determine his continued ability to function on the job, the report must be made available to the employer. Of course, it is hoped that the professional preparing the report will bear in mind that it may find its way into a personnel file. Most personnel staff are not trained to interpret such data adequately without an outside consultant. Nevertheless, the report may well become a permanent part of the record, reposing there long after the crisis has been resolved.

Another source of unsolicited data is the employee himself. If a staff member has done something connected with his work that he is particularly proud of, he may want to submit a brief note for the file to officially docu-

[21]*Ibid.*, p. 277.
[22] *Ibid.*, p. 278.

ment his achievement. However, this can be carried to excess. Some overly zealous employees clutter up their records with copies of papers written for classes, routine recognition for tasks performed that they were required to do anyway, and on and on *ad infinitum*. Such abuse must be discouraged.

Other employees or staff may submit memos or evaluatory comments to an individual's personnel file. They may or may not be in a supervisory position. If no controls are exercised and no screening mechanism is implemented, inappropriate, highly biased and potentially damaging material could find its way into the record.

Employee Access to Personnel Files

Employee access to personnel records has become the standard in personnel practice. In addition, the Federal Privacy Act's definition of an "individual" and of a "record" makes it quite clear that employees in federal programs have the same right of access to their files as do consumers of services. This includes the right to have copies made and submit corrections and additions to the record. Other governmental programs have adopted a similar policy, as have most educational systems and many private businesses. The NASW states its position quite strongly:

> [The personnel record] shall be open and available to the employee and contain no material or information that cannot be shared with the employee.[23]

The benefits of such a policy for the employee are obvious. He can protect himself against unjustified personnel actions. There will be more honest communication and sharing in the performance-evaluation process. If this has occurred, the personnel record should hold no surprises and almost everything in it should already be known to the employee. The staff member thus becomes a participant rather than a passive object in the employment process and relationship. He can also give *informed* consent for release of information from his file if he is able to see the material in question before disclosure, thereby preserving confidentiality of sensitive data.

As might be expected, not everyone agrees that employees should have access to their files. It is interesting to note that the Social Work Vocational Bureau (SWVB) is one organization that insists on absolute secrecy of its files from the individual.

> The record should be reviewed by those in your organization who are in employing positions. The record is NOT to be seen by the individual. Neither the name of the candidate nor any information in this record may be passed on to other organizations or persons.
> The record should not be reproduced. . . .

[23] *NASW Standards for Social Work Personnel Practices* (1975), *op. cit.*, p. 28.

You will recognize the record as being highly confidential material which should be handled accordingly.[24]

Apparently the SWVB's references are collected in absolute confidence and with the understanding that the employee will not see them.

There is also the perennial argument that while the employee should have access to most data, there are some items that he should not see. Reports of investigations and interviews conducted while pursuing a grievance or other official action, salary forecasts, tentative promotional planning, and detailed reports of employer-requested medical examinations might be off-limits to the employee. If an agency must collect such data, it will have to be kept separate from the primary personnel file, but its existence and nature should be made known to the employee. The IBM Corporation, in its testimony before the Federal Privacy Protection Study Commission, questioned the current policies of the Federal Privacy Act concerning consumer access:

> Employees should have some means of access to their personal data, but such rules should contain a clear exception for data considered company confidential. In a merit system, data such as salary plans and promotion forecasts are tentative and subject to continual change. Complete disclosure to employees could lead to unwarranted expectations and misunderstandings.[25]

The list of possible contents of personnel records (pages 173–175) suggests a number of areas that should hold no surprises for staff who exercise a right of access. Items 1, 2, 9, 10, 11, 12, 13, 14, 15, 16, 17, 18, 20, and 23 should already be familiar to the employee if basically sound personnel practices have been followed. Even though the employee may think he knows what his file contains, verification of its accuracy can be important. For example, the clearance for past criminal activities may show an arrest record but not indicate that the case was dismissed or the employee found innocent.

Problems could arise if an agency that once denied employees access to performance-evaluation material suddenly makes it available. Destroying the material is not always possible under federal and state laws. If the data is somewhat negative and a potential source of discomfort or anxiety to the employee, an agency administrator should be present at the time access is acquired in order to help interpret the material and deal with the individual's reactions.

Notes regarding impressions from an employment interview will usually not be familiar to employees who have been with a program for any length

[24] "Regulations for Use" of the Personnel Records sent out by the Social Work Vocational Bureau (a job placement service for social workers), New York, N.Y. Cover memo accompanying one such record received in 1976.

[25] "IBM—The Managing of Employee Personal Information and Employee Privacy," *op. cit.*, p. 11 of transcribed copy.

of time. Since the person was hired, the employer's impressions of him during the interview should be fairly positive; but this is not always the case. The *manner* in which material is presented in personnel files must be considered as well as the content. Social workers' entries can be as judgmental and inappropriate in such files as in consumer case records, and what has been put into black and white may follow a staff member around for many years. (It is not unusual for social-work settings to retain employee files for five to ten years or even longer.) In my own review of hundreds of personnel records and related materials over a ten-year period, some glaring examples of improper recording have stood out. In most instances, the writers had no idea at the time that one day the employee would be reading their entries.

The following example illustrates the pitfalls of the improper, process-style, diagnostic type of recording that all too often is found in employee files maintained by social workers. It was written more than ten years before the employee read it. "Mrs. Roberts" had worked for the setting for a period of time, left, and then returned to the same agency a number of years later. The inappropriate entry was found among material generated by the initial period of employment and was taken from a lengthy report of the first employment interview with the individual:

> Mrs. Roberts appeared for an interview as scheduled. I had not noticed the height and weight on her application and was therefore totally unprepared for her appearance. Mrs. Roberts looks to be every bit of the 200 pounds she recorded on the application. There is a role of fat almost like a hunk across her shoulders and her stomach protrudes, giving a total effect of very poor posture. Her hair, which is cut fairly short, was in disarray and she wore no makeup. She had on a blue cotton dress which was rumpled, and altogether made as unprepossessing an appearance as any college graduate I can remember interviewing.

In the middle of the interview the prospective employer decided to check references and noted:

> During the course of the interview, I went to another office and telephoned Dr. Smith, who was at home. At first he was not familiar with Mrs. Roberts, but when I described her, he immediately remembered her. He thinks she "has a chip on her shoulder," which is undoubtedly related to the problem that is causing her obesity, whatever that is. He promised to call me the next morning and read me the letter that Dr. Appleton had written. (When he called the next morning, he gave an impression without saying so that he thought Dr. Appleton was being very charitable and that he did not envy us our decision.)

Toward the end of that interview, the following comments are recorded:

> I found myself becoming extremely irritated with Mrs. Roberts as I would have to explain some things two or three times. Because I realized I was getting such a negative impression and that this could well be because I was irritated at having the interview take up so much time when I had other things which were pressing,

I asked Mrs. Adams to come in and talk with her while I was on the telephone in the other room.[26]

One wonders why this applicant was hired in the first place! Perhaps the recording was accurate—people do sometimes present the type of physical appearance the interviewer so vividly described. But how much detail belongs in a personnel file? Would there have been a better way of saying the same thing? What if the employee's personal appearance were to change with time? In this case, the employee did not read this entry until many years later, when her ego strength was, hopefully, sufficient to withstand the shock of seeing such material in writing. Suppose she had read it shortly after it had been written? A rather nasty situation could have resulted for both employer and prospective employee. Unfortunately, this example is not unique. Obviously, no one screened the file at the time all records became open. One wonders how many settings will find themselves in for some similarly unpleasant surprises because they are unaware of what was put in their records in the "good old days" when one did not need to worry about the employee ever seeing his file.

Items 4 to 7[27] in the list of possible record contents (pp. 173–175) are rarely used by settings employing social workers. Thus, there should be little concern over employee reactions. If such instruments are used, it should be with the idea that the results will be shared with the employee. Any old material of this nature already in the file should be destroyed or shared with the staff member.

Item 8 (copies of medical and psychiatric reports) can present special problems. Many social workers are highly skilled diagnosticians, and if they are not careful their personnel record entries can become more psychiatrically than personnel-oriented. And social work employers may have an intense interest in an applicant's past medical/psychiatric treatment. The applicant should be considered the primary source of information; if data must be sought from a treating professional, it should be kept as simple as possible. All the employer really needs to know is whether or not the individual is able to work at the job for which he is being considered and whether there are any problem areas that might affect this . Such material should be fully shared with the employee. If additional details are obtained that should not be shared, the report should be destroyed, if circumstances permit, rather than made part of a personnel record whose confidentiality is very difficult to maintain.

Item 19 (information supplied by insurance carriers) does not belong in a personnel record in the first place. Employers should not be soliciting such

---

[26] This excerpt is a word-for-word account taken from an actual personnel file still being actively maintained in a social-work setting. Names have been changed. It is being used with the informed and written consent of the employee involved. The author of the material is deceased.

[27] Psychological tests, lie detector tests, aptitude and IQ tests, and credit reports.

data, and insurance companies should not be releasing it. If the details of medical or psychiatric records are disclosed with employee consent, the consent should be "informed," which would necessitate the individual's seeing the material before it is released to the employer. Thus, its presence in the personnel file should not come as a surprise to the employee. However, even if they are obtained with consent, such reports should be destroyed as soon as possible, rather than preserved in a personnel record.

The final performance evaluation at the time of separation from the agency should be shared with the employee. However, this is often prepared after he has left, and the employer may forget to mail him a copy. Some settings may even discourage sharing the evaluation, as they seek full honesty from the supervisor in stating whether he would rehire the individual or not. Most personnel policies granting employee access permit this both during and after the individual's period of employment. Thus, former staff may reappear some time later, asking to see their files. These requests will increase along with heightened consumer awareness of the right to review one's records.

Settings that hold exit interviews with departing employees usually do so in an effort to give them an opportunity to freely comment regarding their experience. The individual is asked to identify positive aspects and make recommendations for changing negative factors. This discussion takes place virtually as the employee is walking out the door so that he need not fear its having any affect on his final performance evaluation. The results of such interviews are used by administration to identify areas where changes are needed and improve working conditions and the service-delivery system. The results of an exit interview are sometimes placed in the individual's personnel file. However, this should be avoided as it constitutes a violation of the employee's right to confidentiality; most exist interviews are conducted with the promise that "everything you say is very confidential." Once an employee's comments get into black-and-white in a personnel record, they become available to many persons within the agency, perhaps even those whom he criticized. Exit-interview content should therefore be summarized and kept in a separate file with all employee-identifying data removed.

12. "I Have a Question. . . ."

Since many helping professionals are not legally sophisticated, the litigation panel recommends that the different professions spell out guidelines—preferably in answers to a series of hypothetical cases—for each professional confronting the most troublesome kinds of situations. . . .[1]

THE FOLLOWING QUESTIONS either introduce new areas of confidentiality or follow up on aspects discussed in previous chapters. They are based on actual incidents or on questions raised by participants in seminars on confidentiality. The language is deliberately informal because it represents an oral discussion. The "answers" are not legal dicta but reflect the guidelines suggested throughout this book.

I need to release some information regarding my client to another agency, but I have been unable to contact him to get his oral or written consent. His wife told me she is sure he would not mind if I released the information and has, in effect, given me permission on his behalf. Can I act on this?

Probably not. Unless the client has been declared mentally incompetent and his wife appointed guardian, she is not legally authorized to sign a release form in his behalf. Several questions must be considered: Does the wife know exactly what information is to be released and to whom? How would the client feel about her gaining full access to this information, as would be necessary in order for her to give fully informed consent for its disclosure?

If the situation is an emergency and the release is necessary for the immediate protection of the client and/or others, you would probably be safe in releasing it without his permission. However, should you ever be challenged on this at a later date, you must be able to establish that it was a bona fide emergency. If your agency comes under the jurisdiction of the Federal

[1] *Confidentiality: A Report of the 1974 Conference on Confidentiality of Health Records,* American Psychiatric Association (Washington, D.C.: 1975), p. 38.

Privacy Act, those regulations should be carefully reviewed for the specific exceptions which permit information to be released without client consent.

The above guidelines will appear idealistic and impractical to settings that have habitually been releasing information via spouse consent because "it's a lot more convenient for everyone and permits service-provision without so much red tape." Confidentiality guidelines should work to the best interests of the client. There are times when it would appear best to apply them very flexibly in order to expedite services. In reality, this is often done as agencies try to avoid "being so hamstrung with precautionary measures that we can't carry out our purpose." As long as no legal statutes prohibit such behavior, it will undoubtedly continue, perhaps justifiably. However, when these agencies lose sight of the ideal approach and overlook potential confidentiality issues at stake, there is real cause for concern.

I got a phone call from a social worker in another agency asking for a copy of our entire social-service file on a client. That's ridiculous, as it covers five years and is over sixty pages long. She then asked if she could come to my office and read the record. I told her "no," and she got rather upset at the inconvenience I was causing her. Now I'm wondering if I made the right decision — did I?

Yes. The fact that she became annoyed at your decision indicates that she is probably not fully aware of confidentiality ethics and regulations.

Firstly, a request for "a copy of the entire social-service record" covering a five-year period is inappropriate. Few agencies would feel comfortable revealing that much information to another setting. Secondly, it is unknown whether or not the client had given written permission for all this to be disclosed. Neither was the purpose specified for seeking the entire record rather than selected parts. Thus, it was correct to refuse the request. If the consumer has not given permission for his file to be released, or if you do not know whether he has, it would be a violation of his confidentiality for an outside person to read the record.

Your response, however, may have been too rigid. You might have discussed further with the other social worker your reasons for saying no. You could have obtained more details regarding exactly what information was needed and why, and then advised her that if she could obtain an appropriate permission-for-release-of-information form signed by the client, you could then allow her access to the file. You would also want to communicate any requirements the receiving agency must abide by in its use of all confidential material you disclose.

Our agency is part of a large network, and we occasionally have to mail entire case records to distant locations. What's the best way to do this with the least risk of confidentiality violations?

If at all possible, avoid mailing case records and confidential material. However, if this must be done, the record should be carefully wrapped in a regular mail envelope and sealed with gummed (not regular adhesive) tape so that it cannot be easily opened or tear en route. It should be sent by registered mail with a return receipt requested to give the sender proof that the material has been received. Registered (and also insured) materials are easier to trace than regular mail should they become delayed or lost. If the record is difficult or impossible to replace, send a xerox copy rather than the original.

I work in a mental health setting. My patient has just told me that he has been working and deliberately not reporting his income to the welfare department. He has a large family and I'm sure he has to struggle to make ends meet. And I know his welfare check would be cut off if they knew his true income. Naturally he wouldn't want me to tell them what's going on. What's my responsibility here?

As a citizen whose tax money is being used to support public welfare, you can understandably become angry when you find a person who is successfully cheating the system. The initial gut-level reaction may very well be, "I've got to put a stop to that." On the other hand, some social workers have strong negative feelings about welfare policies and side naturally with the client—"I'm glad he's getting the extra money; welfare doesn't give enough to live on anyway." Either extreme is inappropriate.

Several issues must be examined in answering this question. Many practitioners feel that they must have the freedom *not* to report illegal or unethical use of another agency's services in certain situations. Thus, there is a tendency here to protect the client from being caught. This action raises several questions: What if the consumer's behavior is illegal, and the other agency then discovers it and finds out you knew about it and took no action? You might be subject to severe criticism. Secondly, is it really therapeutic, in the long run, for a client to engage in such behavior without having to face the consequences?[2] By siding with him against the "system," you may be reinforcing deviant, maladaptive behavior that, on a long-term basis, will only create additional problems for your client. Finally, what obligations do social workers have towards society as a whole? The last item in the NASW Code of Ethics suggests a possible answer: "I contribute my knowledge, skills *and support* to programs of human welfare" (emphasis added).

What if a social worker is employed in a setting that is part of a larger institution or network of agencies, and he learns that his client is being dishonest with another branch or office *in his own agency*? Most settings

---

[2] The "consequences" could be fine and/or imprisonment and denial of further services from the agency for a period of time, in addition to having financial aid "cut off."

would expect this to be reported; the employee who fails to do so may find himself charged with insubordination. How can an agency deliver services if its own staff will not act to keep its program from being abused? In addition, clients receiving services they are not entitled to are occupying slots and consuming time, energy, and money that could be used for individuals who desperately need the service.

On the other hand, having to report dishonesty to another agency can cause a break in rapport between social worker and client, especially if not handled appropriately. Ideally, it should be the client himself who decides to be honest with whomever he has been cheating. Your role is to help him make this decision by reviewing with him the consequences he can expect if, on the one hand, he continues his dishonesty or, on the other, decides to correct the situation. You can offer support, especially if he chooses to make things right, as it could be a rather humiliating and trying experience (for example, if his welfare funds are cut off he could find himself facing some very real financial pressures as his "reward" for being honest). If you determine that the information must be disclosed, this prospect should be fully discussed with him. If he will not take the action himself, you may have to do it for him. In actual practice, casework skills and the relationship between worker and client can often be used to handle the situation without having to alienate the consumer totally or drag him, screaming objections, to the victimized setting.

If you should find several persons cheating a particular program, you might be able to convey your concern to them without violating the confidentiality of any particular individual. For example, one of the administrators might be contacted and advised very informally that "there seem to be a number of people doing so-and-so" as a means of alerting him to the fact that a problem exists. The difficulty with this approach is that most administrators will not take you seriously unless you back up your statement with specifics—who, what, when, where—and often cannot or will not take action unless this information is provided.

Should I automatically tell every new client that I will keep whatever he tells me confidential, and make this a standard part of my introduction?

Every person you work with has a right to know whether information he shares with you will be handled confidentially. Many agencies and staff are using some version of the contract concept, wherein social worker and consumer outline goals together and establish conditions, limitations, and responsibilities in the helping process. This would be the logical place to introduce the topic of confidentiality. You will not want to go into such detail that it appears like a "big deal," but confidentiality provisions should be communicated so as to seem a natural part of the helping process. One way to do this might be for the agency to print up a brief description of its confidentiality regulations to be given consumers during their first contact with the setting. After a brief discussion, with an opportunity for the individual to raise questions, it probably wouldn't be necessary to discuss confidentiality again until a specific occasion arises for doing so (such as when the consumer's consent for release of information must be obtained).

Be careful not to make broad, sweeping statements promising absolute confidentiality. It is often impossible to keep such a promise. On the other hand, it would not be appropriate to go into a lengthy explanation of all the exceptions and exclusions. Some of the more obvious examples might be mentioned as part of a brief explanation that "there are certain situations where I might be legally required to violate your confidentiality, such as if you were to threaten to harm someone or I were subpoenaed by the court. While this doesn't happen very often, you should be aware that the potential exists." This lets the individual know the rules of the game so he can decide what risks he's willing to take before sharing information with you.

Sometimes a consumer will indicate, directly or indirectly, that confidentiality is of concern to him, thus alerting you to a need for in-depth discussion of this aspect. For example, the consumer might inquire what you intend to do with the information he gives you, or comment that "it's important that my affairs be kept secret," or preface remarks with "I've never told anyone these things before," etc. Thus, although an introduction to confidentiality rights and responsibilities should occur in the beginning of the helping relationship, the topic may need to be dealt with at various points throughout the treatment-process as concerns and incidents arise.

One of my clients made me promise not to tell anyone what he's told me. I rather naively made the promise. Now that I've read this, I realize that one piece of information concerns a matter that I am required to report, which means I'll have to break my promise and violate confidentiality. How can I get myself out of this bind?

In the specific situation you are faced with now, there is probably no choice but to go back to the client and share with him what has happened. At the time absolute confidentiality was promised, it was a sincere promise—you weren't aware then that you couldn't keep it. It might be desirable to share quite frankly the dilemma you are now in, offer any apologies that seem in order (without overdoing it), and solicit the client's cooperation in understanding what must be done. You would then need to use basic counseling techniques to help your client deal with his feelings and reactions to your having to disclose the information he revealed.

The best thing, of course, is to avoid getting into this dilemma in the first place, and there are some specific techniques that can be helpful. Usually a person will give you some indication just before he reveals something he considers highly personal or confidential. He may ask for reassurance regarding the policies of confidentiality, may preface his remarks with "I don't talk about this much to anybody," or may even ask directly, "If I tell you something, will you promise not to tell anyone?" Such comments indicate, of course, that he is about to reveal something he considers highly confidential. It may be something that you view as rather trivial, or it could make you feel you need to tell someone or take other definite action.

If you have forewarning before the person reveals this information, you should let him know what you can and cannot promise him in regard to confidentiality. This lets him know the rules of the game so that he can decide for himself how much, if anything, he wants to disclose. A simple statement can be made, such as, "Now, before you tell me this information, I should advise you that I may not be able to promise that no one else will ever find out. Depending on what it is you are going to say, I may be required by the agency or by law to take certain actions." This should cause the consumer to ask questions such as "What kinds of action?" or "What do you mean?" giving you opportunity to explain further about possible court subpoena of records, privileged communication, and related aspects. This type of discussion is absolutely essential if you feel the client is about to reveal something that cannot be kept confidential, such as an intention to commit a crime. On the other hand, if you have reason to believe that the consumer is going to disclose nothing of this nature but simply an intimate personal detail, it might be unnecessary to enter into a detailed discussion of his confidentiality rights and your responsibilities. This is where the inexperienced social worker or student can get into some tight spots. Inexperience may lead him to conclude that the consumer will not reveal anything earth shaking and hence to promise absolute confidentiality, only to have the client disclose something that requires definite action.

Occasionally the social worker has no advance warning; the client suddenly shares confidential information without prior notice. There may be no way to establish any kind of contract, as he has already decided to reveal the information before exploring the consequences. Honesty is essential. The consumer must be advised when a situation necessitates violation of confidentiality. This approach will also require a certain amount of casework skill to help the individual deal with his feelings about having revealed the information.

During the day I am employed in a large social service agency. At night I work part-time in the emergency room of a hospital as a medical social worker. Last night a man was brought in by the police under heavy guard. He had been injured while engaging in an illegal act. I was horrified when I realized who it was—a social worker in my own daytime agency. The nature of the crime is such that he could be a real danger to our clients. Our agency is large and I don't think he recognized me; he doesn't know that I know about this. I'm not a supervisor. I know I'm supposed to keep things confidential, but I feel strongly that something must be done for the protection of the clients in our agency. I feel I'm going to bust if I don't talk to someone about my problem. What should I do?

Unfortunately, such situations can and do occur. Practitioners and supervisors who have been around for a while can cite a few and may be able to point to some grey hairs they acquired as a result.

You are probably not required to do anything, as you did not receive the information directly—i.e., the person is not your client. But, let's take this apart further to examine some of the issues:

1. An individual being served by the place where you work part-time had a legitimate contact with its service-delivery system.
2. You were not directly involved with the individual, though you are aware of the circumstances because of your capacity as an official employee.
3. The client happens to be a social worker who works for the same agency that employs you full-time during the day.
4. The client engaged in an illegal act and you believe he could be harmful to others.
5. The client was brought in by the police.

This individual is a bona fide client of the hospital where you work part-time. The fact that he also happens to be a social worker should not cause you to apply different rules of confidentiality to him than you would to other patients. So let's pretend that he is instead a small businessman, a cashier in a department store, or an engineer. He is in police custody and may be jailed following necessary treatment for his injuries.

Regardless of what you do, the fact that this individual has gotten himself into difficulty will probably become known to his employer. He will miss work because of his need for medical treatement; undoubtedly he will be held in jail for a period of time or will at least have to miss several hours' work due to posting bond and arranging for legal counsel. All this will raise questions as to what is going on. Adult arrests are often a matter of public record, and there may be news-media publicity. In an agency as large as the one you describe, someone is apt to see it. Thus, even if you did nothing, your problem about protecting the other social workers' clients would probably be resolved.

But let's suppose his questionable activities were not discovered so dramatically. Suppose you learned of them through "the grapevine" or some other unofficial incident or communication. The following item in the NASW Code of Ethics might suggest an appropriate action:

> I accept responsibility to help protect the community against unethical practice by any individuals or organizations engaged in social-welfare activities.

Your question did not indicate the type of criminal activity the other social worker engaged in, but if it were something such as child-molesting or peddling drugs, these activities could certainly harm others. This being the case, and since his activities appear to violate the profession's Code of Ethics, you would be justified in reporting him and taking action to protect his clients. (Many privileged-communication statutes also permit or require reporting of client actions that could harm others.) This should be done as discreetly as possible, calling the problem to the attention of persons having the authority to deal with the situation effectively. They might or might not promise to keep confidential the source of the information you've given them. The chances are that you might become involved in subsequent legal investigations. As long as you are absolutely certain your information is accurate, you should nave little to fear from the courts. However, if your information proves inaccurate and the individual feels your disclosure was malicious and has damaged him in any way, you could be sued for libel or slander.

A client-pair recently sued me for malpractice. I had been doing marital counseling with a young couple on the verge of divorce. During the course of treatment, they decided it would be in their best interest as well as that of their child to go ahead and divorce. They subsequently did, but ran into numerous problems regarding custody of the child and now blame me for "advising them to get a divorce because this has made things worse." In order to defend myself, I feel I must reveal some of the content as well as the process of our counseling sessions together. Can I do so, or could I then be sued for violation of confidentiality?

Any social worker who is sued should seek immediate legal counsel. The attorney will then provide specific guidance on confidentiality issues. You may usually reveal the information necessary to defend yourself without fear of a countersuit for violation of confidentiality, as long as you release only information relevant to the suit. If you are covered by privileged communication, your state law probably has a clause indicating that a client waives his right to privileged communication when he initiates legal action against the professional involved. Thus, you are not legally obligated to keep the information confidential. Also, your clients have already made public the fact that they were in treatment with you and have undoubtedly disclosed some "confidential" material while instituting their suit. This fact may also free you from legal obligations to maintain confidentiality of this same material. Even if your are practicing without privileged-communication coverage, you would still be free to testify, and the court will undoubtedly require you to bring out certain information in order to fully explore the matter. If the court should ask for data that you feel is irrelevant to the issue at hand, you should attempt not to release it.

In the lawsuit brought against me by the couple who divorced, I am concerned about the court's subpoenaing other people to appear as witnesses. For example, I had one contact with the mother-in-law, and saw the teenage child for a period of time. Also, they ran into another couple I am counseling in the waiting room, and if they've given these people's name to the court I'm afraid they'll be subpoenaed. I really don't want all these extraneous people dragged into this mess, too—and it certainly won't be in their best interests therapeutically. Can I prevent this?

Maybe and maybe not. Your attorney should try to convince the court that you should not be required to release the names of any of these persons, or, if the other side has already done so, that they should not be contacted. Whether this succeeds or not will depend on the judge's opinion as to whether these persons' involvement is crucial for a full understanding of the facts in the case. If he thinks not, outside persons may not need to be subpoenaed. Otherwise, there may be little you can do to prevent their appearing. Also, your attorney may recommend that they be involved if he feels it would be helpful to your defense.

I am involved in a lawsuit (as a defendant) that is generating some publicity in our local news-media and social-work community. What can I say that won't violate confidentiality?

Do not say anything unless specifically instructed to do so by your attorney. Defendants are usually advised not to talk to news media but to refer reporters to the attorney. Technically, you could probably talk with anyone about details that have already been made public without violating confidentiality. However, this may not be to your best interest; it could make it more difficult for your attorney to represent you successfully. Thus, it's best not to discuss the situation at all.

The documents involved in most lawsuits are a matter of public record. A file is maintained at the courthouse and, unless it has been sealed by the court, anyone can gain access to it. Routine correspondence and paperwork may be open, while depositions and testimony outside the courtroom may be sealed. State laws vary on the confidential status of material generated by lawsuits; your attorney can provide a more specific interpretation. Thus, some information will be highly confidential and some not. The key issue, then, is not so much confidentiality as an understanding of how to act in your own best interest in this type of situation.

My clients have recently been giving me a lot of negative feedback regarding one particular social worker in our agency, and sometimes they generalize and become critical of the entire program. This places me in a sticky situation. Most people who complain seem to be just ventilating, and I don't think they really want me to do anything with what they tell me except keep it confidential. But I'm beginning to think that something should be done about a certain problem, involving a colleague's approach to clients, that's been brought to my attention. What can I do?

Confidentiality can become an issue here as you wonder, "Should I tell someone or shouldn't I?" You've really touched on two different problems: complaints regarding the agency, and concerns regarding an individual worker.

The agency employing you issues your paycheck and meets many other needs. It is natural to identify closely with the work-setting and its staff, and to react with a certain amount of defensiveness if someone criticizes it. There may be a tendency to feel that perhaps the client is wrong—"things aren't really that bad." In some instances, it may be that the consumer who is angry at the agency was in a bad mood the day when he suffered the supposed inconvenience or injustice. On the other hand, it could have been the agency which was inflicting anger onto the client and gratifying its own needs. A personality clash may have occurred, or perhaps an agency representative really did not treat the consumer with respect. Thus, the complainant deserves a receptive ear. If the problem appears serious, it should be investigated—maybe there was a breakdown in the service-delivery system, and if it affected one person adversely perhaps others less vocal have been and will be affected. You might not investigate the problem personally, but certainly it should be called to the attention of a suitable supervisor or administrator for review. This would be especially important if more than one person is voicing the same complaint.

When complaints are received about another worker, the same basic concepts apply. It may or may not be desirable to keep the incident confidential, even if the consumer asks you to do so. Various possibilities should be explored. A change in counselor, which can be anxiety-producing to the client in the midst of receiving services, may have distorted his view of a previous worker. Perhaps he is projecting feelings of anger onto his former counselor. Or the worker may have been required by the agency to take an action that upset the client, even though it was in accordance with agency policy and/or in the client's behalf. The social worker who receives negative feedback must try to remain objective, avoiding either joining defensively with the ex-worker against the client or tearing down the previous worker. This is most difficult in those situations where you yourself may intensely dislike the other worker and disapprove of the way he relates to his clients. In most situations, it would be quite unprofessional to share your negative views with the client. Ask yourself: If *you* were the other social worker how would you want another worker to respond to a consumer's complaint about you?

The best approach for handling this is based on good casework skills— respond to the feelings being expressed. You may or may not consider them justified; however, it is important to recognize their existence and to show appropriate empathy. Remarks such as, "I can understand that you must be feeling very angry at Mrs. Brown right now," or, "That must have been quite an upsetting experience for you," or "I'd be mad too if that'd happened to me" usually help to communicate a feeling of empathy and encourage ventilation of feelings. As the client verbalizes, you may be able to explore the nature of the problem further and determine if it is his indirect way of trying to communicate a much deeper need, or if something within the agency really did create a problem for him. If the latter is the case, the incident should be discussed with someone in the setting who can explore it further. The fact that you are doing this should be shared with the client.

I have a personal philosophy that when I am asked for evaluations or references, everything I feel and have experienced with that employee and/or student should be put into black and white. This way the person knows what's being said and can defend himself. I'm opposed to all this informal oral exchange that takes place where the person being talked about doesn't know what's being said about him by whom and has no way to defend himself. What do you think of this philosophy?

This attitude seems to be expressed most often by persons who have not been supervising long enough to run into some of the more bizarre, hair-raising situations that many senior supervisors have experienced—the employee caught engaging in illegal or immoral activities, the psychotic social-work supervisee, the individual who personally and perhaps even physically attacks the supervisor, the practitioner who grossly violates basic social-work principles, the staff member with a horrendous personality conflict with someone in the department, the individual who destroys agency property, the employee who brings a lawsuit against his supervisor, the MSW who somehow got through school but who has no usable skills nor any more feeling for people than a block of cement does, and on and on *ad infinitum.* One should never routinely document all the details of these kinds of problems without carefully considering the possible repercussions for the employee, the supervisor, the agency, the clients being served, and the social work profession as a whole. Sometimes when drastic action is required, the supervisor and agency are forced to document literally everything that takes place, for the protection of the agency and its clients and in order to move toward disciplinary action. If such action is not required, however, a detailed account of subjective personality factors, illegal activities, emotional disturbance, and similar problems can prove highly damaging to the employee; it can put a permanent albatross around his neck that can follow him throughout his career, even after the original problem has been resolved. Many records do not document with equal thoroughness the fact that a problem no longer exists. Thus, prospective employers who read the material years later can become biased against an individual who has perhaps worked through his difficulty.[3] Because it is difficult to control who will read highly explosive, confidential material once it has been put into writing, many seasoned supervisors simply do not record delicate subjective data.

The supervisor should advise the employee as to what he will say if he is asked to supply references, and perhaps give his reasons for deciding not to detail all the problems encountered. Most employees are very relieved when a superior chooses not to record all the problem-areas in elaborate detail (granted, he may be motivated by the fact that an employee's ability to retaliate against what is not in writing is more limited). The damage done by documenting highly negative material will usually far exceed any injustices due to failure to document.

Our agency has a number of students in placement from the local school of social work. There are five field instructors, of which I am one. I supervise two students. We get along well, and they are constantly telling me little things about the other students—their personalities, how my students think they are doing in our agency, how they view their supervisors, etc. Some of this is shared very informally; at other times my students will make a point of asking that I treat the information confidentially. Would it be OK for me to share some of these informal comments with the other field instructors? I don't see how this could harm anyone, but I feel uncertain about it.

You would be treading on dangerous ground. You might or might not be violating the students' confidentiality, but other factors must be considered. Once word got around that you were passing on things shared with you informally, you could quickly develop a reputation as someone who cannot be trusted—and then your students would stop coming to you with even the things that they need to be bringing to your attention. Also, it might be appropriate to sit down with your students and take a look at why they are bringing you these bits of information. Is it just informal chatter, or are they trying to prove a point or meet a need through this process? You might want to look at yourself as well. Do you encourage or permit your students' behavior in order to meet a need of your own?

[3] See pages 185–186 for an illustration of "complete recording" where every subjective reaction appears to have been documented. Some other problems associated with this style of recording in personnel files are also discussed there.

As a social work employee, I recently confided in my supervisor about a personal problem and asked that he keep it confidential, and he agreed. I told no one else about it at work. Yesterday I was shocked to overhear two of our clerical staff discussing my personal problem. Someone has violated my confidentiality and I am very angry. What can I do?

If what you say is accurate, you have every right to be angry! It is hard to believe this kind of thing happens, but we would be burying our heads in the proverbial sand if we didn't admit that occasionally such gross violations of confidentiality do occur. Usually the errant individual is lucky because the person involved does not discover what has happened, but that does not make the action any more acceptable.

The most professional approach would be to confront the supervisor with what has happened and how you feel about it. Granted, depending on your personality and that of the supervisor, a very unpleasant scene might result, and this possibility may cause you to avoid direct confrontation. On the other hand, your superior may surprise you and apologize, retract his statement to the clerical staff, and/or take other actions to try to rectify what has occurred. In either event, if you want to stop him from doing it again or at least have the satisfaction of taking action, he will eventually have to find out that you know he violated your confidentiality and that you are upset about it.

One option might be to go over his head and talk with his immediate supervisor, either to register a complaint or seek consultation. Bear in mind, however, that when the supervisor in question finds out that you have done this, he could react even more defensively than if you had gone to him directly.

Employees (or students) who choose to share personal problems with their superiors should bear in mind that some risks are involved. The supervisor is not there to counsel supervisees directly regarding personal matters. When the supervisor is also a professionally trained helping person, it is easy to confuse the roles. If an employee desires full confidentiality protection for discussion of personal problems, he should seek outside counseling, where he can be more fully protected by the formal client-therapist relationship.

HELP! I'm afraid to breathe for fear I'll violate confidentiality. I'm scared to do anything now—my state of blissful ignorance was highly preferable to what I'm feeling after reading this book. Now what?

Well, it *is* possible to overreact, becoming so preoccupied with confidentiality that poor decisions are made and information which should be shared is not freely exchanged, causing problems for everyone and a decline in the quality of services delivered. Basically there are several key points to remember:

1. Read and be familiar with the confidentiality policies of your professional organization and agency, and abide by them.

2. Do not release information regarding your clients without their written permission. If in doubt, consult this text, your agency's procedures, or your supervisor for ideas that can help you decide what to do.

3. If you are employed in a federally funded program, you must become familiar with the federal legislation that affects you and your clients. Administrative staff may have already boiled it down to a digestible form that will answer many of your questions.

4. Be open with your clients and share information with them freely, unless it would be to their obvious detriment to do so.

5. If you are a licensed social worker practicing in a state that treats communications between you and your clients as privileged, study these statutes and be aware of potential problem-areas before a crisis comes. Do not try to memorize all the legislation, but do know roughly what it says and where to go for more details should a situation arise in which you need guidance.

6. Don't talk about your clients' affairs, your supervisees, or the internal workings of your agency to friends and relatives. Share your emotional reactions to these things if you wish, but omit identifying details.

7. Remember—not every consumer or supervisor is going around with a checklist marking down every little move you make to see if you are violating confidentiality. Consumers and superiors are human, too, and a surprising number realize that you're no different. Most people are reasonably tolerant and understanding.

8. Avoid becoming defensive and "up-tight" if someone should ask to see his file—it's not automatically an indication that he wishes to create problems. He may simply be curious and exercising his right to have curiosity satisfied. Save your tense reactions for those few (and they really *are* very rare) instances where it is appropriate to respond with anxiety.

9. Finally, realize that the ideas presented in this text are not a straitjacket. Except for certain legal aspects, they are guidelines only. Hopefully, they will stimulate you to give the topic a little more conscious thought, so that you can arrive at the most effective way of dealing with confidentiality questions that come up in your daily practice.

13. Conclusions

COMPARED TO OTHER PROFESSIONS social work has dealt with the issues of confidentiality and privileged communication on a rather superficial level. Furthermore, some of the existing social work literature on these topics is superficially researched and misleads the reader with inaccurate statements. Readers may be lulled into a false sense of confidence, feeling fully informed, when in reality they are missing much information vital to their daily practice.

Several studies and reports clearly show that there is much inconsistency between individual social work practitioners and social work agencies in the handling of confidential material. The profession lacks a unified approach, and even the National Association of Social Workers has failed to provide specific guidelines that could form the basis for uniform practice and standards.

Studies have also shown that individual social workers and social-work settings are often only dimly aware of the complexities of confidentiality and privileged communication. Knowledge is often scanty and inaccurate, except for a general belief that "we're supposed to keep things confidential." As a result, a sizable number of settings have no written policies pertaining to confidentiality, though many are now hurriedly attacking this deficiency. Because of the profession's failure to develop its own specific, effective internal monitoring mechanisms and standards in the gathering, recording, and dissemination of confidential information, the federal government is now in the process of doing it for us. It may very well be too late for the social work profession to develop a unified approach and have meaningful input into legislation which may force us into living with regulations that are unworkable or anxiety-provoking.

As the right of consumer access to record material becomes an increasing reality, some settings are overreacting and doing away with *all* records as their "solution." This is not the answer. If staff, students, and private practitioners were adequately trained on the intricacies of confidentiality, and if more attention were paid to how data is collected, recorded, and

202

used, many of the supposed nightmares associated with consumer access would never materialize. In addition, if more honesty and sharing of process and content with consumers were to be incorporated into the basic treatment approach, the idea of consumer access to records would be much less anxiety-provoking.

Consumers of social-work services should be permitted access to social work records. However, there should be a way for the professional to withhold material that would be damaging to the individual when a situation necessitates that such information be recorded. Procedures for handling this must not become a "cop-out" by classifying all records in this category, by creating secret files, or by making consumer access so time-consuming and inconvenient that no one would persist in seeing his file. At present, very few clients ask to view their records; however, with federal legislation and increased consumer awareness of privacy rights, this can be expected to change.

The social work profession is now fighting for the right of privileged communication for social-worker–client communications. Again, several studies indicate that the *majority* of social workers do not even know what privileged communication is. Thus, the profession can be said to be fighting for something it does not even fully understand. It appears that we are not yet sufficiently knowledgeable to even determine if privileged-communication statutes are the best answer to the problem of disclosures of confidential information in the courtroom. Until the average social work practitioner becomes better informed, the profession will not be ready to take on the complexities of the privilege.

Privileged-communication statutes are not the ultimate solution that will prevent court-compelled disclosures. Such statutes contain many exceptions, and courts often overrule existing state laws, forcing disclosures because of "society's need to know." Thus, in reality, privileged-communication statutes are often ineffective in stopping such disclosures; frequently factors other than the privilege prevent the professional from having to part with his confidential information.

If, after considerably more research and more general education of social work practitioners on the concept of privileged communication, it is still felt that privilege is desired, the preferred approach would be a general model-statute granting all clients the right to claim the privilege, regardless of the discipline of the helping professional they are consulting.

An area that has received little attention in the literature is that of the confidentiality problems faced by supervisors and administrators, including the handling of personnel record material. Abuses to human dignity and privacy occur daily. Many agencies have storage areas and file cabinets bulging with yellowing files full of material gathered during the "good old days" when no one thought the employee would ever see it. Such settings are in for some unpleasant, perhaps costly, surprises when their files suddenly become available to employees. There is a need to recognize and deal with this bombshell before it explodes.

This text attempts to identify the key issues relevant to confidentiality in social work practice and to offer some guidelines. A comprehenesive study of this nature is long overdue. While of necessity it points up some of the profession's shortcomings, the critique is required to get us moving and to impress upon all concerned the fact that confidentiality and privileged communication are highly complex topics that cannot be treated lightly, cannot be avoided, and will not go away. The social work profession must address these issues with greater depth, specificity, responsibility, and firmness than ever before in its history.

APPENDIXES

Appendix A. Self-Instructional Exercise

Read the following question carefully and select one of the possible "answers" given. They are all based on solutions actually suggested by social workers, educators, and students who were asked to say what they would do in the situation described here. Follow the instructions given for each response until you have worked through the exercise.

PROBLEM

You have been seeing Mr. Jones in treatment for some time. He is obviously quite disturbed. His hatred for his brother has been building.   Today Mr. Jones tells you that he plans to kill him and demands that you not tell this to anyone else. You are now dealing with a confidentiality issue. What should you do?

(1) I'm not going to do anything right now. This man needs continued treatment. Perhaps I can eventually get him to agree to be hospitalized. (If you chose this answer, turn to page 209, middle.)

(2) Try to talk him out of it. (Turn to page 210, top.)

(3) Refer him to a psychiatrist right away. (Turn to page 208, middle.)

(4) Nothing. I can't violate his confidentiality, and if I did, he'd probably sue me. (Turn to page 211, bottom.)

(5) I have to tell his brother, though I know that will make Mr. Jones angry. (Turn to page 211, top.)

(6) I'd use techniques such as reality testing to try and help him cope better, and I'd analyze why he's telling me these things. (Turn to page 211, middle.)

You pick up the morning newspaper and read that your patient has killed a man by the name of Fred Jones—his brother. He's been apprehended and he's telling everyone he's "sick mentally" and, to prove it, he mentioned the fact he was seeing a social worker for treatment. It's only a matter of time before someone will ask about your relationship with the patient and if you knew anything about his intention to commit murder. There's a good chance you'll be considered an accessory after the fact or at least held responsible somehow. Obviously, you should have done <u>something</u>.

Go back to page 207 and select another response.

If you have professional training in social work, especially at the MSW level, one of the things you should be trained to do is assess human behavior. You have an obligation to make a professional judgment as to just how dangerous this man is. You might also want to refer him to a psychiatrist, of course, but that should not be a cop-out to avoid your having to give your own professional opinion.

Since you are the primary treatment person and you are the one to whom Mr. Jones told his threat to kill his brother, you are held responsible for whatever action needs to be taken at this point. However, you go ahead and refer him to a psychiatrist and do nothing further.

Turn to page 210, middle.

NOTE: If you do <u>NOT</u> have advanced professional training in the psychodynamics of human behavior and accompanying treatment skills, please turn to page 209, top.

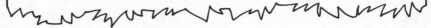

You pick up the morning newspaper and read that your patient has killed a man by the name of Fred Jones—his brother. WHAT HAPPENED?! But the patient <u>promised</u> you he wouldn't do it!

It seems that you fell back on the old, unwritten rule that says, "When you don't know what else to do in a casework situation, give advice." You weren't certain how to deal with this man's extreme hositility towards his brother, so you resorted to advice-giving, which is almost guaranteed to stop the patient from verbalizing his feelings and often produces a superficial promise to go along with what you're advising him to do so you'll get off his back. However, he obviously didn't agree with you, and the approach you used didn't permit him to express how he really felt. So, he went ahead and murdered his brother. The court may hold you partly responsible.

Go back to page 207 and select another response.

If you do not have fairly advanced training in the psychodynamics of human behavior and abnormal psychology, you are not considered competent to judge the
degree of dangerousness of this patient.* Court rulings have supported this.
You should not be attempting to treat this individual because you do not have
the professional treatment skills required. However, you're stuck now—you're
the one he told about wanting to kill his brother. Besides, you have a relationship established with him and you really hate to break it. No one likes to recognize that he isn't qualified to help someone, and the man's threats are probably just manipulative gestures anyway. So, you decide to continue treating
Mr. Jones a little while longer. You've done a lot of reading and you'd like
to see if you can handle it.

Turn to page 213.

---

* Don't despair. There is some question regarding the ability of psychiatrists
to do so also. See page 119.

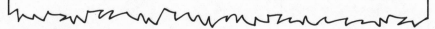

You chose not to do anything drastic, so you continue seeing Mr. Jones in
treatment. He still talks some about wanting to kill his brother, and he continues to emphasize that you are not to tell anyone what he has told you. You
try talking to him about voluntary hospitalization, but he refuses—he doesn't
feel he's that sick. You begin thinking about involuntary hospitalization, but
that gets complicated because of the forms that have to be signed and the medical exam that's required. Besides, you're afraid to even suggest it because
Mr. Jones would just become more upset. More time passes . . . .

Turn to page 208, top.

You have violated Mr. Jones's confidentiality without telling him what you
have done. His brother says to him that evening, "Hey man, you know that
crazy social worker you been seein'—well, he told me today that you're planning to kill me—now isn't that the weirdest thing I've ever heard—man, he's
crazy!" Mr. Jones misses his next appointment with you. You try calling
by phone and leaving messages but he doesn't respond. You're beginning to
wonder what has happened—has he murdered his brother and perhaps been
picked up by the police? No one answers when you call the brother's phone,
which doesn't help your anxiety any. Finally you conclude that the patient
found out what you've done and is so angry he is rejecting you. Would there
have been a better way to handle this?

Turn to page 212.

OK. You and Mr. Jones talk at length about all the reasons why he shouldn't kill his brother. You advise him very strongly against this action. He agrees that it isn't a very good thing to do but he still hates his brother. However, he promises not to kill him, and you feel much better.

Turn to page 208, bottom.

You have avoided the confidentiality issue completely. What exactly do you expect the psychiatrist to do? If he were to report the man's homicidal threat and warn the brother, he could be held liable for violation of confidentiality because he's getting it third-hand and courts won't accept hearsay testimony. It's doubtful Mr. Jones will tell the psychiatrist his plans to kill his brother. You got it first-hand, however. So, in addition to the psychiatric referral, are you going to violate his confidentiality and take some action, or are you going to honor your client's request for confidentiality?

Go back to page 207 and select another response that reflects a definite decision.

You recognize that you're getting in over your head and do not have the knowledge or therapeutic skills to deal with this man's obviously disturbed behavior. You really don't know whether or not he would actually kill his brother, or what action you should take. So, you discuss the situation with your supervisor or with another professional trained in the psychodynamics of human behavior and advanced therapeutic approaches. He advises you that this man is potentially dangerous and that you should warn his brother and also alert the police to the danger. Your supervisor and/or the other professional you consulted also agree to see the patient to help you in your treatment. They may or may not take over the case entirely.

Based on their advice, you go ahead and warn the brother and call the police . . . .

Turn to page 211, top.

You go ahead and tell Mr. Jones's brother that you have been seeing his brother in treatment and that he has threatened to kill him. This is done after you have carefully evaluated the situation and concluded that his threat is real—there is potential that he might actually kill his brother. The brother finds it hard to believe, but thanks you for the warning. You also call the police. However, you are afraid to tell Mr. Jones what you have done because you know he would hate you for it and you're not certain how to handle that; plus, you're a little frightened that he might turn some of his anger against you . . . .

Turn to page 209, bottom.

Well, such techniques might or might not help him to cope better. They sound impressive. Your primary concern is with treatment, so you begin applying these techniques, and time passes . . . .

Turn to page 208, top.

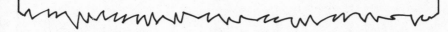

Yes, he might try to sue you but he would probably lose. You are definitely obligated to take action to protect persons that are in danger, when a client whom you are treating expresses what appears to be a serious threat to harm someone. At least one court has held a psychiatrist responsible for failing to take appropriate action to prevent a murder by his client.* Thus, you would probably not be held liable if you violated his confidentiality in this instance.

But, since you chose to do nothing, let's see what happens . . . .

Turn to page 208, top.

---

* See pages 115-121 for a discussion of this type of case and its ramifications for the helping professions.

You know you have to violate Mr. Jones's confidentiality because you need to protect his brother from harm, and you know you could be held responsible if you fail to warn him and notify the proper authorities. You feel you must tell Mr. Jones about it, as he has a right to know that you have decided you cannot keep confidential his verbalized intention to kill his brother. So, you share what you have to do and he becomes very angry—just as you expected. However, it gives you an opportunity to review with him the possible repercussions of his intended actions and to explore a little more his feelings towards his brother. The danger is still there—he may still try to kill his brother, but the sharing has been somewhat therapeutic and you are hopeful that he will remain in treatment, though you realize he may vent his anger towards you by terminating.

You then contact your patient's brother and warn him that he is a possible murder victim. You also order an emergency psychiatric evaluation to determine if the patient can be involuntarily committed if indicated for his own protection or the protection of society. You may also want to notify the police.

You have fulfilled your obligation to society and to the law by taking action to try to prevent a murder from occurring. You have made the right decision as far as the confidentiality issue is concerned. You really had no other choice, and if this patient had gone on to kill his brother you could have been held legally responsible for failing to take action to prevent it.* If you had violated your patient's confidentiality and he never followed through on his threat, you might run a slight risk of him suing you for libel or slander because you "told a lie" about him and violated his confidence. The chances of this happening would be slight; however, if you have carefully documented the reasons why you sincerely felt, in your best professional judgment, that his intentions were real, you might not be held liable.

Exercise completed.

---

* In fact, there has already been one court case where a psychiatrist was held responsible for failure to prevent a murder. See pages 115-121 for a discussion of this type of case and its ramifications for the helping professions.

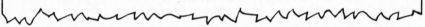

You pick up the morning newspaper and read that your patient has killed a man by the name of Fred Jones—his brother. WHOOPS!

The courts probably won't hold you responsible for doing nothing to try to prevent this (as they might a professionally trained therapist). They will probably determine that you didn't know what you were doing, did not have the training required to accurately assess the situation, and therefore cannot be held responsible. On the other hand, if you were calling yourself a "social work counselor," they may expect you to perform in accordance with your title. Thus, there are some risks for you.

Suppose you didn't violate any laws. Couldn't this murder have been prevented somehow?

Turn to page 210, bottom.

Appendix B-1. Policy on Information Utilization and Confidentiality

Background and Source of Social Work Concern

Questions concerning utilization of information—privacy, confidentiality, privileged communication—have commanded increased attention in both the public and private sectors of our society in recent years. Many factors have combined to make information policy a primary concern of civil libertarians, a subject for legislation and an area of expanding legal action.

The information explosion of the past generation—the advent of the computer, the revolution in data processing, the expanded role of government, the growth of consumer credit, of the insurance industry and of other giant corporate enterprises,—has profoundly affected the lives of all. The "Big Brother" of Orwell's fantasy is becoming a reality a decade sooner than he had foreseen. In this context, officially sanctioned governmental invasions of privacy, the compilation of "enemies" lists, the abuse of FBI functions, the violations of IRS information files, CIA excursions into private lives, the revelation of insurance company data exchange banks, of credit blacklisting, and of countless other intrusions into the personal affairs of virtually every citizen, is cause for alarm. The danger of even greater abuses—deliberate or inadvertent—in collection, maintenance and utilization of personal data by government and industry, pose a threat to our basic liberties of unprecedented dimensions. The Watergate episode with its related disclosures merely dramatizes this danger. The technology and potential for abuse already existed.

National Association of Social Workers, 1975 Delegate Assembly, May 30-June 3, 1975, Washington, D.C. Reprinted by permission. It should be noted that this policy borrows heavily from the November 1973 statement of the National Assembly for Social Policy and Development, especially with respect to specific policies recommended for social welfare agencies and social work practitioners.

Statement of Professional Concern

Recognition of the confidential nature of communications between social workers and their clients has been a cardinal principle of social work from the earliest years of the profession. Legislative protection for social work information in adoption and juvenile court records dates back half a century. The Social Security Act as amended in 1939 required state public assistance plans to "provide safeguards which restrict the use or disclosure of information concerning applicants and recipients to purposes directly connected with the administration of (the program)." The Office of Vocational Rehabilitation issued regulations during the 1940's requiring similar safeguards. Subsequently legislation, regulations and guidelines dealing with various health, welfare and educational programs have in varying degrees recognized the need for limiting and safeguarding the collection and use of personal data.[1]

Within the realm of both public and private social agency practice, confidentiality has been a perennial concern. Although pressures toward gathering, preserving, and at times revealing personal information, are greater within the public sector, both public and private agencies have had to contend with the same basic issues and dilemmas. How is personal privacy to be balanced against the public's need for information, the need for accountability and at times the need for protection? How is the client's privacy to be maintained when there is need for sharing information with 3rd parties, obtaining consultation or otherwise divulging information in conjunction with professional purposes related to the client's interest? To what extent must the protection of individual privacy be balanced against research, knowledge development and teaching needs?

Many of the same issues are present in the sphere of private practice although external pressures for information sharing are likely to be far less on the private practitioner than on the agency. However, insurance carriers often demand detailed diagnostic and other personal data in the name of accountability; private practitioners are occasionally subpoenaed to testify and reveal client confidences in divorce and custody proceedings and in child abuse cases and other domestic suits; and law enforcement agencies have on occasion sought private case record information in the name of the public interest.

In the face of conflicting societal demands regarding information usage, NASW's touchstones in this area as set forth in the Code of Ethics ("I respect the privacy of the people I serve," and "I use in a responsible manner information gained in professional relationships") are insufficient guides.

---

[1] In many other non health, education and welfare areas of broad Federal involvement—e.g., census data, IRS tax return information—restrictions are placed on usage and disclosure of personal information.

The concepts of respect for privacy and responsible use of information must be elaborated more fully in the context of an explicit NASW's public social policy.

Statement of Policy Issue

DELINEATION OF THE POLICY PROBLEM

In the most basic sense, the issue of confidentiality and information usage pits the individual's right of privacy against society's need to know—to ensure accountability, to protect other individuals and to amass information for a variety of social welfare needs (e.g., disease control, research, community planning, etc.). The social worker's central role as the recipient and custodian of personal client information and as a prime agent of social institutions places a prticularly heavy responsibility on the profession and on the individual practitioner to weigh consequences, balance equities and assume responsibility for actions taken.

The profession must be especially mindful of the threat to confidentiality posed by the development of electronic data processing. Precautions which once sufficed to ensure the safety of agency case records may no longer be sufficient when data elements are fed into computer banks or linked to other information systems beyond worker and client control.

Social workers, agency administrators, clients and legislators must be educated to the implications of computer technology and must become aware of both its beneficial and dangerous potentials. Modern data technology also demands that the social work profession re-examine its practices with regard to gathering information and maintaining, sharing, and utilizing case records. We must reassess our policies and ethical base with respect to privacy and consider the need for assuming a more vigorous and active posture in this area including the assumption of new advocacy roles.

Declaration of Policy

NASW policy must be addressed to several levels of activity which at various points intersect and overlap. These levels include the governmental-regulatory agency, business sector,[2] the public and private social welfare agency sector, and the individual social work practitioner.

[2] This would include the several levels of government, law enforcement agencies, insurance carriers and other institutions and systems which, tend to collect, maintain and use personal data banks.

GOVERNMENTAL/REGULATORY AGENCY /BUSINESS SECTOR

With regard to the first level (wherein automated personal data systems are to be found) there is need for adoption of the principles of a Code of Fair Information Practice along the lines recommended in 1973 by HEW's Advisory Committee on Automated Personal Data Systems. NASW therefore recommends that, as appropriate, legislation be enacted, regulations promulgated and policies adopted to ensure that:

a. there be no personal data record-keeping systems whose very existence is secret
b. there be a way for an individual to find out what information about him is in a record and how it is used
c. there be a way for an individual to prevent information about him that was obtained for one purpose from being used or made available for other purposes without his consent
d. there be a way for an individual to correct or amend a record of identifiable information about him
e. efforts be made to curb the proliferation of universal identifiers, including use of Social Security numbers, wherever not currently mandated by law
f. any organization creating, maintaining, using, or disseminating records of identifiable personal data must assure the reliability of the data for their intended use and must take precautions to prevent misuse of the data.

PUBLIC AND PRIVATE SOCIAL WELFARE AGENCIES

NASW recommends that: Each social welfare agency develop and disseminate through its structure, policies and guides that will cover at least the following:

a. What information is to be sought and from whom;
b. What information is to be recorded and in what form;
c. Who has access to case information and under what circumstances;
d. Means for assuring record accuracy or for noting differences;
e. Plans for record retention and disposition.

It should be noted that certain kinds of data—e.g., political beliefs or opinion—should not be recorded at all, even if assumed to have some tangential relevance to the case. "Process recording," if used for teaching purposes, should be promptly disposed of—summarized or expunged—as soon as it has served its purpose. In addition, the agency has the obligation to be sure that the client understands what is being asked, why, and what uses will be made of the information. This is particularly true when the data are to be shared with a third party. Clients must be helped to understand also the possible consequences of refusal to give information required by governmental agencies under law.

It is therefore recommended that:

f. Information about an individual client not be shared with any other individual or agency without that individual's express, informed consent.

g. Case records and related files not be transferred to another agency or individual without the express, informed consent of the client or guardian, and then under rules that the receiving agency provide the same guarantee of confidentiality as the transferring agency.

SOCIAL WORK PRACTITIONERS

Whether as an independent or agency based practitioner, social workers should be guided by the following principles vis-a-vis clients:

a. The client should be used as the primary source of information about himself.

b. Only information which is demonstrably related to the solution of the client's problem should be received, recorded, or released.

c. The client should fully understand the implications of sharing personal information including the ethical obligations of the social worker to respect privacy and protect confidentiality, as well as the legal constraints and limitations which impinge on both client and worker.

d. The client's informed and express consent should be a prerequisite to transmitting or requesting information from 3rd parties.

e. Clients should be apprised of the kind of record(s) maintained by the worker and/or the agency and should have the right to personally verify its accuracy.

Implementation Statement

With respect to governmental and other automated personal data systems NASW should support via technical assistance, testimony, affiliation with other organizations and public interest groups, and such other activities as may be appropriate, legislative and administrative actions which would embody the principles of confidentiality set forth in the proposed Federal Code of Fair Information Practice.

NASW should work with social welfare agencies at the national organizational level and through state and local chapters to gain the support and acceptance of the public and private agency system based on the principles set forth in the Public and Private Social Welfare Agencies part of this statement.

NASW should seek to sensitize and educate its members regarding issues of confidentiality and information usage and should encourage members to be guided by the principles set forth in the Social Work Practitioners section of this statement.

NASW should urge that its members accept advocacy responsibility with respect to protection of privacy as related to clients and vulnerable groups within the population.

Finally, in conjunction with licensing efforts, or if appropriate, independent of such efforts, NASW Chapters should seek enactment at the state level of privileged communication statutes. Such legislation would give clients the legal right to prohibit social workers from being compelled to disclose confidential communications which occur within the social worker-client relationship.

Appendix B-2. A Model Licensing Act for Social Workers

Use of the Statute

The revised model statute should be looked on as a model—as its name states—flexible enough to be adapted by NASW state councils and chapters to the legislative needs of their state. Although the principle of flexibility is urged, it should not be interpreted to mean dilution of basic standards.

Some states may have already achieved legal regulation of social work practice through the issuance of licenses to persons with master's or bachelor's degrees in social work. Those states may want to adapt, change, or amend their statutes to conform with the terminology, descriptions, and other such items that are presented in this model statute. A state that has a "one-level" (e.g., certifying the MSW level only) or "two-level" (e.g., certifying the MSW and BA levels separately) regulation may want to amend its statute to include a "third level"—the social work associate.

The revised model statute, except for certain technicalities of state laws, should be followed when possible; any watering down of the basic standards specified will make the licensing law meaningless.

In the past, NASW has suggested the method of registration as an alternate procedure, if achieving the legal regulation of social work practice was not deemed to be feasible in a specific state. Registration or title protection has proved to be a confusing substitute and has detoured many social workers from attempting to achieve licensing, which is preferred. NASW does not encourage registration as an alternative; it does not suggest that chapters or councils consider the dual option.

Reprinted from "Legal Regulation of Social Work Practice" (Washington, D.C.: National Association of Social Workers, 1973). Copyright © 1973 by the National Association of Social Workers, Inc. Used by permission.

The revised model statute should also be seen as a way to unify practitioners in the social service system. At least three levels of professional and pre-professional practice are acknowledged in the statute, while six levels have been identified in *Standards for Social Service Manpower*.

The relationship between the levels in the model statute and the NASW manpower classification levels in *Standards for Social Service Manpower* is as shown below.

Variations that do not substantially dilute the impact of the manpower classifications or that substantially embody these classifications can be inserted as options in the appropriate sections of the model statute.

A word of caution: legislators and the public can become easily confused by a multiplicity of levels and descriptions. The three levels in the revised model statute consider distinctions in education and experience among the following:

1. Persons with a master of social work degree and above—certified social workers.
2. Bachelor's degree holders with approved undergraduate social service education—social workers.
3. Preprofessionals—social work associates.

Further specification at the topmost level is included for the private, independent practice of social work, specifying at least two years of experience in the method in which the private practitioner wishes to practice, as a certified social worker.

A working definition of social work has been devised for use in the model statute. It is an amalgamation of definitions that have been gleaned from state statutes which either have been passed or are close to passage. These definitions are but working definitions for purposes of law and are not necessarily detailed descriptions of social work practice.

The revised statute includes the term "psychotherapy" in the definition of social work. This addition, coupled with the two-year requirement for

Manpower Classification Level	*The Model Statute*
1. The certified social worker	licenses: social work fellow certified social worker graduate social worker
2. The social worker	licenses: social worker
3. The social work associate	licenses: social work technician social work associate

practice in another social work specialty as a limitation to the private independent practice of social work, will protect the private practitioner. Psychotherapy should be limited to those who are qualified and is one of the recognized specialties under the private independent practice section. For those who are concerned about "third-party" medical insurance payments, the language of the definition is now clear.

If a chapter or council requires further definition of "psychotherapy," the following is suggested:

> "Psychotherapy" is the use of psychosocial and social methods within a professional relationship to assist a person or persons to achieve a better psychosocial adaptation; to acquire greater human realization of psychosocial potential and adaption; to modify internal and external conditions that affect individuals, families, groups, or communities with respect to their behavior, emotions, and thinking and their intrapersonal and interpersonal processes. Forms of psychotherapy include but are not restricted to individual psychotherapy, conjoint marital therapy, family therapy, and group psychotherapy.[1]

A Model Licensing Act for Social Workers

1. Purpose
2. Definitions
3. Practice of Social Work
4. Representation to the Public
5. Titles and Qualifications for Licenses
6. Private, Independent Practice of Social Work
7. Exemption from Requirements
8. Bribery, Fraud, Misrepresentation, and False Statements
9. Duties of State Regulatory Agency
10. Board of Social Work Examiners
11. Grounds for Disciplinary Proceedings
12. Disciplinary Proceedings
13. Renewal of Licenses
14. Fees
15. Privileged Communications
16. Separability Clause

1. PURPOSE

Since the profession of social work profoundly affects the lives of the people of this state, it is the purpose of this act to protect the public by set-

---

[1] This definition is based on the one included in the California Business and Professional Code, Div. 3, Chap. 17, Sec. 9049.

ting standards of qualification, education, training, and experience for those who seek to engage in the practice of social work and by promoting high standards of professional performance for those engaged in the profession of social work.

2. DEFINITIONS

"State regulatory agency"[2] means the (name of the existing professional regulatory body to be charged with the responsibility of this act).[3]

"Board" means the Board of Social Work Examiners established under this act.

3. PRACTICE OF SOCIAL WORK

a. After (date), no person may engage in the practice of social work unless he is licensed under this act as a certified social worker or social worker, and no social work associate may practice except under the supervision of a certified social worker or social worker.

b. For the purposes of this act, "social work practice" is defined as service and action to affect changes in human behavior, a person's or persons' emotional responses, and the social conditions of individuals, families, groups, organizations, and communities, which are influenced by the interaction of social, cultural, political, and economic systems. The practice of social work is guided by special knowledge of social resources, social systems, human capabilities, and the part conscious and unconscious motivation play in determining behavior. The disciplined application of social work values, principles, and methods in a variety of ways includes but is not restricted to the following: (1) counseling and the use of applied psychotherapy with individuals, families, and groups and other measures to help people modify behavior or personal and family adjustment, (2) providing general assistance, information, and referral services and other supportive services, (3) explaining and interpreting the psychosocial aspects of a situation to individuals, families, or groups, (4) helping organizations and communities analyze social problems and human needs and provide human services, (5) helping organizations and communities organize for general neighborhood improvement or community development, (6) improving social conditions through the application of social planning and social

[2] The model statute assumes the existence in your state of a state regulatory agency— usually a department of licensing and registration. However, some states do not have an overall department. In such cases, the act should give the Board of Social Work Examiners the powers and duties indicated for the state regulatory agency.

[3] The material in parentheses indicates information to be inserted by the local NASW committee on legal regulation.

policy formulations, (7) meeting basic human needs, (8) assisting in problem-solving activities, (9) resolving or managing conflict, and/or (10) bringing about changes in the system.

Nothing in this act shall be construed to prevent licensed physicians, surgeons, psychologists, psychotherapists, attorneys, court employees, marriage counselors, family counselors, child counselors, or members of the clergy from doing work within the standards and ethics of their respective professions and callings, provided they do not hold themselves out to the public by title or description of service as being engaged in the practice of social work. Any profession licensed under state law shall be exempt from the purposes of this act. Students enrolled in recognized programs of study leading to social work degrees may practice only under the direct supervision of a certified social worker or a social worker licensed under this act.

Violation of the foregoing shall be a misdemeanor punishable by fine of not less than $(amount) nor more than $(amount), by imprisonment for not less than (period of time), or by both fine and imprisonment.

4. REPRESENTATION TO THE PUBLIC

After (date), no person may represent himself as a social worker by using the titles "certified social worker," "social worker," "registered social worker," "social work associate," or any other title that includes such words unless licensed under this act.

After (date), no person may represent himself as a certified social worker, social worker, registered social worker, or social work associate by adding the letters CSW, SW, RSW, or SWA unless licensed under this act.

Violation of the foregoing shall be misdemeanors punishable by a fine of not less than $(amount) nor more than $(amount), by imprisonment for not less than (time period) nor more than (time period), or by both such fine and imprisonment.

5. TITLES AND QUALIFICATIONS FOR LICENSES

The state regulatory agency shall issue a license as a certified social worker, a social worker, or a social work associate.

a. The state regulatory agency shall issue a license as a "certified social worker" to an applicant who

1. Has a doctorate or master's degree from a school of social work approved by the state regulatory agency.
2. Has passed an examination prepared by the board for this purpose.
3. Has satisfied the board that he is a person of good moral character.

b. The state regulatory agency shall issue a license as a "social worker" to an applicant who

1. Has a baccalaureate degree in a social work or social welfare program approved by the state regulatory agency from a college or university approved by the state regulatory agency or a baccalaureate degree in another field, two years' experience in a social work capacity, and completion of courses equivalent to a social work or social welfare program approved by the state regulatory agency from a college or university approved by the state regulatory agency.
2. Has passed an examination prepared by the board for this purpose.
3. Has satisfied the board that he is a person of good moral character.

c. The state regulatory agency shall issue a license as a "social work associate" to an applicant who

1. Has a baccalaureate degree in a non-social work field or discipline or an associate of arts degree in the human services in a program approved by the state regulatory agency from a junior college, college, or university approved by the state regulatory agency or equivalent as determined by the board.
2. Has passed an examination prepared by the board for this purpose.
3. Has satisfied the board that he is a person of good moral character.

6. PRIVATE, INDEPENDENT PRACTICE OF SOCIAL WORK

a. After (date), no person may engage in the private, independent practice of social work unless he

1. Is licensed under this act as a certified social worker.
2. Has had two years of experience under appropriate supervision in the field of specialization in which the applicant will practice (e.g., psychotherapy, community organization, or planning).
3. Has passed the examination prepared by the board for this purpose.

b. Violation of the foregoing shall be a misdemeanor punishable by a fine of not less than $(amount) nor more than $(amount), by imprisonment for not less than (time period) nor more than (time period), or by both such fine and imprisonment.

7. EXEMPTION FROM REQUIREMENTS

a. From the effective date of this act to (cutoff date), an applicant shall be exempted from the requirement for any examination provided for herein if he satisfies the board that he is and actually has been engaged, for at least two years, in the practice for which the examination would otherwise be required.

An applicant shall be exempted from the requirement for any examination provided herein if

1. He satisfies the board that he is licensed or registered under the laws of a state or territory of the United States that imposes substantially the same requirement as this act.
2. Pursuant to the laws of such state or territory, he has taken and passed an examination similar to that for which exemption is sought.

b. From the effective date of this act to (cutoff date), an applicant shall be exempted from any academic qualifications required herein if he satisfies the board that he is and has been actually engaged, for at least two years, in the practice for which the academic qualifications would otherwise be required or if he has a post baccalaureate degree in a social work program approved by the state regulatory agency from a college or university approved by the state regulatory agency.

8. BRIBERY, FRAUD, MISREPRESENTATION, AND FALSE STATEMENTS

The following shall be misdemeanors punishable by a fine of not less than $(amount) nor more than $(amount), by imprisonment for not less than (time period) nor more than (time period), or by both such fine and imprisonment:

a. Obtaining or attempting to obtain a license, certificate, or renewal thereof by bribery or fraudulent representation.

b. Knowingly making a false statement in connection with any application under this act.

c. Knowingly making a false statement on any form promulgated by the state regulatory agency in accordance with this act or the rules and regulations promulgated under this act.

9. DUTIES OF THE STATE REGULATORY AGENCY

In addition to the duties set forth elsewhere in the act, the state regulatory agency shall

a. Annually publish a list of the names and addresses of all persons who are

1. Licensed certified social workers under this act.
2. Licensed social workers under this act.

3. Licensed social work associates under this act.
4. Eligible to engage in the private, independent practice of social work under this act.

b. Promulgate rules and regulations that set standards for professional practice for certified social workers, social workers, and social work associates and such other rules and regulations as may be reasonably necessary for the administration of this act and to carry out the purposes thereof.

10. BOARD OF SOCIAL WORK EXAMINERS

a. The governor (or appropriate appointing authority) shall appoint a Board of Social Work Examiners consisting of no fewer than (number) certified social workers, (number) social workers, and (number) social work associates, all of whom shall be licensed under the provisions of this act, and (number) others as seemed necessary, except that members comprising the board as first established shall be persons who are eligible for licensing as certified social workers, social workers, and social work associates, (and others) as provided in this act, and their initial term should be for at least two years from the date of initial passage of this act.[4]

b. The term of office of each member of the board shall be for three years, provided, however, that of the members first appointed, (number) shall be appointed for terms of two years, (number) shall be appointed for terms of three years, and (number) shall be appointed for terms of four years.

c. Members of the board can be removed from office for cause in the manner provided by the statutes of (name of state) for public officials who are not subject to impeachment.

d. Compensation for members of the board shall be (to vary with local requirements and compensation afforded similar boards established for the regulation of other professions).

e. The organizations, meetings, and management of the board shall be established in regulations promulgated by the state regulatory agency.

f. In addition to the duties set forth elsewhere in this act the board shall

1. Recommend modifications and amendments to this act to the governor (or another appropriate state agency).
2. Recommend standards of professional practice for certified social workers, social workers, and social work associates to the state regulatory agency.

[4] The board might include certified social workers, social workers, social work associates, consumers of service, board members of voluntary agencies, social work and social service educators, and so forth. It is most important, at least, that there be representation on the board of those licensed at the levels specified in the statute.

3. Recommend modifications of and amendments to its rules and regulations to the state regulatory agency.
4. Recommend prosecutions for violations of this act to the appropriate district attorneys.
5. Act in an advisory capacity to the state regulatory agency in all matters pertaining to the administration and purposes of this act.
6. Recommend to the (attorney general/state attorney) bringing of civil actions to seek injunctions and other relief against violations of this act.

11. GROUNDS FOR DISCIPLINARY PROCEEDINGS

a. The state regulatory agency may refuse to renew, may suspend, or may revoke any license issued under this act on proof after a hearing that the person[5]

1. Is guilty of conduct defined as a misdemeanor in this act.
2. Has been convicted of a misdemeanor under this act.
3. Has been convicted in this or any other state of any crime that is a felony in this state.
4. Has been convicted of a felony in a federal court.
5. Is unable to perform the functions of his license by reason of (a) mental illness, (b) physical illness, or (c) addiction or intoxication.
6. Has been grossly negligent in the practice of social work.
7. Has violated one or more of the rules and regulations of the state regulatory agency.

b. These grounds for disciplinary proceedings may be waived by the state regulatory agency on the advice and counsel of the State Board of Examiners. (This item may be inserted *only* if state law governing professional licensing permits it.)

12. DISCIPLINARY PROCEEDINGS

a. Hearings are to be conducted by a three-man panel of the board. The recommended decision will be determined by majority vote.[6]

[5] This section has been inserted, since most states require this type of section with respect to their professional regulation requirements. Social work practice is oriented to the concept of the rehabilitation of persons. No one should be denied licensing if he is determined to be fit and competent to practice. Your state may have a more lenient set of grounds for disciplinary proceedings in its professional regulations: by all means, use them. The wording suggested in this section is extracted from a typical existing state statute.

[6] Because state administrative laws and practices vary considerably as does the nature of regulation of professions within each state, only the safeguards to be included are listed in this section.

b. Reasonable notice (a minimum of twenty days) of charges shall be given and shall be served personally or by registered mail.

c. The accused shall have the right to counsel.

d. The accused shall have the right to cross-examination of witnesses.

e. There shall be a stenographic record of the proceedings.

f. The accused shall have the right to call witnesses on his own behalf.

g. The accused shall have the right to subpoena witnesses and documents.

h. The state regulatory agency shall review the recommended decision made by the board and shall render the decision, but penalties recommended by the board cannot be increased by the state regulatory agency.

i. Judicial review of the refusal to allow an examination, refusal to grant a license, and review of disciplinary hearings shall be in accordance with state statutes regulating judicial review of administrative action.

13. RENEWAL OF LICENSES

a. All licenses shall be effective when issued by the state regulatory agency.

b. The license of certified social worker, social worker, and social work associate shall expire on the last day of the month in the calendar year that is exactly two years from the calendar year and month in which the license is issued.

c. A license may be renewed by the payment of the renewal fee as set by the board in accordance with Section 14 of this act and by the completion and submission—on a form provided by the state regulatory agency—of a sworn statement by the applicant that he is currently engaged in the practice of social work and that his license has been neither revoked nor is currently suspended.

d. The application for renewal may be made within one year of the expiration of the license.

e. At the time of license renewal, each applicant shall present satisfactory evidence that in the period since the license was issued, he has completed the continuing education requirements specified by the state board of examiners.

14. FEES

Fees shall be as established and published by the Board of Examiners.[7]

All fees under this act are nonrefundable and shall be disposed of (in accordance with your own state's practice).

[7] When possible, do not designate fees. The Board of Examiners will have to return to the state legislature should it decide that a higher or lower fee is indicated. The board should establish and publish its own schedule.

15. PRIVILEGED COMMUNICATIONS

No licensed certified social worker, social worker, or social work associate or his employee may disclose any information he may have acquired from persons consulting him in his professional capacity that was necessary to enable him to render services in his professional capacity to those persons except

a. With the written consent of the person or persons or, in the case of death or disability, of his own personal representative, other person authorized to sue, or the beneficiary of an insurance policy on his life, health, or physical condition.

b. That a licensed certified social worker, licensed social worker, or licensed social work associate shall not be required to treat as confidential a communication that reveals the contemplation of a crime or a harmful act.

c. When the person is a minor under the laws of this state and the information acquired by the licensed certified social worker, licensed social worker, or licensed social work associate indicates that the minor was the victim or subject of a crime, the licensed social worker, the social worker, or the social work associate may be required to testify fully in any examination, trial, or other proceeding in which the commission of such a crime is the subject of inquiry.

d. When the person waives the privilege by bringing charges against the licensed certified social worker, the social worker, or the social work associate.

16. SEPARABILITY CLAUSE

If any section of this act or any part thereof shall be judged by any court of competent jurisdiction to be invalid, such judgment shall not affect, impair, or invalidate the remainder of any other section or part thereof.

Appendix B-3.   Code of Ethics

SOCIAL WORK IS BASED ON humanitarian, democratic ideals. Professional social workers are dedicated to service for the welfare of mankind, to the disciplined use of a recognized body of knowledge about human beings and their interactions, and to the marshaling of community resources to promote the well-being of all without discrimination.

Social work practice is a public trust that requires of its practitioners integrity, compassion, belief in the dignity and worth of human beings, respect for individual differences, a commitment to service, and a dedication to truth. It requires mastery of a body of knowledge and skill gained through professional education and experience. It requires also recognition of the limitations of present knowledge and skill and of the services we are now equipped to give. The end sought is the performance of a service with integrity and competence.

Each member of the profession carries responsibility to maintain and improve social work service; constantly to examine, use, and increase the knowledge on which practice and social policy are based; and to develop further the philosophy and skills of the profession.

This Code of Ethics embodies certain standards of behavior for the social worker in his professional relationships with those he serves, with his colleagues, with his employing agency, with other professions, and with the community. In abiding by it, the social worker views his obligations in as wide a context as the situation requires, takes all the principles into consideration, and chooses a course of action consistent with the code's spirit and intent.

As a member of the National Association of Social Workers I commit myself to conduct my professional relationships in accord with the code and subscribe to the following statements:

Adopted by the Delegate Assembly of the National Association of Social Workers, October 13, 1960, and amended April 11, 1967. Reprinted by permission. The NASW Code of Ethics is in process of revision. Adoption of a new code or changes in the existing one requires approval of the Delegate Assembly, which is next slated to convene in mid-1979.

- I regard as my primary obligation the welfare of the individual or group served, which includes action for improving social conditions.
- I will not discriminate because of race, color, religion, age, sex, or national ancestry and in my job capacity will work to prevent and eliminate such discrimination in rendering service, in work assignments, and in employment practices.
- I give precedence to my professional responsibility over my personal interests.
- I hold myself responsible for the quality and extent of the service I perform.
- I respect the privacy of the people I serve.
- I use in a responsible manner information gained in professional relationships.
- I treat with respect the findings, views, and actions of colleagues and use appropriate channels to express judgment on these matters.
- I practice social work within the recognized knowledge and competence of the profession.
- I recognize my professional responsibility to add my ideas and findings to the body of social work knowledge and practice.
- I accept responsibility to help protect the community against unethical practice by any individuals or organizations engaged in social welfare activities.
- I stand ready to give appropriate professional service in public emergencies.
- I distinguish clearly, in public, between my statements and actions as an individual and as a representative of an organization.
- I support the principle that professional practice requires professional education.
- I accept responsibility for working toward the creation and maintenance of conditions within agencies that enable social workers to conduct themselves in keeping with this code.
- I contribute my knowledge, skills, and support to programs of human welfare.

Appendix B-4. Confidential and Privileged Communications: Guidelines for Lawyers and Social Workers

CONFIDENTIALITY IS A MOST FUNDAMENTAL and essential element in the relationship between client and social worker and between client and attorney; it is inherent in the social worker-client relationship, the provision of services by the individualized service agency, and in the advice and representation by the lawyer.

The non-differentiated use of the terms "confidentiality" and "privileged communication" has been the source of much confusion and misunderstanding in the social work profession. Contributing equally to the misunderstanding between the professions, is the failure on the part of some lawyers to appreciate the confidential relationship between client and social worker. It is therefore important to distinguish confidentiality from privileged communication. Privileged communications are those confidential communications which are protected from disclosure by law.

Communications between social worker and client, attorney and client, physician and patient, priest and penitent, are made in the confidence, or trust, that they will not be disclosed to third persons who are not integral and necessary elements of the particular confidential relationship. The confidential nature of these communications is protected by the Canons of Ethics of the various professions and by the integrity of the professional person to whom the communications are made.

In the law, there are two types of privileged communications, only one of which is related to the discussion of confidentiality and privilege. The

This statement was issued August 1968, by the National Conference of Lawyers and Social Workers with the approval of the American Bar Association and the National Association of Social Workers.

only universal privilege is that which attaches to the client for statements made by him to his attorney in the relationship of attorney and client. Because of the balancing of interests between the protection of the individual and the necessity of society to have a complete revelation of the truth, the extension of this privilege has been greatly restricted by the courts, and where extension has taken place, in the main, it has been by legislation. Generally, such protection has been extended to patients in the patient-physician relationship, a penitent in the penitent-clergy relationship, and in some states where social workers have been licensed, the privilege has been extended to their clients as well.

The protection which the privilege affords the client, patient, or penitent, is that the professional may not be compelled to testify as to those confidential communications made within the relationship, in any judicial or administrative proceeding.

The problem is further complicated for social agencies giving individualized services by reason of the fact that the services they render are supported by the community as a whole, whether through general or special tax revenue or through voluntary contributions. The agency is thus faced with the need to assure the client's right to privacy and, at the same time, to account to the public for the manner in which it expends the funds provided by the public. This not only creates potential conflict in the agency's efforts to perform its functions in a responsible manner, but also difficulty for social workers—who, by and large, practice their profession within and as staff of social agencies—in obtaining the same status of confidentiality as is enjoyed by other professions, in short, the status of privileged communication between social worker and client.

Social services are being made available to more and more people, from all walks of life, and at increasing cost to the public in general. At the same time more and more professional disciplines and auxiliary sources, such as the schools, are becoming involved in the provision of social services in individual cases. Sometimes this leads to different emphases and may involve differences in concept with respect to confidentiality in the sharing of information. Moreover, there is cumulative evidence of increasing concern for the privacy of the individual who seeks and needs the help of social agencies and increased concern on the part of individualized service agencies for safeguarding the concept of confidentiality as one that is basic to the relationship between the client and the social agency.

It is essential therefore to deal with the matter of confidentiality in terms of the:

social agency's dual responsibility to the client and the public;
recognition that the social agency carries responsibility to share, where
    appropriate, information to facilitate provision of client service;
emphasis on the development of the client-social agency relationship

and the role of confidentiality in establishing and maintaining that relationship;

involvement of the social agency with other agencies and professions and disciplines in client service;

heightened concern for the right of privacy of the individual;

acknowledgment that confidentiality, by and large, is not equated with privileged communication.

In view of the above, social agencies providing individualized service should adopt policies in respect to confidentiality which are clear to the worker, the client, and the public. Such policies should undergo periodic review both in terms of their continuing relevance and effectuation in practice.

In recognition of the rights of individuals seeking assistance from our respective professions, and the protection of society, the National Conference of Lawyers and Social Workers recommends to the professions the following principles:

1. Confidentiality assures that disclosures made within the relationship of client and social worker or lawyer will be used constructively in the client's behalf and will not be passed on to others except when required by law, or when authorized by client.
2. After permission is granted to the social worker or to the attorney, by the client, to exchange or divulge information to each other, each should recognize and respect the trust which the client has placed in the other.
3. Except when there is specific permission from the client, or when authorized or required by law, the social worker should not testify nor should the social agency produce its files in any proceeding except when under subpoena, or in defending against claims brought by the client against the social worker or agency.
4. When subpoenaed, the social worker or agency should consult legal counsel as to those matters which are subject to production in court.
5. When records are required to be produced, every effort should be made to limit demands for information to those matters essential for the purposes of the proceeding.

Appendix C. Model "Consent for Release of Information" Form

This model form was developed by the author and incorporates all the principles outlined on pp. 61–62 of Chapter 5.

THE ABC MENTAL HEALTH CLINIC
CONSENT FOR RELEASE OF CONFIDENTIAL INFORMATION

(Name of social worker) of the (social service department) of the ABC Mental Health Clinic requests permission from ___(typed name of client)___ to release certain confidential information about ___(typed name of client)___ . This information will be released to:

Name:_____   Address: _____

Organization:_____   _____

Position:_____   Phone: _____

Material to be released: _____
_____
_____
_____

Purpose of the disclosure: _____
_____

(Name of individual receiving the data) of the (name of organization receiving the data) must abide by the following limitations in his and his agency's use of the information received:
_____
_____

My signature indicates that I know exactly what information is being disclosed and have had opportunity to correct or amend the data to make certain it is accurate and complete. I am also aware of all consequences that might occur as a result of signing this consent form or of my refusal to do so. I am aware that this consent can be revoked (in writing) at any time.

My signature also means that I have read this form and/or have had it read to me and explained in language I can understand. All the blank spaces have been filled in except for signatures and dates.

This consent form expires on ____(date)____ unless revoked by me in writing prior to that date.

_____   _____   _____
(client's signature or "X")   (date signed)   (Witness)

_____   _____   _____
(client's guardian)   (date signed)   (Witness)

_____   _____
(ABC Mental Health Clinic Rep.)   (date signed)

Distribution: ABC Mental Health Clinic files; ____(name of client)____ ;
       (name of individual/agency receiving the data).

Bibliography

General Sources

Aldrick, Robert. *Health Records and Confidentiality: An Annotated Bibliography with Abstracts.* Washington, D.C.: National Commission on Confidentiality of Health Records, October 1977.

American Psychiatric Association. "Official Position Statements of the American Psychiatric Association in Precis Form, 1948-1975." Washington, D.C.: APA (no date given).

_____. "Psychiatry and Confidentiality: An Annotated Bibliography. Library of the American Psychiatric Museum Association." Washington, D.C.: APA, September 1974 (51 pp., mimeographed and organized by subject area).

"Bibliography of Law and Psychiatry." *American Criminal Law Review,* Vol. 10 (Spring 1972), p. 619.

Carroll, James D., and Knerr, Charles R. "Bibliography." Unpublished, mimeographed listing of several hundred references pertaining to confidentiality and research. Obtained from the authors at the University of Texas at Arlington, 1977.

"Confidentiality of Medical Records." National Library of Medicine, Literature Search No. 76-5. January 1973 through December 1975. 106 Citations. Washington, D.C.: U.S. Department of Health, Education and Welfare, Public Health Service, National Institutes of Health.

Harrison, A. "The Problem of Privacy in the Computer Age: An Annotated Bibliography," December 1967. Santa Monica, California: Rand Corporation, Publication No. RM-5495-PR/RC.

_____. "The Problem of Privacy in the Computer Age: An Annotated Bibliography, Volume 2," December 1969. Santa Monica, California: Rand Corporation Publication No. RM-5495/1-PR/RC.

Hunt, K., and Turn, R. "Privacy and Security in Databank Systems: An Annotated Bibliography, 1970-1973. Santa Monica, California: Rand Publication No. R-1361-NSF, March 1974.

National Committee for Citizens in Education, Children, Parents, and School Records (1974). An organization concerned with confidentiality of student records (NCCE). This reference contains a compilation of all relevant state laws regarding privacy of educational records.

Sources of Current Articles

ALR. Found in legal libraries. This Index lists cases by subject area and is updated regularly.

Business Periodicals Index. This is a good source of articles related primarily to computerization of data and confidentiality problems faced by the news media.

Cumulative Index to Nursing

Excerpta Medica: Section 32—Psychiatry

Federal Register

Hospital Literature Index. A key source for references pertaining to confidentiality of medical and psychiatric records.

Index Medicus. Articles might be listed under "Confidentiality," "Privileged Communication" or "Jurisprudence."

Index to Legal Periodicals. Check listings for "Right of Privacy," "Privileged Communication," "Psychiatry," "Psychotherapy," and "Social Welfare."

Management Abstracts. This currently lists very few articles related to confidentiality but is a good source for locating such articles should they appear in the future.

Personnel Literature

Personnel Management Abstracts. This lists very few articles now, but some may appear in future editions.

Privacy Act Digest. Washington, D.C.: Superintendent of Documents, Government Printing Office. Jacket #599-056 (1975 or 1976—no date). It is possible this will be updated from time to time.

Psychological Abstracts. Check listings for "Ethics," "Law," "Privileged Communication," "Confidentiality," "Values," and "Philosophy."

Rx Confidentially. Newsletter published quarterly by the National Commission on Confidentiality of Health Records, Washington, D.C. Reports on conferences, publications, government activities, and other items of interest to people concerned with confidentiality of health records.

Social Sciences and Humanities Index

Social Service Review Index: Volumes 1-40 (1927-1966)

The Social Welfare Court Digest. This Digest reports on court cases pertinent to social work, with heavy emphasis on cases involving minors and publicly funded programs.

Social Work Abstracts

Vocational Rehabilitation Index

Chapter 1: Basic Principles of Confidentiality

American Psychological Association. "Ethical Standards of Psychologists. *American Psychologist*, Vol. 23, No. 23 (May 1968), p. 358.

Beatman, Francis L; Sherman, Sanford N; and Leader, Arthur L. "Current Issues in Family Treatment," *Social Casework*, Vol. XLVII, No. 2 (February 1955), pp. 75-81.

Benjamin, Alfred. *The Helping Interview*. "Honesty Essential," Boston: Houghton Mifflin Co., 1969, pp. 58-60.

Bernstein, Arthur H. "Law in Brief: Unauthorized Disclosure of Confidential Information." *Hospitals*, Vol. 48, No. 121 (November 1, 1974), p. 126.

Biestek, Felix. *The Casework Relationship*. "Principle 7—Confidentiality." Chicago: Loyola University Press, 1957, pp. 120-133.

Briar, Scott, and Miller, Henry. *Problems and Issues in Social Casework*. "Confidentiality." New York: Columbia University Press, 1971, pp. 45-49.

Confidentiality in Social Services to Individuals. New York: National Social Welfare Assembly, April 1958.

Davison, Evelyn H. *Social Casework*. Second Edition. "The Principle of Confidence." Baltimore: Williams and Wilkins, 1970, pp. 33-44, 135-136.

Dubourg, G. O. "Confidentiality in Social Work." Letter to the Editor. *Lancet*, Vol. 1, Part 1 (February 12, 1972), p. 373.

Federal Privacy Act of 1974. Public Law 93-579. December 31, 1974.

Garrett, Annette. *Interviewing: Its Principles and Methods*. Second Edition. New York: Family Service Association of America, 1972.

Hamilton, Gordon. *Principles of Social Case Recording*. New York: Columbia University Press, 1946.

————. *Theory and Practice of Social Casework*. Second Edition. New York: Columbia University Press, 1951.

Johnson, Dorothy E., and Vestermark, Mary J. *Barriers and Hazards in Counseling*. "Anxieties Concerning Confidentiality," Boston: Houghton Mifflin Co., 1970, pp. 117-120.

Kadushin, Alfred. *The Social Work Interview*. "Confidentiality," New York: Columbia University Press, 1972, pp. 54-55, 305-306.

Keith-Lucas, Alan. *Giving and Taking Help*. Chapel Hill: University of North Carolina Press, 1972.

Koestler, Frances A., Ed. *The COMSTAC Report: Standards for Strengthened Services*. New York: Commission on Standards and Accreditation of Services for the Blind, 1966.

Lindenfield, Rita. Letter to the Editor of *Social Service Review*, Vol. 38 (September 1964), pp. 341-342.

McGuinn, Walter, S. J. "The Professional Secret in Social Work," *Boston College School of Social Work Studies*, Vol. I, No. 1 (1938).

"Matter of Confidentiality, The." Editorial note in *Social Casework*, Vol. XXXII, No. 10 (December 1951), pp. 436-437.

National Association of Social Workers. "Code of Ethics of the NASW." Washington, D.C.: NASW, adopted by the Delegate Assembly of NASW, October 13, 1960 and amended April 11, 1967.

_____. *The Sandpiper*, April–May 1973 and June 1973. Newsletter of the South Florida Chapter of NASW, Miami.

National Assembly for Social Policy and Development. "A New Look at Confidentiality in Social Welfare Services." New York: Cambridge Press, November 27, 1973 (pamphlet).

Noble, John H. Jr. "Protecting the Public's Privacy in Computerized Health and Welfare Information Systems." *Social Work*, Vol. 16, No. 1 (January 1971), pp. 35–41.

Olafson, Freya; Ferguson, A., Jr.; and Parker, A. W. *Confidentiality: A Guide for Neighborhood Health Centers*. San Francisco: Pisani Printing Co., 1971.

Pardue, Jerry; Whichard, Willis; and Johnson, Elizabeth. "Limiting Confidential Information in Counseling." *Personnel and Guidance Journal*, Vol. 49, No. 1 (1970), pp. 14–20.

Perlman, Helen Harris. "The Caseworker's Use of Collateral Information." *Social Casework*, Vol. XXXII, No. 7 (July 1951), pp. 325–333.

Principles of Confidentiality in Social Work. Washington, D.C.: Committee on Records, District of Columbia Chapter, American Association of Social Workers, 1947.

Regensburg, Jeanette. "Some Thoughts on Being a Professional Social Worker." *Social Casework*, Vol. XL, No. 3 (March 1959), pp. 220–225.

"Report to Executive Committee, Committee on Confidential Nature of Case Work Information." New York: Family Welfare Association of America, 1943 (mimeographed).

Reynolds, Mildred M. "Threats to Confidentiality." *Social Work*, Vol. 21, No. 2 (March 1976), pp. 108–113.

Roycroft, E. B. "Confidentiality in Social Work." Letter to the Editor. *Lancet* 1 (7910) 797, April 5, 1975.

"Safeguarding the Confidential Nature of Case Records in Public Agencies: A Summary of Statements from a Few Individual Agencies." New York: Family Service Association of America, January 1940.

Schubert, Margaret. *Interviewing in Social Work Practice: An Introduction*. "Privacy and Confidentiality." New York: Council on Social Work Education, 1971, pp. 46–47.

De Schweinitz, Elizabeth, and De Schweinitz, Karl. *Interviewing in the Social Services: An Introduction*. Published for the National Institute for Social Work Training by the National Council of Social Welfare. Distributed in the United States by Council on Social Work Education, September 1962.

Sprafkin, Benjamin R. "A New Look at Confidentiality." *Social Casework*, Vol. XL, No. 1 (January 1959), pp. 87–90.

"Standards of Professional Conduct for Social Workers." *Compass*, Vol. 22, No. 4 (February–March 1941).

Whitebrook, Oscar E. "The Professional Confidence in the Case Work Relationship." *The Family*, Vol. XXVI, No. 6 (October 1945), pp. 250-257.

Wilson, Suanna J. "Confidentiality: Human Rights vs. Effective Service Delivery; Legal Aspects of Privileged Communication and Confidentiality." Invitational Presentation at the 1977 National Association of Social Workers Fifth Biennial Professional Symposium, *Social Work Skills: Humanizing the Human Services*. San Diego, California: November 19-22, 1977.

Wysor, Dorothy E. "Ethics?" *The Family*, Vol. IX, No. 9 (January 1929), pp. 295-297.

Chapter 2: Situations That Often Lead to Confidentiality Violations

American Psychiatric Association. *Confidentiality: A Report of the 1974 Conference on Confidentiality of Health Records*. Washington, D.C.: APA, 1975.

Brodsky, Stanley L. "Shared Results and Open Files with the Client." *Professional Psychology*, Fall 1972, pp. 362-364.

Brown, John R. "Publicity Versus Propaganda in Family Work." *Family*, Vol. VII, No. 3 (May 1926), pp. 75-79.

Crawshaw, Ralph. "Gossip Wears a Thousand Masks." *Prism*, Vol. 2, No. 6 (June 1974), pp. 45-47.

Dillhunt, Elaine. "Employees Learn Importance of Confidentiality." *Hospitals*, Vol. 49, No. 18 (September 16, 1975), pp. 83-84.

Ginsberg, Frances, and Clarke, Barbara. "Patients Need Privacy—and May Sue if They Don't Get It." *Modern Hospital*, Vol. 118, No. 6 (June 1972), p. 110.

Gouldner, Alvin W. "The Secrets of Organizations." *The Social Welfare Forum*, 1963. Ninetieth Annual Forum, Cleveland, Ohio, May 19-24, 1963. New York: Columbia University Press, 1963, pp. 161-177.

Hardy, C. T., Jr. "Is the Wrong Person Listening?" *Hospital Physician*, Vol. 1 (October 1965), pp. 195ff.

Medini, G., and Rosenberg, E. H. "Gossip and Psychotherapy." *American Journal of Psychotherapy*, Vol. 30 (1976), p. 473.

Chapter 3: The Federal Privacy Act of 1974 (and Related Legislation)

ARTICLES AND BOOKS

"A Chapter of Legislative History: Safeguarding the Disclosure of Public Assistance Records: The Legislative History of the 'Jenner Amendment'—Section 618, 1951." *Social Service Review*, Vol. 26, (June 1952), pp. 229-234.

Alves, Joseph T. *Confidentiality in Social Work*. Washington, D.C.: Catholic University of America Press, 1959. Doctoral dissertation available through University Microfilms, Ann Arbor, Michigan.

"APWA and the Release of Public Assistance Information." *Social Service Review*, Vol. 26 (September 1952), pp. 341–343.

Bigelow, Robert P. "The Privacy Act of 1974." *The Practical Lawyer*, Vol. 21, No. 6, (September 1, 1975), pp. 15–24.

Davidson, James H. "The Privacy Act of 1974—Exceptions and Exemptions." *Federal Bar Journal*, Vol. 34, No. 4 (Fall 1975), pp. 323–329.

Eastman, Hope B. "Enforcing the Right of Privacy Through the Privacy Act of 1974." *Federal Bar Journal*, Vol. 34, No. 4 (Fall 1975), pp. 335–339.

Fanning, John P. "Protection of Privacy and Fair Information Practices." *The Social Welfare Forum, 1975*. New York: Columbia University Press, 1976.

"Federal Privacy Act: Disclosure of Medical Reports in Social Security Disability Claims." *Journal of Kansas Medical Society*, Vol. IXXVI, No. XI (November 1975), p. 282.

Metz, Douglas W. "Privacy Legislation: Yesterday, Today and Tomorrow." *Federal Bar Journal*, Vol. 34, No. 4 (Fall 1975), pp. 311–315.

National Bureau of Standards. *Computer Security Guidelines for Implementing the Privacy Act of 1974*. FIPS Publication 41. Washington, D.C.: National Bureau of Standards, 1975.

"News and Notes: Federal Rules Issued on Confidentiality of Drug, Alcohol Records." *Hospital and Community Psychiatry*, Vol. 26, No. 10 (October 1975), pp. 687–691.

"Notes and Comment: Again the Question of 'Opening the Relief Rolls.'" *Social Service Review*, Vol. 25 (September 1951), pp. 392–394.

"Notes and Comment: Secrecy for Relief Rolls." *Social Service Review*, Vol. 25 (June 1951), pp. 239–41.

Sacks, Herbert S. "Editorials: PSRO and the Privacy Act: Progress in Confidentiality Guarantees." *Connecticut Medicine*, Vol. 39, No. 11 (November 1975), pp. 702–703.

Stromberg, R. E. "Medical-Legal Forum: When May a Hospital Release Alcohol or Drug Abuse Treatment Records?," *Hospital Forum* (California), Vol. 18, No. 9 (December 1975), p. 20.

GOVERNMENT PUBLICATIONS

Civil Service Commission. "Adoption of a Notice of Systems of Records." Privacy Act of 1974. *Federal Register*, Vol. 40, No. 226 (November 21, 1975), pp. 54356–54363.

Family Educational Rights and Privacy Act of 1974. Amends Public Law 93–568, effective November 19, 1974 ("The Buckley Amendment").

Federal Privacy Act of 1974. Public Law 93–579, Enacted December 31, 1974 and effective September 27, 1975. *Federal Register*, Part V-VI (October 8, 1975).

"Federal Register Privacy Act Publications: Table of Dates and Pages." *Federal Register*, Vol. 41, No. 21 (January 30, 1976), pp. 4710–4714.

Freedom of Information Act. Title 5, United States Code, Section 552, 1966.

"Privacy Act: Notice of Proposed Rulemaking." Department of Health, Education and Welfare, Office of the Secretary (45 CFR Part 5b). *Federal Register*, Vol. 40, No. 158 (August 14, 1975), pp. 34129–34131.

Privacy Protection Study Commission. "Final Recommendations of the Privacy Protection Study Commission as Contained in the Final Report." Washington, D.C.: Privacy Protection Study Commission (no date). This is a summarized version of *Personal Privacy in an Information Society*.

_____. "Notice of Hearings: Public Assistance and Social Services." Draft Recommendations of the Privacy Protection Study Commission. *Federal Register* (December 8, 1976).

"Privacy Rights of Parents and Students," Part II. Department of Health, Education and Welfare, Office of the Secretary. Final Rule on Education Records. *Federal Register* (June 17, 1976), pp. 24662–24675.

Protecting Your Right to Privacy—Digest of Systems of Records, Agency Rules, Research Aids. Office of the *Federal Register*, National Archives and Records Service, General Services Administration. Government Printing Office Publication No. G54.107/9. Washington, D.C.: no date—but it appears to be February 1976.

"Public Welfare—Title 45," Subtitle A. Department of Health, Education and Welfare, General Administration. Part 5b—Privacy Act Regulation. *Federal Register*, Vol. 40, No. 196 (October 8, 1975).

"Record Retention Guide." Section 4 concerns the Social Security Administration (pp. 19447–19448); Section 5 the Social and Rehabilitative Service (pp. 19448–19449) and Section XLI concerns the Veteran's Administration (p. 19503). *Federal Register*, Vol. 41, No. 93 (May 12, 1976).

"Safeguarding Information; Protective and Vendor Payments." Title 45—Public Welfare. Chapter II, Social and Rehabilitative Services (Assistance Programs), Department of Health, Education and Welfare: Financial Assistance. *Federal Register*, Vol. 40, No. 217 (November 10, 1975), pp. 52375–52376.

U.S. Government Printing Office. *Personal Privacy in an Information Society*. Washington, D.C.: July 1977.

LETTERS AND WRITTEN STATEMENTS SUBMITTED TO THE PRIVACY PROTECTION STUDY COMMISSION

American Humane Association. Letter to the Commission dated January 4, 1977, from Milton C. Searle, Executive Director.

Carroll, James D., and Knerr, Charles R. "Written Statement Prepared for Submittal to the Federal Privacy Protection Study Commission Public Hearings, Research and Statistical Records, January 5–6, 1977." Prepared December 1976.

Child Welfare League of America, Inc. Letter to the Commission dated January 3, 1977, from Clara J. Swan, Associate Director of Field Operations.

Community Service Society (New York). Letter to the Commission dated January 12, 1977, from Alvin L. Schorr, General Director.

Family Service Association of America. Letter to the Commission dated January 5, 1977, from an individual with an illegible signature.

Mental Health Law Project (sponsored by the American Civil Liberties Union Foundation et al.). Letter to the Commission dated January 7, 1977, from Edward P. Scott, Attorney.

National Council on Crime and Delinquency (Hackensack, New Jersey). Letter to the Commission dated December 27, 1976, from Frederick Ward, Jr., Executive Vice-President.

Salvation Army, Booth Memorial Home (Anchorage, Alaska). Letter to the Commission dated December 30, 1976, from the "social service staff" of the Home.

Salvation Army (Massachusetts Divisional Headquarters in Boston). Letter to the Commission dated December 23, 1976, from Hilton J. Friesen, Envoy, Community Services Coordinator.

State Department of Public Welfare, Austin, Texas. "Comments on Draft Recommendations of Privacy Protection Commission," January 10, 1977.

State of Michigan Department of Social Services. Letter to the Commission dated January 7, 1977, from John T. Dempsey, Director, with addendum.

YWCA of the National Capital Area (Washington, D.C.). Letter to the Commission dated January 6, 1977, from Mrs. Regina H. Saxton, President, Board of Directors.

TESTIMONY BEFORE THE PRIVACY PROTECTION STUDY COMMISSION

Blue Cross and Blue Shield of Florida, Testimony on May 20, 1976, by J. Dan Lewis, Jr., Senior Vice President in Charge of Benefits Administration during hearings on insurance practices.

Blue Cross Organizations. "Statement on Behalf of the Blue Cross Organizations" presented before the Commission's hearings on insurance practices, May 20, 1976.

Community Council of Greater New York (New York, N.Y.). Statement of Jerry A. Shroder, January 13, 1977.

Department of Health, Education, and Welfare—Social and Rehabilitation Service. Testimony of Nicholas Norton on Behalf of Robert Fulton, Administrator, January 13, 1977.

Food Stamp Division, Food and Nutrition Service, United States Department of Agriculture. Testimony of Mrs. Nancy Snyder, Director, January 11, 1977.

Governor's Council on Drug and Alcohol Abuse, State of Pennsylvania. Testimony of Peter S. Pennington, Acting Executive Director, January 13, 1977.

Hennepin County Welfare Department, Minnesota Department of Public Welfare. Testimony of Dennis Erickson, Assistant Director of Special Services and two other representatives on Tuesday, January 11, 1977.

IBM Corporation. "IBM—The Managing of Employee Personal Information and Employee Privacy." Oral Statement (December 10, 1976) of Walton E. Burdick, Vice President, Personnel Plans and Programs, IBM Corporation, during the hearings on employment and personnel record-keeping practices.

Middlesex County Welfare Board, New Brunswick, New Jersey. Testimony of Carol A. Puleio, Deputy Director, January 13, 1977.

National Association of Social Workers. Testimony of Dolores Delahanty, member and Co-Chairman, National Conference of Lawyers and Social Workers, January 12, 1977.

National Urban League. Testimony of Maudine R. Cooper, Deputy Director, January 12, 1977.

National Welfare Fraud Association (Harrisburg, Pennsylvania). Testimony of Dorothy M. Forney, Immediate Past President, January 13, 1977.

Special State Prosecutor for Health and Social Services of the State of New York. Testimony of James Bryan, Counsel to the Special State Prosecutor for Health and Social Services.

State of California, Department of Benefit Payments. Testimony presented January 13, 1977.

Supplemental Security Income Program (SSI). Social Security Administration, Office of Program Operation, Bureau of S.S.I. Testimony of Barry Powell, Acting Deputy Assistant Bureau Director, January 11, 1977.

Chapter 4: Confidentiality of Case Record Materials

American Medical Association. "Confidentiality of Health Care Information: Model State Legislation" (reference Committee B, p. 337). Adopted by AMA's House of Delegates at the 1976 Annual Convention (June 27–July 1, 1976, Dallas, Texas, 125th Annual Convention).

American Medical Record Association. "Position Paper on the Confidentiality of Medical Information." October 1975.

American National Red Cross. "The American National Red Cross Guidelines for Service to Military Families: Confidentiality. For the Use of SMF in Applying the Principle of Confidentiality in Services to People." ARC 2049, October 1974 with two attachments: (1) "Establishment, Maintenance and Disposition of Case Records" and (2) "Release of Confidential Information" (form).

American Orthopsychiatric Association. "Position Statement on Confidentiality of Health Records," June 1975.

American Psychiatric Association, Task Force on Automation and Data Processing. "Automation and Data Processing in Psychiatry." Washington, D.C.: APA, 1971.

Angell, Stephen L., and Greving, Frank T. "A New Look at the Social Service Exchange." *Social Work*, January 1955.

Arleigh, R. (pseud.). "Could You be Sued for Invasion of Privacy? Suit Involving Teaching Records." *Medical Economist*. Vol. 50 (April 2, 1973), pp. 77-83.

Behnke, Roy H. "The Confidentiality of the Patient Record." *Journal of the Florida Medical Association*, Vol. 62, No. 2 (February 1975), p. 40.

Berger, M. M.; Sherman, B.; Spalding, J.; and Westlake, R. "The Use of Videotape with Psychotherapy Groups in a Community Mental Health Service Program." *The International Journal of Group Psychotherapy*, Vol. 18 (1969), pp. 504-515.

Blackey, Eileen. "The Use of Audio Visual Aids in Training." *Family*, Vol. 31, No. 2 (November 1950), pp. 366-371.

Bristol, Margaret Cochran. "Ethics of Recording," in *Handbook on Social Case Recording*. Chicago: University of Chicago Press, 1936, pp. 197-207.

Castendyck, Elsa, and Fenlason, Anne F. "The Confidential Nature of Social Case Records in Public Relief Agencies." *The Family*, Vol. XVI, No. 10 (February 1936), pp. 308-310.

Computer Security Guidelines for Implementing the Privacy Act of 1974. FIPS Publication 41. Washington, D.C.: National Bureau of Standards, 1975.

Confidentiality: A Report of the 1974 Conference on Confidentiality of Health Records (Key Biscayne, Florida). Washington, D.C.: American Psychiatric Association, 1975.

"Confidentiality of Alcohol and Drug Abuse Patient Records—General Provisions." Department of Health, Education and Welfare, Public Health Service. *Federal Register*, Vol. 40, No. 127 (July 1, 1975), Part IV.

"Confidentiality of Medical Information." Joint statement of the American Medical Association Committee on Health-Care Financing and the Medical Relations Committee of the Health Insurance Council of America. February 1974. Statement adopted by the House of Delegates of the AMA and by the Board of Directors of the Health Insurance Association of America.

"Confidentiality of Welfare Records." *Annotated Law Reports*, Vol. 54, 3d 769 (1973).

Converse, M. E. "Photocopying Patient Records." *Hospitals*, Vol. 39 (June 1, 1965), p. 16.

Curran, William J.; Laska, Eugene M.; Kaplan, Honora; and Bank, Rheta. "Protection of Privacy and Confidentiality." *Science*, Vol. 182 (November 23, 1973), pp. 797-801.

Cutler, A. Budd. "Legal Problems in Health Care." Talk given at the Florida Chapter of the Society for Hospital Social Work Directors, Orlando, Florida, November 12, 1976.

Czajkoski, E. H. "The Use of Videotape Recordings to Facilitate the Group Therapy Process." *The International Journal of Group Psychotherapy*, Vol. 18 (1968), pp. 516-524.

Ervin, Senator Sam J., Jr. "Civilized Man's Most Valued Right." *Prism*, Vol. 2, No. 6 (June 1974), pp. 15ff.

Federal Privacy Act of 1974. Public Law 93-579, December 31, 1974.

Foster, L. M. "Do You Want to Share Your Therapy Tapes with the Court?" *Professional Psychology*, Vol. 5 (1974), pp. 369-373.

Gabriel, E. R., Chairman. Joint Task Group on Confidentiality of Computerized Medical Records. "Ethical Guidelines for Data Centers Handling Medical Records." Adopted by the House of Delegates of the Medical Society of the State of New York, March 1975; adopted by Board of Directors, Society for Computer Medicine, November 1975, and also adopted by the National Association of Blue Shield Plans.

Gobert, J. J. "Accommodating Patient Rights and Computerized Mental Health Systems." *North Carolina Law Review*, Vol. 54 (January 1976), pp. 153-187.

Godwin, William F., and Booade, Katherine Anne. "Privacy and the New Technology." *Personnel and Guidance Journal*, Vol. 50, No. 4 (December 1071), pp. 298-304.

Harrison, Annette. "The Problem of Privacy in the Computer Age: An Annotated Bibliography." Santa Monica, California: The Rand Corporation, December 1967.

"Health and Privacy: Patient Records—a Report of Current Practices with Recommendations for Changes." Commonwealth of Massachusetts, Governor's Commission on Privacy and Personal Data. Adopted November 22, 1974.

Hill, Gareth S. "Ethical Practices in the Computerization of Client Data: Implications for Social Work Practice and Record Keeping." Washington, D.C.: National Association of Social Workers (early 1970's).

Hofmann, Adele D. "Confidentiality and the Health Care Records of Children and Youth." *Psychiatric Opinion*, Vol. 12, No. 1 (January 1975), pp. 20-28.

Holton, F. "What Other Nations Are Doing to Protect Personal Information." *Prism*, Vol. 2, No. 6 (June 1974), pp. 60-66.

Jackson, Carmault B., Jr. "Considerations of the 'Active Working Record' versus the 'Permanent Record': The Preliminary View of the American Society of Internal Medicine." *Psychiatric Opinion*, Vol. 12, No. 1 (January 1975), pp. 29-33.

Jackson, Carmault B., Jr. "Guardians of Medical Data." *Prism*, Vol. 2, No. 6 (June 1974), pp. 38-44.

Kadushin, Alfred. "Interview Observation as a Teaching Device." *Social Casework*, Vol. XXXVIII, No. 7 (July 1956), pp. 334-341.

Katz, David. "Videotape Programming for Social Agencies." *Social Casework*, Vol. 56, No. 1 (January 1975), pp. 44-51.

Kedward, H. B., et al. "Computers and Psychiatric Data Recording: Rationale and Problems of Confidentiality." *Comprehensive Psychiatry*, Vol. 14, No. 2 (March-April 1973), pp. 133-137.

Kelley, V. R., and Weston, H. B. "Civil Liberties Guidelines for Computerized Management Information Systems of Mental Health Facilities." *American Journal of Orthopsychiatry*, Vol. 44, No. 2 (1974), p. 279.

Kelley, Verne R., and Weston, Hanna B. "Civil Liberties in Mental Health Facilities." *Social Work*, Vol. 19, No. 1 (January 1974), pp. 48-54.

Kelley, Verne R., and Weston, Hanna B. "Computers, Costs, and Civil Liberties." *Social Work*, Vol. 20, No. 1 (January 1975), pp. 15–19.

Lassers, Willard. "Availability of Records." Chapter 7 in *Confidentiality of Health and Social Service Records: Where Law, Ethics and Clinical Issues Meet.* Proceedings of the Second Midwest Regional Conference. Chicago: University of Illinois at Chicago Circle, December, 1976, pp. 144–166.

Mason, E. A. "Filmed Case Material: Experience of Exposure?" *American Journal of Orthopsychiatry*, Vol. 39 (January 1969), pp. 99–108.

McGill, G. A., and Thrasher, J. W. "Videotapes: The Reel Thing of the Future." *Trial*, Vol. 11 (S/O 1975), pp. 43ff.

McLaren, H. C. "Confidentiality in Gynaecology." Letter to the Editor, *Lancet*, Vol. 1 (February 26, 1972), p. 487.

Miller, Arthur R. "The Assault on Privacy." *Psychiatric Opinion*, Vol. 12, No. 1 (January 1975), pp. 6–14.

"Must Social Workers Be Informers Too?" *NASW News*, December 1972.

National Assembly for Social Policy and Development. "A New Look at Confidentiality in Social Welfare Services." New York: Cambridge Press, November 27, 1973 (pamphlet).

National Association of Blue Shield Plans. "Guidelines on Preserving Confidentiality of Medical Records," approved September 3, 1975. Chicago, Illinois.

National Association of Social Workers. "Policy on Information Utilization and Confidentiality." Policy adopted at the NASW 1975 Delegate Assembly, May 30–June 3, 1975, Washington, D.C.

"News of the Societies: National Federation of Societies for Clinical Social Work: Ethical Standards of Clinical Social Workers." *Clinical Social Work Journal*, Vol. 2, No. 4 (Winter 1974), pp. 312–315.

Noble, John H., Jr. "Protecting the Public's Privacy in Computerized Health and Welfare Information Systems." *Social Work*, Vol. 16, No. 1 (January 1971), pp. 35–41.

"Notes and Comments: An Issue." *Social Service Review*, Vol. 31, (March 1957), pp. 84–85.

Nye, Sandra G. "Model Law on Confidentiality of Health and Social Service Information." Appendix B in *Confidentiality of Health and Social Service Records: Where Law, Ethics and Clinical Issues Meet*, Proceedings of the Second Midwest Regional Conference. Chicago: University of Illinois at Chicago Circle, December 1976, pp. 260–282.

Pascoe, J. "MIB: It Has 12 Million Americans at Its Fingertips." *Prism*, Vol. 2 (1974), p. 28.

Philadelphia Chapter American Association of Social Workers, Committee on Use of Case Records. "The Use of Case Records." *The Compass*, Vol. XXIV, No. 1 (November 1942), pp. 9–16.

Pinkus, Helen. "Recording in Social Work," in *Encyclopedia of Social Work*, Washington, D.C.: National Association of Social Workers, 1977, pp. 1161–1168.

Rand Corporation. "A Bibliography of Selected Rand Publications: Privacy in the Computer Age." Santa Monica, California: The Rand Corporation, August 1976. SB-1047.

Reinitz, Freda A. "The Social Service Exchange and the Challenge of the '60's." *Journal of Social Work Process*, Vol. 13, (1962), pp. 51-70.

Richmond, Mary E. "The Confidential Exchange," in *Social Diagnosis*. Reprint. New York: Free Press, 1965, pp. 303-308.

Richmond, Mary E. "Why Case Records." *Family*, Vol. 6 (November 1925), pp. 214-216.

Serota. "The Protection of Case Material." *The Compass* (May 1939), p. 8.

Society for Hospital Social Work Directors. "Guidelines of Social Work Recording in Medical Charts." Oregon Chapter of the Society, June 1, 1976, final draft.

Spitzer, R. L., and Endicott, J. "Automation of Psychiatric Case Records: Will It Help the Clinician?" *Clinical and Basic Research*, Vol. 31, No. 11 (1970), pp. 45-46.

"Statement of Principles Concerning the Confidentiality of Medical Information of the Health Insurance Association of America," statement developed by the Government Relations Committee of the Health Insurance Association of America. Transmitted by Legislative Bulletin Special No. 1-74—October 24, 1974. Chicago: Health Insurance Association of America.

Swan, P. N. "Privacy and Record Keeping: Remedies for the Misuse of Accurate Information." *North Caroline Law Review*, Vol. 54, (1976), pp. 585-621.

Teicher, Morton I. "Let's Abolish the Social Service Exchange." *Social Work*, Vol. 33, No. 1 (January 1952).

Towle, Charlotte. "The Client's Rights and Use of the Social Service Exchange." *Social Service Review* (March 1949), pp. 15-20.

Tropman, Elmer. "Social Service Exchange." *Community* (June 1959).

_____. "The Social Service Exchange—Yes or No?" *Community* (June 1959), p. 165.

_____. "What's Happening to the Exchange," *Community* (April 1954).

U.S. Department of Health, Education and Welfare. "Records, Computers and the Rights of Citizens." Report No. (OS) 73-94. Washington, Government Printing Office, 1973.

Volkman v. Miller, 383 N.Y.S. 2d 95 Supreme Court, May 13, 1976.

Watson, Andrew S. "Levels of Confidentiality in the Psychoanalytic Situation." *Journal of American Psychoanalytic Association*, Vol. 20, No. 1 (January 1972), pp. 156-176.

Whitebrook, Oscar. "Comments on the Use of Case Records." *The Compass*, Vol. 24, No. 2 (January 1943), pp. 9-10.

Williams, Kenneth J. "Social Service Exchanges." *Social Work Year Book, 1957*. New York: National Association of Social Workers, 1957, pp. 547-553.

Williams, Kenneth I. "Social Service Exchanges." *Social Work Yearbook, 1960*, Vol. 14. New York: National Association of Social Workers, 1960, pp. 559-563.

Wilner, H. A. "Television as a Participant Recorder." *American Journal of Psychiatry*, Vol. 124 (March 1968), pp. 1157-1163.

Wilson, Suanna J. *Recording: Guidelines for Social Workers.* To be published by The Free Press, New York, 1978.

Wilson, Dolores Y. P. "Computerization of Welfare Recipients: Implications for the Individual and the Right to Privacy." *Rutgers Journal of Computers and Law*, Vol. 4, No. 1 (1974), pp. 163-208.

Youngdahl, Benjamin E. "A Civil Liberties Problem?" Letter to the Editor, *Social Work Journal*, Vol. 5, No. 4 (October 1960), pp. 109-110. Also the reply by Alan Reitman, Associate Director of the American Civil Liberties Union, pp. 109-110.

Chapter 5: Release of Information to Others

"Abortion: Parental and Spousal Consent Requirements Violate Right to Privacy in Abortion Decision." *Kansas Law Review*, Vol. 24 (Winter 1976), pp. 446-462.

Ad Hoc Committee on Ethical Standards in Psychological Research (American Psychological Association). "Ethical Principles in the Conduct of Research with Human Participants." Washington, D.C.: American Psychological Association, 1973.

Allan, R. "Silence Is Golden or Is It?" *Mental Hygiene*, Vol. 57, No. 1 (1973), pp. 21-27.

American Hospital Association. *Hospital Medical Records: Guidelines for Their Use and Release of Medical Information.* Chicago: American Hospital Association, 1972.

American National Red Cross. "The American National Red Cross Guidelines for Service to Military Families: Confidentiality. For the Use of SMF in Applying the Principle of Confidentiality in Services to People." ARC 2049, October 1974, with two attachments: (1) "Establishment, Maintenance and Disposition of Case Records," (2) "Release of Confidential Information" (form).

American Psychiatric Association. "American Psychiatric Association Position Statement on the Confidentiality of Medical Research Records." *American Journal of Psychiatry*, Vol. 130, No. 6 (June 1973), p. 739.

_____. *Confidentiality: A Report of the 1974 Conference on Confidentiality of Health Records.* Washington, D.C.: APA, 1975.

Astin, A. W., and Boruch, R. F. "A 'Link' System for Assuring Confidentiality of Research Data in Longitudinal Studies." *American Educational Research Journal*, Vol. 7, No. 4 (1970), pp. 615-624.

Barton, Walter E. "Should a National Commission for the Preservation of Confidentiality of Health Records be Established?" *Psychiatric Opinion*, Vol. 12, No. 1 (January 1975), pp. 15-17.

Baruch, R. F. "Strategies for Eliciting and Merging Confidential Social Research Data." *Policy Sciences*, Vol. 3, No. 3 (1970), pp. 275-297.

Behnke, Roy H. "The Confidentiality of the Patient Record." *Journal of Florida Medical Association*, Vol. 62, No. 2 (Fall 1975), p. 40.

Bergen, Richard P. "Keeping the Patient's Secrets," *Connecticut Medicine*, Vol. 37, No. 9 (September 1973), pp. 481–482.

Bernstein, Arthur H. "Law in Brief: Access to Physician's Hospital Records." *Hospitals*, Vol. 45 (September 1, 1971), pp. 148–152.

———. "Unauthorized Disclosure of Confidential Information." *Hospitals*, Vol. 48 (November 1, 1974), p. 126.

Breckler, I. A. "Informed Consent: A New Majority Position." *Journal of Legal Medicine*, Vol. 1 (July–August 1973), pp. 37–41.

Bruno, Frank J. "Cooperation in Social Work." *The Family*, November 1929, pp. 195–201.

Butler, R. N. "Privileged Communication and Confidentiality in Research." *Archives of General Psychiatry*, Vol. 8 (1963), p. 139.

Carroll, James D. "Confidentiality of Social Science Research Sources and Data: The Popkin Case," *Policy Sciences*, Vol. 6, No. 3 (Summer 1973), pp. 268–280.

———. "The APSA Confidentiality in Social Science Research Project: A Final Report." *Policy Sciences*, (Fall 1976), pp. 416–418.

Carroll, James D., and Knerr, Charles R. "A Report of APSA Confidentiality in Social Science Research Data Project." *Policy Sciences* (Summer 1975), pp. 258–261.

"CASE NOTES: *Roe v. Doe*: A Remedy for Disclosure of Psychiatric Confidences." *Rutgers Law Review*, Vol. 29, (Fall 1975), pp. 190–209.

"Children's Court Records—Confidential." *Application of Lascaris*. Supreme Court of New York, January 5, 1971. *The Social Welfare Court Digest*, Vol. 16, No. 7 (July 1971), p. 5.

Chodoff, Paul. "The Effect of Third Party Payment on the Practice of Psychotherapy." *American Journal of Psychiatry*, Vol. 129 (November 1972), pp. 540–545.

Clark, K. E. "Privacy and Behavioral Research." *International Journal of Psychiatry*, Vol. 5, No. 6 (1968), pp. 496–502.

"Confidentiality of Alcohol and Drug Abuse Patient Records—General Provisions." Department of Health, Education and Welfare, Public Health Service. *Federal Register*, Vol. 40, No. 127 (July 1, 1975), Part IV.

Confidentiality of Health and Social Service Records: Where Law, Ethics and Clinical Issues Meet. Proceedings of the Second Midwest Regional Conference, December, 1976. Chicago: University of Illinois at Chicago Circle, 1976.

Creighton, Helen. "Legal Implications of PSRO's." *Supervisory Nurse*, Vol. 6, No. 5 (May 1975), pp. 18–20.

Cutler, A. Budd. "Legal Problems and Health Care." Talk given at a meeting of the Florida Chapter of the Society for Hospital Social Work Directors, Orlando, Florida, November 12, 1976.

Dade-Monroe Professional Standards Review Organization Inc. "Confidentiality Policy." Miami, Florida, November 1976.

"Disclosure of Reports." *British Medical Journal*, Vol. 4 (November 3, 1973), pp. 305–306.

Errara, Paul. "Common-Sense Approaches to Confidentiality." *Hospital and Community Psychiatry* 1968, Vol. 19, No. 11 (November 1968), pp. 347-349.

Family Service Association. *The Lawyer and the Social Worker: Guides to Cooperation.* New York: Family Service Association of America, February, 1959.

Federal Privacy Act of 1974. Public Law 93-579, December 31, 1974.

Fischer, Constance T. "Consent to Release of What?" *Professional Psychology*, Summer, 1970, p. 424.

Fuller, J. S. "Confidentiality and Collusion: Ethics in the Treatment of Adolescents." Master's thesis in social work, *Smith College Studies in Social Work*, Vol. 43, No. 1 (1972).

Grossman, Maurice. "Insurance Reports as a Threat to Confidentiality." *American Journal of Psychiatry*, Vol. 128, No. 1 (1971), pp. 64-68.

Hall, J. H., and Shore, M. F. "Current Ethical Issues in Mental Health. Rockville, Maryland: National Institute of Mental Health, 1973.

"Health and Privacy: Patient Records: A Report of Current Practices with Recommendations for Changes." Commonwealth of Massachusetts, Governor's Commission on Privacy and Personal Data, adopted November 22, 1974.

Hirsh, Harold L. "Difficulties the Attorney Encounters in Procuring Medical Documents." *Forum*, Vol. 10, No. 1 (Fall 1974), pp. 361-374.

Hofmann, Adele D. "Confidentiality and the Health Care Records of Children and Youth." *Psychiatric Opinion*, Vol. 12, No. 1 (January 1975), pp. 20-28.

_____. "Consent, Confidentiality, the Law and Adolescents." *Delaware Medical Journal*, Vol. 45 (February 1973), pp. 35-39.

_____. "Is Confidentiality in Health Care Records a Pediatric Concern?" *Pediatrics*, Vol. 57, (1976), pp. 170-172.

Hollender, Marc H. "The Psychiatrist and the Release of Patient Information." *American Journal of Psychiatry*, Vol. 116 (January 1960), pp. 828-833.

Hospital Law Manual, Attorney's Volume. Germantown, Maryland: Health Law Center, Aspen Corporation, 1974. With February 1976 quarterly update.

"Invasion of Privacy—Former Criminal's Name Entitled to Protection." *Briscoe v. Reader's Digest Association, Inc.*, Supreme Court of California, 4-2-71. *Social Welfare Court Digest*, Vol. 16, No. 6 (June 1971), p. 1.

Lampos, Jeffrey J. "Third-Party Access: Blue Cross and Blue Shield Plan Practice as an Example." Chapter 2 in *Confidentiality of Health and Social Service Records: Where Law, Ethics and Clinical Issues Meet.* Proceedings of the Second Midwest Regional Conference (Chicago), December 1976. Chicago: University of Illinois at Chicago Circle, 1976, pp. 53-78.

Levine, Richard Steven. "Child Protection Records: Issues of Confidentiality." *Social Work*, Vol. 21, No. 4 (July 1976), pp. 323-324.

Lindenfield, Rita. "Letter to the Editor," *Social Service Review*, Vol. 38 (September 1974), pp. 341-342.

Mariner, Allen S. "The Problem of Therapeutic Privacy." *Psychiatry*, Vol. 30, No. 1 (1967), pp. 60-72.

Marsh, John J., and Kinnick, Bernard C. "Let's Close the Confidentiality Gap." *Personnel and Guidance Journal*, Vol. 48, No. 5 (1970), pp. 362–365.

Menninger, Walter W., and English, Joseph T. "Confidentiality and the Request for Psychiatric Information for Non-therapeutic Purposes." *American Journal of Psychiatry*, Vol. 122 (December 1965), pp. 638–645.

Miller, Arthur R. "The Assault on Privacy." *Psychiatric Opinion*, Vol. 12, No. 1 (January 1975), pp. 6–14.

"Minor's Right to an Abortion—Statutory Requirement of Spousal Consent, or Parental Consent in the Case of an Unmarried, Minor Female, Is an Unconstitutional Deprivation of a Woman's Right to Determine Whether to Undergo an Abortion." *Hofstra Law Review*, Vol. 4 (Winter 1976), pp. 531–547.

National Assembly for Social Policy and Development. "A New Look at Confidentiality in Social Welfare Services," New York: Cambridge University Press, November 27, 1973 (pamphlet).

National Association of Social Workers. "Legal Regulation of Social Work Practice." New York: NASW, 1973.

———. "Policy on Information Utilization and Confidentiality." Policy adopted at the NASW 1975 Delegate Assembly, Washington, D.C., May 30–June 3, 1975.

Nejelski, Paul, and Finsterbusch, Kurt. "The Prosecutor and the Researcher: Present and Prospective Variations on the Supreme Court's *Branzburg* Decision." *Social Service Review*, Vol. 21, No. 1 (Summer 1973), pp. 3–21.

Nelson, Scott H., and Grunebaum, Henry. "Ethical Issues in Psychiatric Follow-up Studies." *American Journal of Psychiatry*, Vol. 128, No. 11 (November 1972), pp. 1358–1362.

"N.Y. Court Rules Hospital Board Member Not Free to Examine Patient Records." *Hospitals*, Vol. 38 (August 16, 1964), p. 132.

Office of Professional Standards Review. "PSRO's and Medical Information—Safeguards to Privacy." Washington, D.C.: Department of Health, Education, and Welfare, 1974.

Paul, E. W.; Pilpel, H. F.; and Wechsler, N. F. "Pregnancy, Teenagers and the Law, 1974." *Family Planning Prospectives*, Vol. 6 (1974), p. 142.

Perlman, Helen Harris. "The Caseworker's Use of Collateral Information," *The Social Welfare Forum, 1951.* 78th Annual Meeting, Atlantic City, New Jersey, May 13–18, 1951. New York: Columbia University Press, 1951, pp. 190–205.

Principles of Confidentiality in Social Work. Washington, D.C.: Committee on Records, District of Columbia Chapter, American Association of Social Workers, 1947.

"Privacy and Behavioral Research: Preliminary Summary of the Report of the Panel on Privacy and Behavioral Research." *Science*, Vol. 155 (January–March 1967), pp. 535–538.

"Report on the Grievance of the Committee for Client's Rights Against the State Department of Social Welfare." Unpublished report of the Golden Gate Chapter of the National Association of Social Workers, San Francisco, September 1968.

Resnick, Reuben B., and Balter, Harry Graham. "Withholding Information from Law Enforcement Bodies." *Social Service Review*, Vol. 8, No. 4 (December 1934), pp. 668–677.

"Revisions and Addenda to Transmittal No. 16—Effective upon Issuance." PSRO Transmittal No. 41 Dated October 6, 1976. Rockville, Maryland: Department of Health, Education and Welfare, Public Health Service, Health Services Administration, Bureau of Quality Assurance.

Rumsey, John M. "Confidentiality: The Patient's Trust Must Be Protected." *Prism*, Vol. 2, No. 6 (June 1974), pp. 22–26.

Sadoff, Robert L. "Informed Consent, Confidentiality and Privilege in Psychiatry: Practical Applications." *Bulletin of the American Academy of Psychiatry and Law*, Vol. 11, No. 2 (June 1974), pp. 101–106.

———. "The Importance of Informed Consent." *Journal of Legal Medicine*, Vol. 1, No. 2 (May/June 1973), pp. 25–27.

Shapiro, Jeffrey G.; Krauss, Herbert H.; and Truax, Charles B. "Therapeutic Conditions and Disclosure Beyond the Therapeutic Encounter." *Journal of Counseling Psychology*, Vol. 16 (1969), pp. 29–294.

Simcox, Beatrice R. "The Social Service Exchange: Part II—Its Use in Casework." *Social Casework*, Vol. 27, No. 9 (October 1947), pp. 388–396.

Simmons, D. D. "Client Attitudes Toward Release of Confidential Information Without Consent." *Journal of Clinical Psychology*, Vol. 24, (July 1968), pp. 364–365.

Smith, A. B., and Berlin, L. "Self-Determination in Welfare and Corrections: Is There a Limit?" *Federal Probation*, Vol. 38 (December 1974), pp. 3–7.

Spalty, E. R. "Juvenile Police Record Keeping," in *Legal Rights of Children: Status, Progress and Proposals*. Fairlawn, New Jersey: Burdick, 1973, pp. 173–196.

"Specifications for Confidentiality Policy on PSRO Data and Information." PSRO Transmittal No. 16 dated February 14, 1975. Rockville, Maryland: Department of Health, Education and Welfare, Public Health Service, Health Services Administration, Bureau of Quality Assurance.

Springer, Eric W. "Professional Standards Review Organizations: Some Problems of Confidentiality." *Utah Law Review*, Vol. 1975 (Summer 1975), pp. 361–380.

"Statement of Policy on the Protection of Confidential Information on the Seeking and Releasing of Information, A." Philadelphia-Camden Social Service Exchange, Bulletin No. 38, March 1950.

Sussman, Alan. "The Confidentiality of Family Court Records." *Social Service Review* (December 1971), pp. 455–481.

Szasz, Thomas S. "The Problem of Privacy in Training Analysis." *Psychiatry*, Vol. 25, No. 1 (February 1962), pp. 195–207.

Teitelbaum, Lee. "The Use of Social Reports in Juvenile Court Adjudications." *Journal of Family Law*, Vol. 7 (1967–1968), p. 425.

Turn, Rein. "Classification of Personal Information for Privacy Protection Purposes." Santa Monica, California: Rand Publication No. P-5652, April 1976.

Ware, William H. "Legislative Issues Surrounding the Confidentiality of Health Records." Santa Monica, California: The Rand Corporation, Publication No. P-5355, January, 1975.

Weed, Lawrence L. "Confidentiality: The Public's Needs Must Be Met." *Prism*, Vol. 2, No. 6 (June 1974), pp. 22–26.

Chapter 6: Consumer Access to Record Materials

"Adult Adoptee's Constitutional Right to Know His Origins." *South California Law Review*, Vol. 48 (May 1975), pp. 1196–1220.

Alves, Joseph T. "Confidentiality and the Right to Know." *American Ecclesiastical Review*, Vol. 155, No. 5 (November 1966), p. 310.

Baran, Annette; Pannor, Reuben; and Sorosky, Arthur D. "Adoptive Parents and the Sealed Record Controversy." *Social Casework*, Vol. 55, No. 9 (November 1974), pp. 531–536.

Boyd, Robert E., and Heinsen, Richard D. "Problems in Privileged Communication." *Personnel and Guidance Journal*, Vol. 50, No. 4 (December 1971), pp. 276–279.

Brodsky, Stanley L. "Shared Results and Open Files with Clients." *Professional Psychology* (Fall 1972), pp. 363–364.

Brody, Eugene B. "The Right to Know: On the Freedom of Medical Information." *Journal of Nervous and Mental Disease*, Vol. 161, No. 2 (August 1975), pp. 73–81.

Chaiklin, Harris. "Honesty in Casework Treatment." *The Social Welfare Forum, 1973*. NCSW, Atlantic City, May 27–31, 1973. New York: Columbia University Press, 1974, pp. 266–274.

"Confidentiality of Alcohol and Drug Abuse Patient Records—General Provisions," U.S. Department of Health, Education and Welfare, Public Health Service. *Federal Register*, Vol. 40, No. 127 (July 1, 1975), Part IV.

"Discovery Rights of the Adoptee—Privacy Rights of the Natural Parent: A Constitutional Dilemma." *University of South Florida Law Review*, Vol. 4 (Spring 1975), pp. 65–83.

"Ethical Guidelines for Data Centers Handling Medical Records." Joint Task Group on Confidentiality of Computerized Medical Records, E. R. Gabriel, Chairman. Adopted by House of Delegates of the Medical Society of the State of New York, March 1975, and the Board of Directors of the Society of Computer Medicine, November 1975. It it also a position statement of the National Association of Blue Shield plans.

Fisher, Constance T. "Paradigm Changes Which Allow Sharing of Results." *Professional Psychology*, Fall, 1972, pp. 364–369.

"Federal Privacy Act: Disclosure of Medical Reports in Social Security Disability Claims." *Journal of Kansas Medical Society*, Vol. 76, No. 11 (November 1975), p. 282.

Gordon, Richard E., and Barnard, George W. "Why a Patient Should Never Get a Copy of His Psychiatric Report." *Consultant*, Vol. 14, No. 12 (December 1974), pp. 110–111.

Kaiser, Barbara L. "Patients' Rights of Access to Their Own Medical Records: The Need for New Law." *Buffalo Law Review*, Vol. 24 (Winter 1975), pp. 317–330.

Kelly, Lucie Young. "The Patient's Right to Know." *Nursing Outlook*, Vol. 24, No. 1 (January 1976), pp. 26–32.

National Association of Social Workers. "Policy on Information Utilization and Confidentiality." Policy adopted at the NASW 1975 Delegate Assembly, Washington, D.C., May 30–June 3, 1975.

Rose, Earl F. "Pathology Reports and Autopsy Protocols: Confidentiality, Privilege, and Accessibility." *American Journal of Clinical Pathology*, Vol. 57, No. 2 (February 1972), pp. 144–155.

Sorosky, Arthur D. "Adoptive Parents and the Sealed Record Controversy." *Social Casework*, Vol. 55, No. 9 (November 1974), p. 531.

Teitelbaum, Vivien Stewart, and Goslin, David A. "The Russel Sage Guidelines: Reactions from the Field." *Personnel and Guidance Journal*, Vol. 50, No. 4 (December, 1971), pp. 311–317.

Webster's New Collegiate Dictionary. Springfield, Mass.: G. & C. Merriam, 1961.

Chapters 7–9: Privileged Communication

ARTICLES—GENERAL

Arnold, Selma. "Confidential Communication and the Social Worker." *Social Work*, Vol. 15, No. 1 (January 1970), pp. 61–67.

Bangs, Arthur J. "Privilege and the Counseling Profession." *Personnel and Guidance Journal*, Vol. 50, No. 4 (December 1971), pp. 270–274.

Bell, Cynthia, and Mulniec, Wallace J. "Preparing for a Neglect Proceeding: A Guide for the Social Worker." *Juvenile Justice*, Vol. 26 (November 1975), p. 29.

Bellamy, William A. "Malpractice Risks Confronting the Psychiatrist: A Nationwide Fifteen-Year Study of Appellate Court Cases, 1946–1961." *American Journal of Psychiatry*, Vol. 118 (March 1962), pp. 769–780.

Bernstein, Arthur H. "Protecting Psychiatric Records." *Hospitals*, Vol. 47 (October 1, 1973), pp. 100–103.

_____. "Unauthorized Disclosure of Confidential Information." *Hospitals*, Vol. 48 (November 1, 1974), p. 126.

Bernstein, Barton E. "The Social Worker as a Courtroom Witness." *Social Casework*, Vol. 56, No. 9 (November 1975), pp. 521–525.

Bloom, V., and Dobie, S. I. "The Effect of Observers on the Process of Group Therapy." *International Journal of Group Psychotherapy*, Vol. 10 (1969), pp. 79–87.

Boyd, Robert E., and Heinsen, Richard D. "Problems in Privileged Communication." *Personnel and Guidance Journal*, Vol. 50, No. 4 (December 1975), pp. 20-28.

Carroll, James D., and Knerr, Charles R. "A Report of APSA Confidentiality in Social Science Research Data Project." *Policy Sciences* (Summer 1975), pp. 258-261.

————. "The APSA Confidentiality in Social Science Research Project: A Final Report." *Policy Sciences* (Fall 1976), pp. 416-418.

"Confidential and Privileged Communications: Guidelines for Lawyers and Social Workers," in *Law and Social Work: Statements Prepared by the National Conference of Lawyers and Social Workers*. Washington, D.C.: National Association of Social Workers, 1973.

"Court Says MD's Must Warn Possible Victims of Patients: California." *Hospitals*, Vol. 49 (February 1, 1975), p. 176.

"Court Upholds Confidentiality of Social Work Communications." *Hospitals*, Vol. 48 (February 16, 1974), p. 116.

Creighton, Helen. "Legal Implications of PSRO's." *Supervisory Nurse*, Vol. 6, No. 5 (May 1975), pp. 18-20.

Curran, William J. "Law-Medicine Notes—Confidentiality and the Prediction of Dangerousness in Psychiatry." *New England Journal of Medicine*, Vol. 293, No. 6 (August 7, 1975), pp. 185-186.

Diamond, B. L., and Weihofen, H. "Privileged Communication and the Clinical Psychologist." *Journal of Clinical Psychology*, Vol. 9 (1953), pp. 388-390.

"Doctor Loses Libel Action." *British Medical Journal*, Vol. 3 (July 21, 1973), pp. 181-182.

Dubey, Joseph. "Confidentiality as a Requirement of the Therapist: Technical Necessities for Absolute Privilege in Psychotherapy." *American Journal of Psychiatry*, Vol. 131, No. 10 (October 1974), pp. 1093-1096.

Feldman, M. J. "Privacy and Conjoint Family Therapy." *Family Process*, Vol. 6, No. 1 (January 1967), pp. 1-9.

Foster, L. M. "Privileged Communication: When the Psychiatrists Envy the Clergy." *Journal of Pastoral Care*, Vol. 33 (1976), pp. 116-121.

Foster, Leila M. "Confidentiality of Group and Family Psychotherapy Records." Chapter 6 in *Confidentiality of Health and Social Service Records: Where Law, Ethics and Clinical Issues Meet*. Chicago: University of Illinois at Chicago Circle, December 1976, pp. 121-143.

————. "Group Psychotherapy: A Pool of Legal Witnesses?" *International Journal of Group Psychotherapy*, Vol. 25, No. 1 (January 1975), pp. 50-53.

Geiser, Robert L., and Rheingold, Paul D. "Psychology and the Legal Process: Testimonial Privileged Communications." *American Psychologist*, Vol. 10, No. 11 (November 1964), pp. 831-837.

Ginsberg, Frances, and Clarke, Barbara. "Patients Need Privacy—and May Due if They Don't Get It," *Modern Hospital*, Vol. 118, No. 6 (June 1972), p. 110.

Hofmann, Adele D. "Confidentiality of the Health Records of Children and Youth." *Psychiatric Opinion*, Vol. 12, No. 1 (January 1975), pp. 20-28.

Holder, Angela Roddey. "How Much Would You Tell a Lawyer?" *Prism*, Vol. 2, No. 6 (November 1974), pp. 52–55.

Holmes, George W. Letter to the Editor. *Social Service Review*, Vol. 38 (June 1964), p. 221.

Hoover, Edgar J. "Let's Keep America Healthy." *American Medical Association Journal*, Vol. 144 (1950), p. 1094.

Huffman, Arthur V. "Confidentiality of Doctor-Patient Relationship in Relation to Court-Ordered Psychotherapy." *Corrective Psychology and Journal of Social Therapy*, Vol. 18 (1972), p. 3.

"Invasion of Privacy—Former Criminal's Name Entitled to Protection." *Briscoe v. Reader's Digest Association Inc.*, Supreme Court of California, April 2, 1971. Reported in the *Social Welfare Court Digest*, Vol. 16, No. 6 (June 1971), p. 1.

Kohler, Max J. "Privileged Confidential Character of Information Imparted to Social Workers." *Jewish Social Service Quarterly*, Vol. 10, No. 4 (June 1934), pp. 253–257.

Lewis, Melvin. "Confidentiality in the Community Mental Health Center." *American Journal of Orthopsychiatry*, Vol. 38, No. 5 (October 1967), pp. 946–955.

MacCormick, Austin. "A Criminologist Looks at Privilege." *American Journal of Psychiatry*, Vol. 115 (June 1959), pp. 1068–1070.

MacDonald, Jonathan B. "Confidentiality of Patient Information: A New Basis of Physician Liability?" *Journal of Medical Association of Georgia*, Vol. 63 (December 1974), pp. 480–482.

Mariner, Allen S. "Psychotherapists' Communications with Patients' Relatives and Referring Professions." *American Journal of Psychotherapy*, Vol. 25, No. 4 (October 1971), pp. 517–529.

Markowitz, Irving. "Confidentiality in Group Therapy." *Mental Hygiene*, Vol. 51, No. 4 (1967), pp. 601–613.

McCaffrey, Sister Mary P. "The Implications of Confidentiality in the Doctor-Patient Relationship." *Hospital Progress*, Vol. 54 (December 1973), pp. 62–63.

McGarry, Louis A., and Kaplan, Honora A. "Overview: Current Trends in Mental Health Law." *American Journal of Psychiatry*, Vol. 130, No. 6 (June 1973), pp. 621–630.

Morrison, J.; Frederic, M.; and Rosenthal, H. J. "Controlling Confidentiality in Group Psychotherapy." *Forensic Psychology*, Vol. 7 (1975), pp. 4–5.

Mykel, Nan. "The Application of Ethical Standards to Group Psychotherapy in a Community." *International Journal of Group Psychotherapy*, Vol. 21 (1971), p. 248.

Nejelski, Paul, and Finsterbusch, Kurt. "The Prosecutor and the Researcher: Present and Prospective Variations on the Supreme Court's *Branzburg* Decision." *Social Service Review*, Vol. 21, No. 1 (Summer 1973), pp. 3–21.

"News of the Societies: National Federation of Societies for Clinical Social Work: Ethical Standards of Clinical Social Workers." *Clinical Social Work Journal*, Vol. 2, No. 4 (Winter 1974), pp. 312–315.

Nye, Sandra G. "Model Law on Confidentiality of Health and Social Service Information." Appendix B in *Confidentiality of Health and Social Service Records: Where Law, Ethics and Clinical Issues Meet.* Chicago: University of Illinois at Chicago Circle, December 1976, pp. 260-282.

———. "Privilege." Chapter 3 in *Confidentiality of Health and Social Service Records: Where Law, Ethics and Clinical Issues Meet.* Chicago: University of Illinois at Chicago Circle, December 1976, pp. 80-99.

Plank, Robert. "Our Underprivileged Communications." *Social Casework,* Vol. 46, No. 7 (July 1965), pp. 430-434.

Plaut, Eric A. "A Perspective on Confidentiality." *American Journal of Psychiatry,* Vol. 131, No. 9 (September 1974), pp. 1021-1024.

"Position Statement on Guidelines for Psychiatrists: Problems in Confidentiality." *American Journal of Psychiatry,* Vol. 126 (April 1970), pp. 1543-1549.

"Principles of Medical Ethics with Annotations Especially Applicable to Psychiatry, The." *American Journal of Psychiatry,* Vol. 130, (September 1973), pp. 1058-1064.

Rappaport, R. G. "Group Therapy in Prison." *International Journal of Group Psychotherapy,* Vol. 21 (1974), pp. 489-496.

"Review of Medical Professional Liability Claims and Suits." *Journal of the American Medical Association,* Vol. 167, No. 2 (May 10, 1958), pp. 227-229.

Reynolds, Mildred M. "Threats to Confidentiality." *Social Work,* Vol. 21, No. 2 (March 1976), pp. 108-113.

Rose, Earl F. "Pathology Reports and Autopsy Protocols: Confidentiality, Privilege and Accessibility." *American Journal of Clinical Pathology,* Vol. 57, No. 2 (February 1972), pp. 144-155.

Rosenheim, Margaret Keeney. "Privileged Communication for Psychiatrists." *Social Service Review,* Vol. 27, No. 1 (March 1953), pp. 100-102.

Rubin, Bernard. "Prediction of Dangerousness in Mentally Ill Criminals." *Archives General Psychiatry,* Vol. 27 (1972), p. 397.

———. "Psychiatry and the Law." Chapter 44 in *American Handbook of Psychiatry,* 2nd ed., Volume V: *Treatment.* Daniel X. Freedman and Jarl E. Dyrud, eds. New York: Basic Books, 1975, pp. 853-898.

Rumsey, John M. "Confidentiality: The Patient's Trust Must Be Protected." *Prism,* Vol. 2, No. 6 (June 1974), pp. 22-26.

Shah, Saleem B. "Privileged Communications, Confidentiality and Privacy." *Professional Psychology,* 1970. Part I: "Privileged Communication"—Vol. 1, No. 1, pp. 56-69; Part II: "Confidentiality"—Vol. 1, No. 2, pp. 159-164; Part III: "Privacy"—Vol. 1, No. 3, pp. 342-352.

Simonaitis, Joseph E. "Documents Filed in Lawsuits are Privileged Communication." *Journal of the American Medical Association,* Vol. 228, No. 10 (June 3, 1974), p. 1332.

Siporin, Max. "Letter to the Editor." *Social Service Review,* Vol. 32 (March 1958), pp. 72-73.

Slawson, P. F. "Patient-Litigant Exception: A Hazard to Psychotherapy." *Archives General Psychiatry,* Vol. 21, No. 3 (1969), pp. 347-352.

Slovenko, Ralph. "Group Therapy: Privileged Communication and Confidentiality." Paper presented at the Annual Meeting of the American Group Psychotherapy Association, San Francisco, February 3, 1977.

_____. "Interview of Group on Confidentiality." Unpublished transcript obtained from the author, dated January 5, 1977.

_____, and Usdin, Gene L. "Privileged Communication and Right of Privacy in Diagnosis and Therapy." *Current Psychiatric Therapies*, Vol. 3. New York: Grune and Stratton, 1963, pp. 277–319.

Smith, Delafield A. "Privileged Communications: The Confidentiality of the Agency-Client Relationship." Washington, D.C., Chapter of the American Association of Social Workers, 1943.

_____. "Reintegrating our Concepts of Privileged Communication." *Social Service Review*, Vol. 16, No. 2 (June 1942), pp. 191–211.

Stern, Henry Root. "The Problem of Privilege: Historical and Juridicial Sidelights." *American Journal of Psychiatry*, Vol. 115, No. 12 (1959), pp. 1071–1080.

Ware, Martha L. "The Law and Counselor Ethics." *Personnel and Guidance Journal*, Vol. 50, No. 4 (December 1971), pp. 305–310.

Weinberger, Paul, and Weinberger, Dorothy. "Legal Regulation in Perspective." *Social Work*, Vol. 7, No. 1 (January 1962), pp. 67–75.

"When Does Confidentiality End?" Notes and Comments in *Social Service Review*, Vol. 38 (March 1964), pp. 74–75.

ARTICLES—LEGAL PERIODICALS*

Ayres, R. J., Jr., and Holbrook, J. T. "Law, Psychotherapy and the Duty to Warn: A Tragic Trilogy?" *Baylor Law Review*, Vol. 27 (Fall 1975), pp. 677–705.

Braman, Robert Jay. "NOTE: Group Therapy and Privileged Communication." *Indiana Law Journal*, Vol. 43 (Fall 1967), pp. 93–105.

Cassidy, Patrick Sean. "Liability of Psychiatrist for Malpractice." *University of Pittsburgh Law Review*, Vol. 36 (Fall 1974), pp. 108–137.

"CF NOTE: Confidential Relationships: Does the Law Require Silence Outside the Courtroom?" *Utah Law Review*, Vol. 6, No. 3 (Spring 1959), pp. 380–390.

Coburn, D. R. "Child-Parent Communications: Spare the Privilege and Spoil the Child." *Dickinson Law Review*, Vol. 74 (Summer 1970), p. 590.

"Confidential Communications to a Psychotherapist: A New Treatment Privilege." *Northwestern University Law Review*, Vol. 47 (1952), pp. 384–389.

Cross, W. "Privileged Communication Between Participants in Group Psychotherapy." *Law and Social Order, 1970*, Vol. 1970, pp. 191–211.

Davis, Danny G. "EVIDENCE: Privileged Communication—A Psychiatrist Has a Constitutional Right to Assert an Absolute Privilege Against Disclosure of Psy-

*References are given in the usual social sciences format rather than the format normally used for legal references. This should make the references more comprehensible to the average reader. All journals cited can be obtained through a law library.

chotherapeutic Communications." *Texas Law Review*, Vol. 49, (May 1971), pp. 929–942.

"Devil's Advocate, The." *Bulletin of the American Academy of Psychiatry and Law*, Vol. II, No. 4 (December 1974), pp. 271–273.

Diamond, Bernard L. "Psychiatric Prediction of Dangerousness." *University of Pennsylvania Law Review*, Vol. 123 (December 1974), pp. 439–452.

"EVIDENCE: Privileged Communication Between Husband and Wife." *Tennessee Law Review*, Vol. 41 (Summer 1974), pp. 943–949.

"EVIDENCE: Privileged Communication in Divorce Actions: Psychiatrist-Patient and Presence of Third Parties." *Tennessee Law Review*, Vol. 40 (Fall 1972), pp. 110–118.

Ferster, E. Z. "Statutory Summary of Physician-Patient Privileged Communication Laws," in *Readings in Law and Psychiatry*, R. C. Allen and E. Z. Ferster, eds. Baltimore: Johns Hopkins, 1975.

Fisher, Robert M. "The Psychotherapeutic Professions and the Law of Privileged Communication." *Wayne Law Review*, Vol. 10 (1963–1964), pp. 609–654.

Fleming, John, and Maximov, Bruce. "Patient or His Victim: The Therapist's Dilemma." *California Law Review*, Vol. 62 (May 1974), pp. 1025–1068.

Glassman, Michael. "Recent Cases—Privileged Communication—Psychiatry: Psychotherapist Has a Duty to Warn an Endangered Victim Whose Peril Was Disclosed by Communications between the Psychotherapist and Patient." *University of Cincinnati Law Review*, Vol. 44 (1975), pp. 368–375.

Goldstein, Abraham, and Katz, Jay. "Psychiatrist-Patient Privilege: The GAP Proposal and the Connecticut Statute." *Connecticut Bar Journal*, Vol. 36 (1962), pp. 175–189.

Grossman, Maurice. "The Psychiatrist and the Subpoena." *Bulletin of the American Academy of Psychiatry and Law*, Vol. 1, No. 4 (December 1973), pp. 245–253.

"Group Therapy and Privileged Communication." *Indiana Law Journal*, Vol. 43 (1967), pp. 93–105.

Joling, Robert J. "Informed Consent, Confidentiality and Privilege in Psychiatry: Legal Implications." *Bulletin of American Academy of Psychiatry and Law*, Vol. 11, No. 2 (June 1964), pp. 107ff.

Kennedy, Craig. "Psychotherapist's Privilege." *Washburn Law Journal*, Vol. 12 (Spring 1973), pp. 297–316.

Latham, Joseph L., Jr. "TORTS: Duty to Act for the Protection of Another—Liability of Psychotherapists for Failure to Warn of Homicide Threatened by Patient." *Vanderbilt Law Review*, Vol. 28 (April 1975), pp. 631–640.

"Legal Response to Child Abuse, The." *William and Mary Law Review*, Vol. 11, (1970), p. 960.

Logatto, Rev. Anthony F. "Privileged Communication and the Social Worker." *Catholic Lawyer*, Vol. 8, No. 5 (Winter 1962), pp. 5–19.

Louisell, David W., and Sinclair, Kent, Jr. "The Supreme Court of California 1969–70; Forward—Reflections on the Law of Privileged Communication—The Psychotherapist-Patient Privilege in Perspective." *California Law Review*, Vol. 59 (1971), pp. 30–55.

Love, George H., Jr., and Yanity, Gerald J. "Psychotherapy and the Law." *Medical Trial Quarterly* (Spring 1974), pp. 405–429.

Meldman, J. A. "Centralized Information Systems and the Legal Right to Privacy." *Marquette Law Review*, Vol. 52 (1969), p. 343.

Mironi, Mordechai. "Confidentiality of Personnel Records: A Legal and Ethical View." *Labor Law Journal*, Vol. 25, (May 1974), pp. 270–292.

Nejelski, Paul, and Lerman, L. M. "A Researcher-Subject Testimonial Privilege: What to Do Before the Subpoena Arrives." *Wisconsin Law Review* (1971), p. 1085.

"NOTE: The Social Worker-Client Relationship and Privileged Communications." *Washington University Law Quarterly*, Vol. 1965 (1965), pp. 362–395.

"NOTES: Group Therapy and Privileged Communication." *Indiana Law Journal*, Vol. 43 (Fall 1967), pp. 93–105.

"NOTES AND COMMENTS: Functional Overlap between the Lawyer and Other Professionals: Its Implications for the Privileged Communication Doctrine." *Yale Law Journal*, Vol. 71 (May 1962), pp. 1226–1273.

Paulsen, M. G. "Child Abuse Reporting Laws: The Shape of the Legislation." *Columbia Law Review*, Vol. 67 (1967), p. 223.

Perr, Irwin N. "Current Trends in Confidentiality and Privileged Communications," *Journal of Legal Medicine*, Vol. 1, No. 5 (November–December 1973), pp. 44–47.

Perr, I. "Problems of Confidentiality and Privileged Communications in Psychiatry," in *Legal Medicine Annual*, C. H. Wecht, ed. New York: Appleton-Century-Crofts, 1971.

"Privileged Communications: A Case by Case Approach." *Maine Law Review*, Vol. 23 (1971), pp. 443–462.

"Psychiatrist Has No Constitutional Right to Assert an Absolute Privilege Against Disclosure of Psychotherapeutic Communications." *Texas Law Review*, Vol. 49 (1971), p. 929.

"Psychiatrist-Patient Privilege: A Need for the Retention of the Future Crime Exception." *Iowa Law Review*, Vol. 52, No. 6 (June 1967), pp. 1170–1186.

Rappeport, Jonas R. "Psychiatrist as an Amicus Curiae," Parts I and II. *Medical Trial Technique Quarterly*, 1972 Annual, pp. 183–189, 297–313.

"*Roe v. Doe*: A Remedy for Disclosure of Psychiatric Confidences." *Rutgers Law Review*, Vol. 29 (Fall 1975), p. 195.

Slovenko, Ralph. "Psychiatrist-Patient Testimonial Privilege: A Picture of Misguided Hope." *Catholic University Law Review*, Vol. 23 (1974), pp. 649– 673.

_____. "Psychiatry and a Second Look at Medical Privilege." *Wayne Law Review*, Vol. 6, No. 2 (Spring 1960), pp. 175–207.

_____. "Psychotherapy and Confidentiality." *Cleveland State Law Review*, Vol. 24 (1975), pp. 375–396.

"Suggested Privilege for Confidential Communications with Marriage Counselors, A." *University of Pennsylvania Law Review*, Vol. 106, No. 2 (December 1957), pp. 266–278.

"Tarasoff and the Psychotherapist's Duty to Warn." *San Diego Law Review*, Vol. 12 (July 1975), pp. 32–51.

"Tarasoff v. Regents of the University of California: Psychotherapist, Policeman and the Duty to Warn—An Unreasonable Common Law?" *Golden Gate University Law Review*, Vol. 6 (Fall 1975), pp. 229–248.

"Tarasoff v. Regents of University of California: The Psychotherapist's Peril." *University of Pittsburgh Law Review*, Vol. 37 (Fall 1975), pp. 155–168.

"TORT LAW: Psychotherapist-Patient Privilege, Patient's Dangerous Condition, Confidentiality, Legal Duty to Warn Potential Victim." *Akron Law Review*, Vol. 9 (Summer 1975), pp. 191–198.

"TORTS: *Tarasoff v. Regents of the University of California*—The Dangerous Psychiatric Patient—the Doctor's Duty to Warn." *Land and Water Law Review*, Vol. 10 (1975), pp. 593–606.

"Underprivileged Communications: Extension of the Psychotherapist-Patient Privilege to Patients of Psychiatric Social Workers." *California Law Review*, Vol. 61 (June 1973), pp. 1050–1071.

BOOKS

Alves, Joseph. *Confidentiality in Social Work*. Washington, D.C.: Catholic University of America Press, 1959. Doctoral dissertation available through University Microfilms, Ann Arbor, Michigan.

American Psychiatric Association. *Confidentiality: A Report of the 1974 Conference on Confidentiality of Health Records*. Washington, D.C.: APA, 1975.

_____. *Confidentiality and Third Parties*, Task Force Report 9. Washington, D.C.: APA, June 1975.

Army Social Work. TM 8-241, Department of the Army Technical Manual, Headquarters, Department of the Army, January 1958.

Confidentiality in Social Services to Individuals. New York: National Social Welfare Assembly, April 1958.

Dewitt, Clinton. *Privileged Communications Between Physician and Patient*. Springfield, Ill.: Thomas, 1958.

Group for the Advancement of Psychiatry. *Confidentiality and Privileged Communication in the Practice of Psychiatry*. Report No. 45. New York: GAP, June 1960.

Richmond, Mary. *What is Social Casework?* New York: Russell Sage Foundation, 1922.

Slovenko, Ralph. *Psychiatry and Law*. Boston: Little, Brown, 1973.

_____., and Usdin, Gene L. *Psychotherapy, Confidentiality and Privileged Communication*. Springfield, Ill.: Charles C. Thomas, 1966.

Wigmore, John H. *Evidence in Trials at Common Law*, Vol. 8 (revised by J. T. McNaughton). Boston: Little, Brown, 1961.

CASES

A. B. v. C. D. 7F (Scott) 72 (1905).

Berry v. Moench 8 Utah 2d 191, 331 p.2d 814 (1958).

Bogust v. Iverson, 10 Wisconsin 2d 129 N.W.2d 228 (1960).

Carr v. Watkins, 227 Me. 578 177 A.2d 841 (1962).

Clarke v. Geraci, 208 N.Y.S.2d 564 (Supreme Court 1960).

Ellis v. Ellis, 472 S.W.2d 741 (Tennessee Appeals Court 1971).

Felber v. Foote, 321 F. Supp. 85 (D. C. Conn. 1970).

Furness v. Fitchett (*New Zealand Law Review* 396, 1958).

Griffin v. Medical Society of N. Y. 11 NYS 2d 109 (1939).

Hall v. Alameda, 20 Cal. App. 3d 362 (1971).

Hammonds v. Aetna Casualty and Surety Co., 243 F. Supp. 793 (D.C. Ohio, 1965).

Horne v. Patton, 287 So. 2d 824 (Alabama 1973).

Humphrey v. Norden, 359 N.Y.S. 2d 733 (Sup. Court 1974).

In re: Cathey, 55 Ca. 2d 679, 361 p.2d 426 (1961).

In the Matter of the City of N. Y. (Sup. Court Bronx County) 91 N.Y.L., February 1, 1934, p. 529, Col. 7 (reversing Perlman).

Iverson v. Frandsen, 237 F2d 898 (Utah Court of Appeals 1956).

Leyra v. Denno, 347 U.S. 556 (1954).

Oaks v. Colorado 371 p.2d 443 (Colorado 1962).

People v. Fenerstein (1936) 293 N.Y. Supp. 239.

People v. Quinn 61 Cal. 2d 551, 39 Cal. Rptr. 393, 393 p.2d 705 (1964).

Perlman v. Perlman, Index No. 5105, N.Y. Supreme Court, Bronx County, June 30, 1939.

Queen v. OrtMeyer, N.Y. (Supr. Court, 1962).

Re: Kryschuk & Zulynik, 14 D.L.R. 2d 676 (Sask., Canada Magis. Court 1958).

Re: Lifschutz, 2 Calif. 3d 415 (1970).

Rhodes v. Metropolitan Life Ins. Co., 172 F.2d 182 (5th Cir. 1949).

Roberts v. Superior Court of Butte County, 9 C.3d 330 (Calif. Supr. Court, April 11, 1973).

Simrim v. Simrim, 43 Cal. Rptr, 376 (Dist. Court App. 1965).

State v. Driscoll 193 N.W.2d 851 (Wisconsin 1972).

Tarasoff v. Regents of the University of Calif., 13 Ca. 3d 177 (1974).

U.S. v. Kansas City Lutheran Home Association, 297 F. Supp. 239 (D.D. Mo. 1969).

Yoder v. Smith, 112 N.W. 2d 862 (Iowa 1962).

MISCELLANEOUS

American Bar Association. "Canon Four: A Lawyer Shall Preserve the Confidences and Secrets of a Client." *Code of Professional Ethics*. Chicago: American Bar Association, 1975, pp. 21c–23c

Barneis, Ruth S., and Wilson, Suanna J. "A Study of Social Attitudes Towards Epilepsy." Unpublished master's thesis, Syracuse University School of Social Work, June 1968.

"Confidentiality in Social Work." *NASW News*, Vol. 19, No. 3 (March 1974), p. 9.

Fearqueron, Margaret Elizabeth. "A Study of Selected Aspects of Privileged Communication as Related to School Counselors, with Particular Reference to Florida." Unpublished doctoral dissertation, Florida State University, Tallahassee, December 1973.

"Indecent Liberties with His Wife's Daughter—Conviction Affirmed: *State v. Driscoll*, 193 N.W. 2d 851 (Wisconsin), Supreme Court of Wisconsin, in February 3, 1972." *Sex Problems Court Digest*, Vol. 3, No. 5 (1972), p. 5.

National Association of Social Workers. "Memorandum—Summary of NASW Chapter Activity on State Regulation of Social Work." April 1976. Washington, D.C.: NASW.

_____. "Model Licensing Act for Social Workers." Washington, D.C.: NASW, 1973.

_____. "State Comparison of Laws Regulating Social Work." July 1976. Washington, D.C.: NASW, 1973.

Schroeter, Gerd. "An Exploratory Analysis of Privileged Communication." Unpublished master's thesis in sociology, Vanderbilt University, January 1966.

_____. "Protection of Confidentiality in the Courts: The Professions." *Social Problems*, Vol. 16 (Winter 1969), pp. 376–385.

U.S. Department of Health, Education and Welfare, News Release, *HEW News*, August 8, 1974.

Chapter 10: Confidentiality Problems Faced by Supervisors and Administrators

Miller, Pauline. "The Confidential Relationship in Social Work Administration." *Proceedings, National Conference of Social Work*. New York: Columbia University Press, 1942, pp. 574–583.

National Association of Social Workers. *Manual for Adjudication of Grievances*. Washington, D.C.: NASW, 1973.

_____. "Standards for Social Service Manpower: Professional Standards," NASW Policy Statement 4. Washington, D.C.: NASW, 1973.

_____. *NASW Standards for Social Work Personnel Practices*. New York: NASW, 1958.

_____. *NASW Standards for Social Work Personnel Practices*. Washington, D.C.: NASW, 1975.

Chapter 11: Confidentiality of Personnel Records

American Psychiatric Association. *Confidentiality and Third Parties*. Task Force Report 9. Washington, D.C.: APA, June 1975.

"Federal Genesis of Comprehensive Protection of Student Educational Record Rights: The Family Educational Rights and Privacy Act of 1974." *Iowa Law Review*, Vol. 61, No. 1 (October 1975), pp. 74–133.

Hermann, Donald H. J., III. "Privacy, the Prospective Employee, and Employment Testing: The Need to Restrict Polygraph and Personality Testing." *Washington Law Review*, Vol. 47 (October 1971), pp. 73–154.

"IBM's Guidelines to Employee Privacy: An Interview with Frank T. Cary." *Harvard Business Review* (September 10, 1976), pp. 82–90.

"IBM—The Managing of Employee Personal Information and Employee Privacy." Oral statement of Walton E. Burdict, Vice President, Personnel Plans and Programs, IBM Corp. Presented before the Privacy Protection Study Commission Hearings on Employment and Personnel Record-Keeping Practices, December 10, 1976.

Madsen, Rex E. *"EEOC v. University of New Mexico*—Tenth Circuit Reduces Standards for Production of Employee Personnel Files in EEOC Investigation." *Utah Law Review* (Spring 1975), pp. 264–278.

Mattessich, Carole Marie. "Buckley Amendment: Opening School Files for Student and Parental Review." *Catholic University Law Review*, Vol. 24 (Spring 1975), pp. 588–603.

Miner, Mary G. "Pay Policies: Secret or Open? and Why?" *Personnel Journal*, Vol. 53, No. 2 (February 1974), pp. 110–115.

Mironi, Mordechai. "Confidentiality of Personnel Records: A Legal and Ethical View." *Labor Law Journal*, Vol. 25, (May 1974), pp. 270–292.

"Privacy of Information in Florida Public Employee Personnel Files." *University of Florida Law Review*, Vol. 27, No. 2 (Winter 1975), pp. 481–501.

Wangler, Lawrence A. "The Employee Reference Request: A Road to Misdemeanor?" *Personnel Administrator*, Vol. 18, No. 6 (November 12, 1973), pp. 45–47.

Wright, Robert R. "Current Confidentiality Policy Provisions for Personnel Records." *College and University Personnel Association Journal*, Vol. 24, No. 2 (March 1973), pp. 60–66.

Yoder, Dale. *Personnel Management in Industrial Relations*, 6th ed. Englewood Cliffs, N.J.: Prentice-Hall, 1970.

Index

Absence of records, 47–54
Absolute confidentiality, 3, 192
ACSW examination, x
Administrative confidentiality problems, 155–171; *see also* References; Personnel records

Blanket consent forms, 58–60
Buckley Amendment: *see* the Family Educational Rights and Privacy Act

Case record: *see* Records
Client: *see* Consumer
Complaints regarding colleagues, 197–198
Computerized data, 42–47
  bibliographies of readings, 238
  extent of use, 27, 42–43, 72
  legal challenges to maintaining, 43–44
  privacy violations associated with, 42–47
  requirements for preserving confidentiality of, 45–47
Confidential information
  discussing with friends and relatives, 9–10
  gathering of under Privacy Act, 20–21, 23, 26
  handling the need to talk about, 15–16
  shared within agency, 11, 67, 68, 131–132, 180–181, 199

social worker's ability to handle responsibly, 28, 151–153, 202–203
Confidentiality: *see also* Confidential information
  absolute, 3, 192
  of case records: *see* Records
  in client lawsuits, 195–196
  common types of violations, 9–14
  of computerized data: *see* Computerized data
  dealing with violators of, 14–15
  definition of, 1–2
  of employee references: *see* References
  in employee/student grievances, 167–170
  of internal agency affairs, 6, 79
  issues facing supervisors and administrators, 155–171
  leaks in an agency, 166–167
  as part of casework contract, 191–192
  in personnel lawsuits, 170–171
  of personnel records: *see* Personnel records
  persons bound by, 6–7
  problems when client swears social worker to secrecy, 192–193
  relative, 3–4
  requirements for social work students, 5, 7, 35–36
  of tape and video recordings: *see* Tape recordings; Video recordings

of various kinds of information, 4-6
violations by supervisors, 199-200
Consent for release of information: *see*
"Informed consent"; Release of
information
Consumer access to case records; *see
also* Personnel records
arguments against, 86-93
arguments favoring, 93-96
concerning adoptions, 85
under Federal Privacy Act of 1974,
19-20, 24, 84, 89
as fraud deterrent, 28
reactions to record material, 27,
87-89
readings, 256-257
recommendations, 95-96
recommendations before Privacy
Protection Study Commission
hearings, 26-28
as requirement for "informed consent," 63
Criminal acts, confidentiality issues involved in, 115-121, 207-213,
230

Dangerousness, prediction of,
119-120, 207-213
Destruction of records, 35
Disclosure: *see* Release of information
Dual records, 49-52
Duty to warn: *see* Privileged com-
munication

Employee confidentiality rights, 164-
166, 193-195; *see also* Personnel records; Confidentiality,
issues affecting supervisors and
administrators
Exceptions to privileged communication statutes: *see* Privileged
communication

Family Educational Rights and Privacy Act (the Buckley Amendment), 110, 159-160
Federal Privacy Act of 1974
impact on personnel record-keeping,
176

implications for social work, x,
17-18
paperwork generated by, 28-29
proposed revisions, 23-25
provisions of, 3, 17-23, 33, 76
related regulations, 18*n*, 242-244
Federal Privacy Protection Study
Commission
draft recommendations of, 23-25
responsibilities of, 22-23
testimony given in hearings, 25-29,
30*n*, 244-246

Guardianship, as related to confidentiality issues, 64, 65
Grievances, 167-170
confidentiality of material in, 168
and legal action, 169-170
Group therapy: *see* Privileged communication

"Informed consent"
as applied to personnel records, 181
conditions necessary for, 57
and the "Consent for Release of Information Form," 57-64, 237
definition, 56
withdrawal of, 63
Insurance reports, 71-72, 182-183

Lawsuits involving confidentiality
issues; *see also* corresponding
footnotes on each page listed
against social workers for violating
confidentiality, 144-145
alcoholic airplane pilot, 124
blanket consent form found invalid,
142*n*
cases, list of, 264-265
client introduces privileged information into litigation, 113
client pressured to disclose information to counselor, 140
client waiver of privilege, 112-113
regarding computerized data, 43-44
from consumers upon seeing record
materials, 98-91
court did not need social worker's
information, 138*n*

court's need for disclosure of confidential information is greater than injury to professional relationship, 114-115

court's need for disclosure of confidential information is *not* greater than injury to professional relationship, 99, 113-115, 137-138*n*

did social worker promise confidentiality to the client?, 114

duty to warn, 116-121

over employee reference material, 157-158

federal law overturns state privileged communication statute, 128

following a grievance, 169-170

forced disclosure of drug users, 123-124

and group therapists, 133-134

over improper release of information, 60-61, 144

inappropriate hallway discussion upsets patient, 145

maintaining confidentiality in, 195-196

malpractice, 115, 143-144, 170-171, 195-196

in personnel matters, 170-171

suicide of client, 121-122

Licensing of social workers, 220-230

Litigation: *see* Lawsuits

Malpractice: *see* Lawsuits

MIB (Medical Information Bureau), 72

Minors

child abuse/neglect, 123, 230

special confidentiality considerations for, 122-123, 130-131, 230

Model statutes, 50-51, 65*n*, 109, 135-136, 140-141

MSIS (Multi-State Information System), 45

NASW confidentiality guidelines

for client access to records, 85

Code of Ethics, 4-5, 231-232

regarding computerized data, 43, 46-47, 217

regarding confidentiality in grievances, 168-169

critique of, xii, 33, 47, 55, 177, 202

regarding employee access to personnel files, 183

Guidelines for Lawyers and Social Workers, 233-235

Model Licensing Act for Social Workers, A, 220-230

for obtaining consents for release of information, 60, 65-66, 218

regarding personnel records, 176-178

concerning privileged communication, 115, 118, 126, 230

regarding references, 158-159

One-way mirror, ethical issues in use of, 41

Periodicals containing confidentiality articles, 239

Personnel policies regarding confidentiality under Federal Privacy Act, 21

Personnel records, 172-187

employee access to, 183-187

guidelines for maintaining confidentiality of, 178-180

information contained in, 172-175

and privileged communication, 181

protecting confidentiality of, 176-180

release of information from, 180-182

outside the agency, 181-182

within the agency, 180-181

Physically safeguarding records, 33

Privacy Act of 1974: *see* Federal Privacy Act of 1974

Privacy Protection Study Commission: *see* Federal Privacy Protection Study Commission

Privileged communication, 97-154

conditions a profession must meet to obtain it, 99-100

confidentiality contract, 134-135

death of the client's effect upon, 125-127

definition of, 2, 97–100, 233–234
and discrimination against the poor,
    150
effectiveness of, 153–154
exceptions to state statutes, 111–142
    affiliation with other disciplines
        not covered by privileged com-
        munication, 131–132
    bill collecting by therapist,
        127–128
    child abuse, 123, 230
    client introduces privileged
        material into litigation, 113
    client sues counselor, 115, 130
    client threatens or commits crimi-
        nal act, 115–121, 207–213, 230
    client threatens to harm therapist,
        122
    client waiver of privilege,
        111–113, 230
    client's condition makes his em-
        ployment hazardous to others,
        124, 193–195
    commitment, 125
    communication does not meet
        Wigmore's criteria, 113–115,
        147–150
    counselor moves to another state,
        129
    court-ordered examination,
        124–125
    disclosure needed to save client's
        life, 130
    drug usage, 123–124
    fact client is seeing counselor is
        not privileged, 129–130
    federal government requires
        disclosure, 128–129
    information is learned outside
        professional treatment relation-
        ship, 128
    information shared in presence of
        third person, 128, 133–137
    life/accident insurance claims, 133
    medical conditions must be
        reported, 122
    military setting, 132

    minor involved in criminal activ-
        ity, 122–123, 230
    pre-sentence investigation reports,
        131
    protection of a minor, 130–131,
        230
    suicidal client, 121–122
    treasonous activities of client, 131
and federal privacy legislation, 28
and group therapy, 133–137
non-privileged situations where con-
    fidentiality still may be pre-
    served, 137–142
    agent of counselor covered by
        privileged communication may
        also be covered, 140–141
    blanket consent form signed, 142
    a communication meets Wig-
        more's criteria, 137
    data can be obtained elsewhere,
        138–139
    documents filed in lawsuit, 142
    hearsay information, 141
    incompetent witness, 139–140
    involuntary disclosure from client
        to counselor, 140
    lack of relevancy, 137–138
    society expects the communication
        to be privileged, 139
    special communications declared
        privileged, 138–139
and personnel records, 181
and pet-master communications, 108
readings on, 257–266
    cases, 264–265
    legal articles, 261–264
social work's ignorance concerning,
    151–153, 203
Wigmore's four conditions for, 99,
    113–115, 137, 147–150
who has it, 100–110
    attorneys, 101–102
    clergymen, 103–104
    client, 109, 111–113
    other professions, 106–108
    physicians, 102–103
    psychiatrists, 104

psychologists, 104–105
social workers, 105–106, 146–153
PSRO's (Professional Standard Review
   Organization), 72–75

Recording
   of frustrating incidents, 38–39
   legal aspects of, 39–40
   in personnel records, 175, 185–186
   process (narrative) style, 37
   as related to quality of care, 53–54
   what not to record, 36–40
Records
   arguments for and against doing
      away with, 47–54
   client access to: *see* Consumer access
   definition of, 31
   destruction of, 35
   maintaining confidentiality of,
      31–54
   maintaining dual records, 49–52
   material that does not belong in,
      36–40
   personnel, 172–187
   physically safeguarding, 33
   readings pertaining to confidentiality
      of, 246–251
   traditional written case record, 32
References, 155–162
   employee access to, 158–160
   on employees who have been fired,
      157–158, 160, 161–162
   how gathered, 156–157
   solicited and unsolicited, 156–157
   verbal, 161
   writing of when problems exist,
      198–199
Relative confidentiality, 3–4
Release of information, 55–82
   from agencies for use in classroom,
      35–36
   to attorneys, 80–81; *see also*
      Privileged communication; Sub-
      poenas
   to computers: *see* Computerized
      data

concerning and to minors, 66, 70,
   122–123, 130–131
to consumers: *see* Consumer access
   to records
to the court, 82; *see also* Privileged
   communication; Subpoenas
regarding employees, 162–163
to family and friends of client,
   68–70
to the general public, 70
"informed consent" as prerequisite
   for, 56–64; *see also* "Informed
   consent"
to news media, 5*n*, 78–80
to other agencies/disciplines, 70–71
to other social workers, 67–68,
   189–190
from personnel files: *see* Personnel
   records
to police, 81–82
to PSRO's, 72–75
in published reports, 80
readings, 251–256
release of information form, 57–64,
   237
   abuses to use of, 58–61
   blanket consent forms 58–60
   content of, 61–62
   example of, 237
   guidelines for use of, 61
   who can obtain client's signature,
      63–64
   who can sign it, 64, 188–189
to researchers, 75–78
to third-party payers, 71–72
under Federal Privacy Act regulations, 19–22
to unions, 181–182
when client appears non-alert, but
   has no legal guardian, 65–66
when client is cheating another agency, 190–191
without client consent, 64–67, 130,
   188–189, 190–195; *see also* Privileged communication
Relevancy issue in privileged communication, 137–138

Social service exchange, 45; *see also* Computerized data
Social workers
  and knowledge of privileged communication statutes, 151–153
  and right of privileged communication, 146–153
Students, special confidentiality requirements for, 5, 7, 35–36
Subpoenas
  of case record materials, 52
  definition of, 145–146
  of group therapy members, 133–134

of research data, 78, 108n
responding to, 52–53, 145–146
Suicidal client, 121–122
Suits: *see* Lawsuits

Tape recordings, 40–52
Third-party payers: *see* Release of information

Video recordings, 40–42
Violations of confidentiality, 9–14, 199–200; *see also* Lawsuits